CONNECTING
— with —
GOD
Our Stories, Your Journey

CONNECTING
with
GOD

Our Stories, Your Journey

RIVER STREET PRESS

Connecting with God

Copyright © 2023 by River Street Press

Published by River Street Press
5104 Bigelow Commons, Enfield, CT 06082

All rights reserved.

Printed in the United States of America on recycled paper.

Library of Congress Control Number: 2023913177
Hardcover ISBN: 978-1-7326132-3-2
Paperback ISBN: 978-1-7326132-4-9
e-Book ISBN: 978-1-7326132-5-6

DEDICATION

This book is dedicated to women determined to create a meaningful and successful life. By sharing their stories and experiences, these women are shaping not only a better future for themselves but also for others. *Connecting with God—Our Stories, Your Journey* is intended to support and inspire others on their faith journey. May it provide a platform for women to connect deeply with God and find guidance and solace in their shared experiences.

CONTENTS

Answered Prayers	1
Blessings	21
Bravery	59
Communion with God	87
Commitment to God	117
Diet	135
Encouragement	157
Fitness	173
God's Love	225
Giving	273
Hope	283
Holy Spirit	301
Home	309
Nature	337
Miracles	379
Marriage & Relationships	395
Reflection	431
Success	455
Surrender	481
Thankfulness	537
Trust	557

ACKNOWLEDGMENTS

This book is a testament to the divine inspiration behind its creation. It came to fruition with the initial God-given idea. I am deeply grateful for the courageous contributors who shared their most personal and intimate stories, making this book a collection of profound experiences.

The tireless dedication of Evelyn Marrero and Patricia Reed, who worked to bring everything together, and the keen insight of my friend Rico Hill were instrumental in shaping the final product. Their contributions have made this book possible and have added depth and richness to its pages.

In Appreciation,

Sandra A. Sergeant

FOREWORD

I experienced a challenging period during my journey with God when I felt isolated and unsupported. I would pray, seeking solace in the hope that God would send me a companion who truly understood my struggles. However, I soon realized that God's responses to my prayers rarely unfolded as I anticipated. To my surprise, His responses often exceeded my expectations.

The answer to my prayer manifested in reading a book that captivated and compelled me to finish it within a few days. The narratives within were sincere and exquisite. Even though I had not personally encountered everything described, the emotions expressed by the author resonated with me. I, too, had experienced similar fears and joys and witnessed others going through similar experiences. Immersing myself in these stories reassured me that I was not alone in my challenging season. The book illuminated the fact that while our journeys are diverse, each person's story has a distinct destination.

Another response to my prayer emerged through first of all rediscovering my relationship with myself and then tapping into the sisterhood that had always been present yet escaped my attention.

What started as one woman's divinely inspired idea has transformed into this remarkable book, thanks to the tenacity of numerous women and the support of both men and women alike. We sincerely pray that what we have shared here will be a blessing to you as you read, just as it has been a blessing for us to commit our stories to these pages.

Connecting with God is a compilation of stories from women of various backgrounds and life stages. They have endured profound heartaches, celebrated immense joys, and cherished those quiet moments that are rarely discussed. We hope you find encouragement as you engage with their life experiences. May you come to realize that you are not alone on your life's journey. Through these stories, may you rediscover the woman God intended you to be and may your faith, and hope in God grow exponentially.

Kelley Matieriene

Answered Prayers

*It shall come to pass that before they call,
I will answer; and while they are
still speaking, I will hear.*

—ISAIAH 65:24, AMP—

Dumb Faith

BY KAREEN WILSON

And Jesus answered them, "Truly, I say to you, if you have faith and do not doubt, you will not only do what has been done to the fig tree, but even if you say to this mountain, 'Be taken up and thrown into the sea,' it will happen. And whatever you ask in prayer, you will receive, if you have faith."

—MATTHEW 21:21–22, ESV

"True faith manifests itself through our actions."

—FRANCIS CHAN

As the woman tried to remember her doggy paddle in the deep blue sea, she sent up a prayer. "Please, Dear God, I need Your help! Save me! I have faith that You will save me."

As she felt the water around her face, she heard the sounds of a coast guard boat approaching. As they attempted to reach her, she waved them on and shouted, "God will save me. I'm good!"

ANSWERED PRAYERS

A few minutes later, a loud helicopter hovered overhead, the wind from the rotors churning the water into choppy waves. The woman looked up at the rope hanging down from the helicopter and shouted back, "I do not need you to rescue me. God will save me!" She let the helicopter go.

Before long, the waves were too high and her legs too weak. She felt the water overtake her. When she arrived in heaven, she asked God why He did not save her. She explained that her faith had been strong, and she had known that He was certainly able to save her.

God replied, "I sent a boat and a helicopter, and you sent both of them away."

This story reminds us of how our faith is at times. God can choose to answer our prayers in many ways, but we can become so fixed on how we expect God to answer that we miss the answer when it comes.

Our faith can move mountains, and we need to maintain a close relationship with God so that we can discern God's answers when they arrive. God's answers are sometimes unexpected, so faith requires believing that even the most unlikely person, situation, or thought can be the answer to our prayer. He can answer through great loss or in a rather mundane way. God sent a stuttering old man named Moses to rescue the Israelites from Egypt. Israel's first king was a young shepherd boy. The Israelites had faith that they would be a great nation, but that evolved in surprising ways.

Always be conscious that God can bless you in either mysterious or simple ways. Ask God to enable you to see His working in your life regardless of how He chooses to answer.

Praise, Repentance, and Petitions

BY ANANDI MOSES

Do not be anxious about anything, but in everything by prayer and pleading with thanksgiving let your requests be made known to God.

—PHILIPPIANS 4:6, NASB

While prayer has many aspects, two important basic elements are relationship and petition.

The relationship side of prayer involves thanksgiving and/or praise as well as repentance. We first need to turn our focus on God by contemplating His beauty and praising and thanking Him for the many blessings He has given us. This helps remind us of the goodness and mercy of God. These moments when we look at God's work in our lives take the focus off of ourselves and help our faith to grow.

When we have filled our souls with the love of God through contemplating His wondrous works and praising and thanking Him for them, we can then straighten out our relationship with God in areas where we have failed Him. We can ask for forgiveness of our sins and enjoy the assurance of pardon from God. Praise and worship as well as repentance and forgiveness are necessary to maintain a strong relationship with our Father.

Once the relationship is in order, God is very pleased to hear our petitions. Our needs and desires are important to Him. He desires to provide us with everything that is good for us. Yet we can become so caught up in the relationship aspect of prayer that we fail to realize our needs are important enough to bring before God's throne. We feel our problems will seem petty to God, or we feel unworthy of His help—but God never sees it that way.

On the other hand, some of us may be so burdened by our needs that it is hard to take our eyes off them and look to Jesus with praise and worship. We miss out on a huge blessing either way.

Regarding prayer, we cannot depend on moods and feelings. We need to trust God and come to our prayer time willing to turn our eyes on Him and praise Him, find forgiveness for our sins, and place our needs in His hands.

Prayer Focus

BY ANANDI MOSES

And you will seek Me and find Me when you search for Me with all your heart.

—JEREMIAH 29:13 , NASB

The discipline of prayer is hard to cultivate. Most Christians earnestly try, but for those like me with a wandering mind, it is tough.

Prayer is communication. How does a person communicate in real life? Think about it. There is a speaker and a listener. There is a conversation going back and forth. There is speaking, listening, clarifying, questioning, agreeing, empathizing, etc. There is tone of voice, pitch, and body language. These are cues for us to continue the conversation in different directions. Coordination and understanding are present in conversations even when people disagree. Now, imagine if you will, you can neither see nor hear the person with whom you're talking. Just how engaging do you think that conversation would be?

Sin has raised a veil between God and us. We no longer have the luxury that Adam had in speaking directly to God. For us, praying sometimes feels like a one-way conversation. No doubt, God hears our prayers! But we can't see Him nodding in acknowledgment or reflecting our feelings. So, prayer can feel like a monologue. It's easy to get distracted. Hard to focus.

I used to struggle to pray for more than a few minutes without my mind wandering. One day, I realized that I write when I want to think. My mind slows down, and my thoughts become organized and flow when I write. I make important decisions after I sit down to write out my thoughts. It helps to have my eyes and fingers coordinate with my mind in the process of thinking. With that thought, I was impressed that I should write my prayers, which proved to be a great blessing! What was once a few words spoken at the speed of thought transformed into a time of organized communication involving worship, praise, thanksgiving, petition, and sometimes simply lingering in God's presence.

What is your most effective way of organizing your thoughts? What do you do when you think about important ideas? What do you do when you need to communicate an important message? You can use the same tool to focus on God while praying. Some people need to take a walk. Some speak their thoughts out loud. Maybe you have a special place to pray or a posture to assume. Ask God to show you your personal prayer tool. As simple as it seems, using that tool will facilitate the spiritual aspects of praying.

Why Should We Pray

BY ANANDI MOSES

L̲o̲r̲d̲, You have searched me and known me.
You know, when I sit down and when I get up;
You understand my thoughts from far away.
You scrutinize my path and my lying down,
And are acquainted with all my ways.
Even before there is a word on my tongue,
Behold, L̲o̲r̲d̲, You know it all.

—PSALM 139:1–4, NASB

"Prayer is like talking to your best friend." Most of us have heard this assertion before, and it is true that when we talk to a friend, we need not fear being judged. A good friend will not use what we say against us. A friend has good intentions and wishes for our well-being. All of these same qualities are true about God. However, even a true friend is only human. God is very different from anyone we know here on earth. That is why praying is unlike talking to anyone else we know.

Consider that God knows everything; He is omniscient. He even knows what we don't know about ourselves. What does that mean?

It means that when we pray, it is pointless to pretend or try to act worthy and dignified in God's presence. Since God knows everything, we can let go of our reservations when we engage with the world outside. We have no need for inhibitions when we kneel in front of God. We can lay before Him the innermost essence of who we are.

While our transparency doesn't add anything to God's understanding of us, it helps us access the truth about ourselves that may be hard to lay bare in any other space, even to ourselves. It helps us accept that we are sinners in need of grace; it reinforces our understanding that God is love. It helps us shed our own false righteousness and allow God to cover us with His perfect righteousness. It allows the Holy Spirit to show us our needs. It is one thing for God to know us because He is omniscient, but it is another to stand before God and open ourselves to be known. Being utterly transparent before Him makes us willing for God to work on us.

The space to open yourself to God is created in your hour of prayer not simply because God is omniscient but also because God is omnibenevolent. God is love. He not only knows you fully but loves you anyway. His love is the healing balm to the sin-crushed heart, and that balm is available to us at the altar of prayer every day. We are given the privilege of looking up to an awesome God who loves us unconditionally even though He knows exactly who we are. That privilege helps us to experience acceptance that leads to change. Talk to Him today; He is waiting.

Thank You, Jesus!

BY SARA E. BAYRÓN

*This is the confidence we have in approaching God:
that if we ask anything according to his will, he hears us.*

—1 JOHN 5:14, NIV

It was New Year's Day in 2011, which fell on a Saturday that year. It was my turn to teach Sabbath School that morning, and I was driving Grandpa and a friend to church. The roads were empty of cars. I suppose that people were probably still sleeping from celebrating the night before. On the way, I passed by a street where a detention center is located and saw a dark-skinned woman walking down the street in the distance. As I approached her, I noticed she was wearing a black see-through dress with very little clothing underneath. When I stopped at the traffic light, she approached my car and knocked on my window, asking me to drive her home.

I hesitated a bit as I was shocked and apprehensive, but the woman kept asking and saying, "I was asking God to send someone to give me a ride home, and when I saw you, I knew God was listening to me." I learned that she had been picked up by the police the night before and spent the night in the detention center. I saw desperation and panic in her face, and I didn't want anything wrong to happen to her, so I agreed to give her a ride home. She got in the car and, though she didn't talk much on the drive to her house, through her tears, I could hear her saying "Hallelujah" and "Thank You, Jesus." She praised God for listening to her and sending an angel to help her.

When we reached her neighborhood, she instructed me to drop her off before crossing the railroad tracks, but I refused since it was a dangerous area. I crossed the tracks to the side of town that was not the safest place to be and dropped her off in front of her house. As she got out of the car, she was dispensing blessings to everyone in the car with me, but to me, she said, "I know that you are one of God's angels, so you are already blessed."

Needless to say, I was late to Sabbath School that day and unable to teach the lesson, but God was using me to bless this woman that morning. Although I was willing to help her, I felt that I needed to talk seriously with God because of what was happening in my own life.

"Lord, I have been praying for a long time for You to answer my request, and I still don't see the answer. But this lady who is neither doing right nor serving You prays to You, and You use me to answer her prayer right away. What do You want to teach me about this?"

God quickly reminded me that He came to save imperfect people and that when I do something for someone in need, I do it for Him.

I got up from my prayer time with a fresh realization of my need to trust God with all my heart. He knows what is best for me. I am satisfied that if I trust in Him, He will answer. I will wait for my answer to come.

Answered Prayers

BY SARA E. BAYRÓN

The prayer of a righteous person is powerful and effective.

—JAMES 5:16B, NIV

I lived in Florida, and my brother lived in Michigan then. We often talked on the phone, and I knew he had heart problems. Doctors planned to catheterize the heart, and I was waiting for the results.

Heart catheterization is a standard procedure, but once my brother's was finished, the doctor indicated that open heart surgery was immediately necessary because 90% of some arteries were blocked. The doctor also told my brother he was in danger of having a significant heart attack and dying if he left the hospital without surgery.

My brother's wife called me to tell me the news, and I immediately fell on my knees and prayed for God to guide the surgeon's hands. I did not want to go to Michigan, but I prayed that God would make it happen if I needed to be there.

I told my husband what was happening, and he told me to fly to Michigan to be with my brother. I thought it unnecessary, but I booked a flight that involved a connection and a very late arrival. Since the flight was a last-minute decision, I arrived at the airport very close to my departure time As I waited in line, a man cut in front of me, pushing me aside and saying that he was in a hurry and afraid that he would miss his flight. When I reached the counter, the flight attendant told me my flight had closed its doors.

That missed flight meant I would be getting to Michigan even later. The counter agent had seen the man push me aside, so when I told her why I was going to Michigan, she said, "Let me see if I can get a direct flight for you."

I did get that direct flight, which meant I saw my brother as soon as he was out of the surgery. He had been very depressed about the surgery and was very happy to see me. He confessed that he had been praying I would be there when he awoke I was thankful I could be with him at such a critical time.

God listens. And He answers. He heard my prayers for smooth travel and, most of all, a successful surgery for my brother. God heard my brother's prayer and brought me to Michigan when, if it had been up to me, I might not have gone. God used my husband to make that happen. Don't ever doubt that our God is the God who answers the prayers of His children.

God Will Provide

BY GLARIBEL PINERO-AMARO

*Therefore do not worry about tomorrow,
for tomorrow will worry about itself.
Each day has enough trouble of its own.*

—MATTHEW 6:34, NIV

My parents divorced during my childhood. My mom, after being in an abusive marriage for almost a decade, had enough courage to get out of that relationship, but that decision put a heavy load on her shoulders. However, despite being ill, she believed she had made a wise decision.

She was a strong woman. I rarely ever saw her cry, even though I believe she did cry almost every day. Looking back, I can imagine how scared she was. But she was a woman of faith—faith that kept her going until the day she passed away.

After the divorce, she couldn't return to work because of a heart condition. The abuse had affected her both physically and mentally. Thankfully, several organizations provided aid, and she took advantage of everything available to our family. She went to school and created a small childcare business in our home to sustain us.

Even though money was always scarce, she managed to put food on the table every day for her family.

She had asked God to save her from her suffering and from continuing in a miserable life, and He did. She taught us to wait on the Lord and follow His ways even when it is hard, though there were moments when our faith was tested.

I remember one Friday evening when our meal consisted of white rice with her homemade dressing and bean broth—and we had no food in the house to eat the next day, nor did we have any money. The three of us (my youngest sibling, mom, and I) ate our last meal in silence that evening, our minds in turmoil. The only thing my mom told us that afternoon was "God will provide for us."

Yeah, right! I thought. I was almost fifteen years old. We had Vespers and went to bed silently. The following day, while we were getting ready for church, the father of one of the babies my mom cared for stopped by our house with a loaf of bread. I'll never forget his words: "Gladys, I went to the bakery this morning, and I brought this bread for you and your children." God had provided breakfast. We gave thanks to God and went to church. At the end of the service, the church treasurer asked to speak to Mom in private and told her to unlock the trunk of her car. On our way home, my brother and I couldn't believe our eyes. The boxes in our trunk contained rice, meat, beans, and vegetables…everything we needed for at least a week. The next day was Sunday, and another father stopped by our house to pay my mom for the previous week of babysitting. We had money for gas!

Mom made it her goal to remind me of God's provision every single time He answered her prayers, and now I remind you that God will provide, always, no matter what.

Praying Like Breathing

BY ESTHER PELLETIER

Pray without ceasing.

—1 THESSALONIANS 5:17, KJV

I was there for my first niece's birth. Her head slipped out and, after a lull, her shoulders and the rest of her tiny body. She was blue at first. Suddenly, her lungs filled as she took her first breath with a big gasp. Instantly, her skin tone turned pink. My sister says she thought maybe the ceiling was leaking at that moment because she felt drops of water splashing onto her leg. Those were my tears. Watching a new human life enter the world fills us with powerful emotions!

Was it like that for God as He breathed the breath of life into Adam in the Garden of Eden? As Adam's body shuddered to life, did God feel like crying with joy? His vision had come to fruition. Humans are the only creatures into which God breathed directly. We are told Jesus again breathed onto humans. Still, this time it was His fearful disciples locked in a room, His new body of believers who desperately needed His Holy Spirit to come alive as new creatures in Him (John 20:22; 2 Corinthians 5:17).

ANSWERED PRAYERS

Breathing in oxygen is our body's most important physical need. So perhaps our breathing can teach us some lessons about our walk with God.

1. Just as breathing must be non-stop to sustain life, our communication with God is non-stop if we are to remain alive spiritually. Sometimes we think of prayer as words we say with our eyes closed, but prayer can occur every second we are awake. At any moment, we can take a deep breath and maybe practice the 4-7-9 method (in for a count of 4, hold for a count of 7, out for a count of 9). As we slow down, we are aware of God's breath and growing work in us and our constant connection to Him.

2. When we breathe in, we receive fresh oxygen. In exchange, we breathe out toxins and poisons that our body does not need, carbon dioxide. Just so, in prayer, we offer God all of ourselves, including the parts we need to expel from our spiritual selves. He takes all that we offer Him and, in exchange, gives us the purity we need. It's an ongoing cycle of receiving and giving back.

How does your constant prayer life invigorate you? Is Jesus breathing on you to move you out of a place of hiding? Are there any breathing and prayer habits you would like to improve to live more fully in God's expansiveness?

Prayers Heard

BY MEGAN BLACKMORE

Before they call I will answer;
while they are still speaking, I will hear.

—ISAIAH 65:24, NIV

I sometimes struggle, wondering if God is hearing my prayers, if the words I utter on my knees reach His ears, and if He actually will answer them if He does hear.

Sometimes I feel as if I am going through the motions of prayer out of Christian obligation, and my heart doesn't feel connected to the sentences I am streaming together for the Lord. Sometimes I even dread praying, for I feel I have to say certain things or else the opposite will happen.

Praying is supposed to be a simple communication between our Creator and us, but we have complicated the matter a hundredfold. God simply wants to hear our voices, to hear from us. He's looking for nothing fancy, nothing long even, and nothing specific every time.

Still, for whatever reason, my mind often doesn't grasp this concept, and I feel my prayers are becoming rehearsed rather than heartfelt.

Isaiah 65:24 brought to my attention that the Lord not only hears my prayers but is answering them too. This thought then reminds me that it isn't about what I say when I pray but how I communicate with Him verbally. In that verse, God says that before we call on His name, He will answer us, and even while we are still praying, He hears us. God hears every word, every utterance, every silent prayer, and every cry. And He not only hears, but He also answers.

Praying need not be a task we simply check off our to-do list before bed or when we wake up in the morning, and this is something I am currently learning. Instead, praying is just a natural and genuine conversation with the Lord throughout the day…quick check-ins with the One who created us, our thoughts, and our vocabulary.

So, if you're like me and struggle to pray heartfelt prayers to the Lord, start small, start with a simple, "Hi, Lord," and allow the conversation to flow naturally from there as you talk to God while you go about your day.

And remember, out of the millions and billions of prayers the Lord encounters every second of the day, He still hears your voice loud and clear as if you were the only one talking to Him.

Blessings

May God be gracious to us and bless us and make his face shine on us.

—PSALM 67:1, NIV—

Tired of Waiting? (Part 1)

BY ZORAIDA VELEZ-DELGADO

> "Lord," Martha said to Jesus,
> "if you had been here, my brother would not have died.
> ²² But I know that even now God will
> give you whatever you ask."
>
> —JOHN 11:21–22, NIV

When I get to heaven, I will look for Lazarus because he has an amazing story to tell.

The Bible doesn't really specify how many times Lazarus was present when Jesus worked miracles. We just know that Lazarus' sisters knew that Jesus could perform them. They had witnessed the power Jesus had received from His Father and how He had used that power to heal others. Now, imagine what went through Lazarus' mind when he became ill. I love how Jesus said, after learning that the one He loved was sick, "This sickness will not end in death. No, it is for God's glory so that God's Son may be glorified."

We know what happened next. Jesus arrived too late to "save" Lazarus. Upon his arrival, Jesus was told that Lazarus had already been in the tomb for four days.

"Lord," Martha said to Jesus, "if you had been here, my brother would not have died. But I know that even now God will give you whatever you ask." That, my friends, is faith in the power of God.

You know how the story ends, but I wonder if you know how it relates to you. How many times have you prayed for something but see no response from God? Yes, we have learned that His response is sometimes *yes,* sometimes *no,* or sometimes even *wait.* In a world where our attention span is less than a goldfish's, we want responses now! Answer my prayer now, tell me now, do it now.

(To be continued)

Tired of Waiting? (Part 2)

BY ZORAIDA VELEZ-DELGADO

> *"Lord," Martha said to Jesus,*
> *"if you had been here, my brother would not have died.*
> *²² But I know that even now God will*
> *give you whatever you ask."*
>
> —JOHN 11:21–22, NIV

The power of God doesn't always translate into what He can do, but in what He chooses to wait to do. Jesus could have dropped everything to see Lazarus when he was sick; after all, Bethany was less than two miles from Jerusalem. But the key is what Jesus expressed when He learned about Lazarus' illness. "It is for God's glory so that God's Son may be glorified." Even when we think some problem is about us, it isn't. It is about the bigger picture. It is not for our salvation but for the salvation of our brothers and sisters.

Imagine being there when Jesus called Lazarus out of the grave. What a picture, what a miracle, what a decisive moment! Lazarus was not healed, but he was resurrected! Oh, I'm sure Lazarus' life was never the same after that moment!

How many prayer requests have you elevated recently? What kind of response are you receiving? If the Lord has not answered your prayer yet, it may be a no, but it could also be that He is waiting to give you a decisive moment. You didn't get the job you prayed for? Wait; He may want you to start a business. You were not accepted at the school of your choice? Wait. You may shine more at a small university. Are you not getting back together with that boyfriend? Wait; he was good, just not right for you. Someone better is coming!

Waiting can be frustrating, but remember, the God we serve loves to surprise us with magical moments. Yours is coming!

Blessings in Unexpected Ways

BY AVALEY FRANCES MATIERIENE

And my God will meet all your needs according to the riches of his glory in Christ Jesus.

—PHILIPPIANS 4:19, NIV

As I began nursing school, one significant obstacle stood in my way—I didn't have a car. However, my faith in God's provision propelled me forward, knowing that He could make a way where there seemed to be none. With $2,000 in savings, I embarked on a journey filled with unexpected blessings and valuable lessons.

Borrowing my mother's car for transportation, I stumbled upon a 15-year-old Volkswagen Jetta available for purchase at $1,999. This serendipitous encounter felt like a divine sign, a doorway to independence. Despite my lack of experience driving a stick shift, my stepfather generously offered to teach me in just one day, solidifying my decision to acquire the Jetta.

With a heart of gratitude, I embarked on my nursing school journey, relying on the Jetta to transport me to and from classes and even on long clinical trips. Although the car had its share of challenges, such as non-closing doors and a leaking cooling system, I embraced these imperfections, recognizing that having a reliable mode of transportation was a blessing.

However, after a year and a half, the brakes failed, and my mechanic delivered unexpected news—the bottom of the car was rotted out, rendering it beyond repair. Uncertainty loomed over me, but I turned to the place of purchase with hope. Astonishingly, the seller agreed to take back the car without question and provided me with $1,000 in return.

This experience taught me a profound lesson in gratitude and unexpected blessings. It reminded me that God's provision often comes in surprising ways, and His timing is always perfect. As we navigate through life's challenges, we can trust that God sees our needs and is faithful to provide, whether it be through a reliable car, unexpected financial blessings, or the strength to persevere.

Let us embrace each season of life, knowing that God's provision extends far beyond our expectations. Just as He turned my initial investment into a new opportunity, He can transform our trials into blessings, reminding us of His faithfulness and grace. May we approach every hurdle with unwavering faith, believing that God's blessings are waiting to be revealed in the most unexpected ways.

Unexpected Blessings in Unlikely Places

BY AVALEY FRANCES MATIERIENE

*Every good and perfect gift is from above,
coming down from the Father of the heavenly lights,
who does not change like shifting shadows.*

—JAMES 1:17, NIV

As an exchange student in the Philippines, I had the privilege of living with a host family associated with the local Rotary Club. It was an arrangement to ensure that the exchange student would be accommodated in a wealthy household during their stay. Little did I know that amidst the differences in wealth and status, God had a unique lesson in store for me.

One fateful night, a water main break caused a flood in the house where I was staying. The rising waters turned my temporary shelter into a chaotic scene. In the darkness of the night, I found myself swimming through muddy currents, desperately seeking higher ground. It was in that moment of fear and uncertainty that God guided my steps to a humble two-room nipa hut, where a poor family welcomed me with open arms.

This family, with hearts overflowing with compassion, offered me shelter, dry clothes, and warmth. They embraced me as their own, providing solace and comfort amidst the chaos. Their kindness reminded me that God's provision knows no boundaries and often comes from unexpected sources. It was a poignant lesson that wealth and status do not define the richness of a person's heart or their willingness to help.

Reflecting on this experience, I am reminded of James 1:17, which affirms that every good and perfect gift comes from above. Our Heavenly Father, the source of all blessings, does not change like shifting shadows. He works through various channels, often using ordinary people to extend His grace and provision. This encounter served as a profound reminder that our circumstances do not limit God's blessings but flow abundantly when we least expect them.

The Blessings

BY KAREEN WILSON

> [24] *The L*ORD *bless you and keep you;*
> [25] *the L*ORD *make his face shine on you*
> *and be gracious to you;*
> [26] *the L*ORD *turn his face toward you*
> *and give you peace.*
>
> —NUMBERS 6:24–26, NIV

Imagine being in a beautiful place while on vacation. Your mind is transported to perfection, and your surroundings are lovely. You are calm and feel at peace, and the world's stress drops off you. Perhaps you are on a tropical island beside crystal blue water with clear blue skies overhead and white sand beneath your feet. You look up to feel the warmth of the sun shining down on you. Can you feel its rays penetrating your skin and creating a feeling of awe?

Now imagine God's love. The sunshine can feel like God's love, which is even brighter, warmer, and more robust. This love surrounds you and provides immunity to the virus around you. The vitamin enriches your mind and body and heals your soul. You feel peace as you bask in the sun's (or Son's) rays.

Aaron spoke the blessing in Numbers on the people of Israel. God had given these words to Moses, and even though God blesses us spiritually, emotionally, and materially, words are a powerful way to invoke the love of God. When we say words of encouragement and praise, we encourage others. The blessings are like sunshine that blesses and bestows peace in everything it touches. The face of God looks down and shines love, peace, and joy all around you. You can feel the sun's warmth and God's grace showing up in all aspects of your life.

Pronouncing this prayer to your family, friends, coworkers, and people in your church can be a simple way to let them know that you love them and wish them God's love whenever you see them or they need hope and encouragement.

Who can you bless and encourage today?

The Man Named Jabez

BY KAREEN WILSON

*Jabez cried out to the God of Israel,
"Oh, that you would bless me and enlarge my territory!
Let your hand be with me and keep me from harm so that
I will be free from pain." And God granted his request.*

—1 CHRONICLES 4:10, NIV

Here, the prayer of Jabez is powerful and bold. I can imagine him on his knees with his hands held high and tears of joy and love mingled with frustration running down his face. He is claiming his place with God, and he knows who he is and to whom he belongs.

Let's look at the history of this man named Jabez. His story begins in a seemingly mundane part of the Bible where the writer lists names. A history lesson, if you will. However, when we get to Jabez, there is more to his story. First, his mother named him Jabez because she bore him in pain. Are not all children born in pain, especially back in Bible times? So, what was so special about his birth that she would give him that name? Living with a name that meant pain could not have been easy. The text does say that he was more honorable than his brothers. Jabez was a great guy and a writer, and God noticed.

How does this reflect your situation? You are not what the world labels you to be. Your mother can give you a name, or people can characterize you, but that does not define who you are. Pray a prayer that connects you to God, and a new creation is born. "Create in me a new heart." Jabez did not let his name deter him from being something extraordinary. He was more honorable than his brothers. As Christians, we are to give everyone we encounter love, peace, and joy. Whatever our past story or name, we can be better and more loving. God notices honorable people. God inspired the writer of the Chronicles to write about Jabez. God sees Jabez. His actions and prayers are written in Scripture for all to see for generations. God sees you. You are unique to the Creator and will impact this world and everyone in it. Be righteous and loving.

So, what about this prayer? I have simplified it, and the prayer sounds like this: Bless me, indeed! Expand my territory and put your hands upon me so I may not cause or feel pain."

Tomorrow, we will expand on the prayer and discover how it can be applied to our lives.

Bless me, indeed! My blessings today are:

The Prayer of Jabez

BY KAREEN WILSON

*Jabez cried out to the God of Israel,
"Oh, that you would bless me and enlarge my territory!
Let your hand be with me, and keep me from harm so that
I will be free from pain." And God granted his request.*

—1 CHRONICLES 4:10, NIV

Today, let's break down Jabez's prayer. This passage has so much depth and inclusion that I am sure you will see how it can impact your life. I am going to use the following translation simply for ease of explanation.

Bless me, indeed! Expand my territory and put your hands upon me so I may not cause or feel pain.

Bless me indeed: Jabez is very confident in his request for a blessing. He is sure that God will touch him and that only God provides blessings. Material blessings are included but not the focus. This man desires spiritual wisdom and supernatural blessings. Like Solomon, Jabez knows that true blessings like knowledge, strong moral character, and love between family and friends are worth more than earthly possessions.

Expand my territory: This can pertain to land and houses, which are important, but influence is the focus. Expand my reach. How can I influence more people for the kingdom of Heaven? Influencers on social media want to reach more people and have more followers. This is what Jabez is thinking. How can I expand to reach more people and help them see God's goodness?

Put your hand on me: The hand of God is a symbol of guidance. God is leading you toward the ideas and issues where you can help. Listen to God's guidance. When the hand of God is on you, nothing is impossible.

I may not cause or feel pain: Jabez's very name translates into "He that causes pain." He did not want that name anymore, plus he asked for God to help him be the type of person who has empathy and does not hurt people physically or emotionally. Many will say he is asking to have no difficulty and feel no pain, but we all know this is not possible. Jabez is asking that he does not have to "feel the pain." As we go through a difficult time, God can help us put things into perspective so that we feel less of the pain. I can think of times in my life when I was hurting. The distress of life disabled my heart and body. Then I prayed, and the pain was still there, but it was less, and I could see victory on the other side. Prayer gave me hope, and the pain went away.

Commit this prayer to memory. When you need support from God, this little prayer will bring you comfort and peace.

How Well Does God Know You?

BY KAREEN WILSON

You know when I sit and when I rise;
you perceive my thoughts from afar.
You discern my going out and my lying down;
you are familiar with all my ways.
Before a word is on my tongue you,
*L*ORD*, know it completely.*

—PSALM 139:2–4, NIV

Netflix knows me. I watch one show, and as I browse, it recommends many other shows that I also enjoy. Netflix uses artificial intelligence and machine learning to keep me on a Netflix binge so that, if I am not careful, four hours will go by before I even realize what happened. Google, Amazon, and Facebook all use algorithms that keep us buying, watching, and following people. You have to be vigilant not to get stuck in its web. All of these companies are improving their science every day.

The only safety from the prying eyes of Netflix is to not get on the platform. Do not shop on Amazon; it will not know what influences you to buy. Don't log into Facebook and post your story and search to find out what everyone on your friend list is doing in their life. That is the only way to stay out of the big brother's eyes of these media groups.

If all these companies are so good at reaching me, what about God? Even though God is always there, am I spending enough time in God's Word and interacting with Him for the Spirit to know my heart and desires? Remember those four hours spent binge-watching Netflix? What if we spend that time reading God's Word and meditating on His goodness instead? Would not God bring me more blessings and wisdom if He knew what I was searching for?

Every time you focus on building your relationship with God, it grows stronger, and your prayers get answered. More blessings show up. An attitude of gratitude produces more of the things for which you are grateful.

What media platforms could you switch out for reflection time with God?

The Sea of Galilee

BY KAREEN WILSON

> *As Jesus was walking beside the Sea of Galilee, he saw two brothers, Simon called Peter and his brother Andrew. They were casting a net into the lake, for they were fishermen.*
>
> —MATTHEW 4:18, NIV

As I stepped out of the bus and walked to the grounds where history indicates Jesus delivered the Beatitudes, I was amazed by the grandeur of the lake and the beauty of the area. I imagined how Jesus gave a message of hope that inspired humanity forever. Jesus must have been excited to share ideas and concepts that were very new and a blessing to people suffering under Roman rule and religious dogma.

Today, an eight-sided church there represents the eight Beatitudes or eight blessings. Groups come to church for worship, and the church grounds contain a meeting house, a monastery, and a hostel.

The Sea of Galilee is a lake surrounded by a resort town. The lake has trendy shops and hotels to host many visitors looking for relaxation. The Town of Tiberias has a boardwalk and areas to dock many boats.

Looking at the lake, I imagine Peter walking on the water and Jesus holding out His hand. I think of the disciples leaving their lives as fishermen to become fishers of men.

The Sea of Galilee is part of so many stories, and to see it in person helps to give life and meaning to the events in the Bible.

Blessed are the poor in spirit, for theirs is the kingdom of Heaven. As I look out over the lake, I reflect on this Beatitude and recognize my need for the Savior in my life. I desire for God to enter my heart and bless me.

I encourage you to read the Beatitudes and reflect on how each blessing impacts your life.

If you visited the Sea of Galilee, what would you do while you were there? What would your emotions be?

He Really Does Care

BY KELLEY MATIERIENE

> *⁶ Therefore humble yourselves under the mighty hand of God, that He may exalt you in due time, ⁷ casting all your care upon Him, for He cares for you.*
>
> —1 PETER 5:6–7, NKJV

One of the things I like to do when life grows hectic is have a cup of tea. That may sound odd but hear me out. A cup of tea forces us to slow down and exercise patience. We have to wait for the water to boil, wait for the tea bag to steep, and then wait a little while before we drink the tea so we don't burn our mouths. It's the very exercise of waiting for something so you can fully enjoy it.

Imagine then when I found myself working eighty- plus hours a week from home in a house with no kitchen and my kettle packed up in a box somewhere between Connecticut and North Carolina. I was beside myself. Every day that passed, I promised myself that I would just buy a new kettle through Amazon, but I never found the time. When a friend of mine offered me one, I accepted with excitement only to find out I would have to wait two weeks for them to bring it to me because shipping it was not worth it in their opinion.

One day I was sitting at work and said a little prayer. "Lord, You know I don't have time or energy to find a tea kettle online. Lord, You also know I don't want to pay three dollars for tea at Starbucks or Panera. Help me." I said, "Amen," and went about my busy day. The prayer was forgotten and once I started really focusing on work, so was the tea. The next day, I sat down to work after a night of little sleep wishing once again that I had a cup of tea, and I heard a knock at my door. Standing on my porch holding her tea kettle in her outstretched hand was my mother.

"What about you?" I asked, but she reassured me that she had a stove and could make tea while I did not, and then she left to start her busy day. I closed the door as my eyes welled with tears, but I'm not sure whether I cried because I was exhausted or because when I realized how much God cares and how He really does hear the prayers we pray, I was overwhelmed. It was probably a bit of both.

It's the prayers where we tell God our cares, yet don't suggest to Him how to fix the issues or go about trying to rectify them after we say "Amen." The ones where we really give God the space to move as we patiently wait. He never fails to show up. He never fails to move. Admittedly, He doesn't always show up with a yes by granting the request, and He often takes longer than my human mind deems necessary. Yet He always shows up, always on time, and always reminds me that He means what He says when He says to pray about everything. \

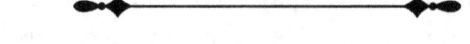

Renewed Youth Promised

BY SANDRA A. SERGEANT

*Who satisfieth thy desire with good things,
So that thy youth is renewed like the eagle.*

—P 103:5, ASV

This was the worst encounter with the flu virus I had ever experienced. It began very mildly but soon progressed to extremely high fevers, total loss of appetite, weakness, severe headaches, and overall body pain. It was as if I had been suddenly hit by a large boulder out of nowhere.

One of my favorite authors says, "Disease begins and ends in the mind." And the battle between my mind and body began. I crawled out of bed each morning and forced myself to prepare my homemade remedies; when friends and family called to check on me, I told them I was getting better. Determined not to give in, I forced myself to back my car into the garage. This act had challenged me in the past. During this time, I encountered our focus text, the last part of the verse, which states that "my youth will be renewed like an eagle." An eagle? How so? And so began my search to discover the true meaning of the renewal process of the eagle.

Here is what I discovered. The Hebrew word for *renew* is *kered*, meaning to repair and build. According to Jewish understanding, the eagle is a long-lived bird of prey that can reach seventy years of age under certain conditions. But when the eagle reaches the age of forty, it becomes weaker because its nails have become long and no longer as flexible. The bird cannot quickly grab its prey. Also, the long sharp beak becomes very curved so that it cannot pierce its prey, while the wings become heavy causing the feathers to become very thick and attached to the breast. At this point the eagle has difficulty flying and has two choices; die or undergo a painful renewal process.

The eagle flies to the mountains and beats its beak against a rock until it is broken off, then waits until it grows back, then plucks out all of its feathers, then waits for new feathers to grow back; the final step in the process is the plucking out of the nails, and then waiting for the regrowth. In all, this process takes about six months, but an eagle can live for another thirty years after this renewal is complete.

The eagle imagery in this verse is powerful. Eagles are also known for their strength, agility, and ability to soar to great heights. God desires to renew our strength and vitality. He rejuvenates our spirits, giving us the endurance and resilience to face life's challenges with confidence. It is through our relationship with God that we find true renewal.

This verse resonates with me; God has promised that in times of deep despair, sickness, or confusion, though painful, He will fill us with good things and renew our lives like the eagle. Be encouraged today.

When the Storms Come

BY KELLEY MATIERIENE

*He who dwells in the secret place of the Most High
Shall abide under the shadow of the Almighty.*

—PSALM 91:1, NKJV

"Who would like to read a Bible passage?" my mom asked. All the kids looked at one another, none of us daring to raise our hands or make eye contact. I don't know which is greater: the fear of being called out by your peers for raising your hand or being singled out by the adult in the room to do something you would rather not do. Either way, I was "voluntold" to read. And on this occasion, my grandmother was in attendance. I adored my grandmother; she had the best laugh, and we got the best food when she came to visit. I was asked to read Psalm 91. We all groaned...why does it always have to be a long passage when we want to go do something more fun? But I wondered silently because I dared not voice my frustration out loud.

As I began reading, my grandmother started reciting. This annoyed me even more...why did I have to read it if she knew the words and could recite them? Honestly!

Looking back, I can laugh at that scene now, but I also realize the reading of it was for me. I needed to hear the words to try to grasp what it means to seek refuge in God. The reading was for each of us kids with our brief lives to that point who felt like we were invincible and knew it all. Even my grandmother reciting it was a lesson for us: to make it to her age, we had better hold on to some verses in the Bible that would help us through. The verses reminded us of who we are and where we can go for help.

If the adults had tried to explain this to us as children, we wouldn't have understood, just as my children now don't understand the importance of hiding God's Word in their hearts. However, it is my duty to model it and to assist them in doing so. It may take many years for them, as it did for my generation, but the lesson is too great to not be taught.

Psalm 91 (NKJV) ends in a promise; it's one I cling to when the storms come:

> [14] *"Because he has set his love upon Me,*
> *therefore I will deliver him;*
> *I will set him on high because he has known My name.*
> [15] *He shall call upon Me, and I will answer him;*
> *I will be with him in trouble;*
> *I will deliver him and honor him.*
> [16] *With long life I will satisfy him,*
> *And show him My salvation."*

Life is going to throw all sorts of unexpected happenings your way. Remember who you are and what He promises. Today, write out your favorite promise, share it with someone you love, and place it somewhere that you are sure to see it.

Living in the Shadow

BY MEGAN BLACKMORE

*For we know that our old self was crucified with Him
so that the body ruled by sin might be done away with,
that we should no longer be slaves to sin—
because anyone who has died has been set free from sin.*

—ROMANS 6:6–7, NIV

There are often moments that remind us of the "good ol' days," if you can call it that. Certain events, songs, shows, or triggers bring us right back to a place that once was.

This can be a good thing, provoking happy memories, or it can be a more morbid experience, reminding us of mistakes, challenges, or the "not-so-good-ol' days."

I often think of this as living in the shadow of our old selves.

It can sometimes be difficult to disconnect from the old self, to forgive yourself for what you've done, or even to just acknowledge the choices you've made that have impacted your life.

When we live in this shadow of the old self and allow our past to control and affect us in the present, we have defeated the purpose of the life created anew that the Lord has given us.

The verse for today reads that our old self was crucified with Him so that the body ruled by sin might be done away with and that we should no longer be slaves to sin. It's such a powerful message, but I don't think we fully grasp it.

To have our old self die means our old self no longer exists. To put it simply, in layman's terms, if something is dead, there is no way it can continue on. When we look at our old self and what is still lurking in the shadows to remind us of our shortcomings or who we used to be, we do not understand the death in that old self.

When we live in the shadow of who we used to be before we were raised again in the Lord, we are telling God that the sacrifice Christ made for us wasn't good enough. It's like saying, "The old me is still around, and I can't get rid of her!" But all the while, God is telling us through verses like today's, "That person is already gone!"

We've already been created anew, we have already been raised again with Christ, and the old us has no power anymore. What's dead is dead; let it lie.

The enemy wants us to be caught up in our old self because, when we are caught up in that shadow, we can't live in the light already provided for us. It's like seeing the light at the end of the tunnel but not moving your body toward it to escape the darkness.

It's time to accept God's message and promise simply for what it is. The old you is no more, and you, yes you, are a new being entirely in Christ. Own it, embrace it, praise the Lord for it.

A Letter to the President

BY EVELYN RAQUEL DELGADO MARRERO

Ask and it will be given to you; seek and you will find; knock and the door will be opened to you.

—MATTHEW 7:7, NIV

In 1951, my father was called to serve in the United States Army. He had just moved his family from Puerto Rico to New York City in search of better living conditions. His family consisted of a wife and three young children, the oldest being three years old and the youngest only a few months old. He had just found a job working as an auto paint technician. He made repairs to vehicles that had been in collisions and, being somewhat of a perfectionist, he became very skilled at his job. He was earning a good amount of money.

When he received the letter asking him to report for active duty, life was in an uproar. Mom was living in a new country, learning a new language, and dealing with three little children. On top of that, she had to find a way to earn a living to sustain the family if her husband was not going to be there. So, her mom came to live with her to help with the children while she worked as a seamstress. Life had suddenly become very hard for her.

My mother was a very determined and resourceful woman. She confided in God's promises. She asked my father's boss to write a letter indicating that he was an essential person at his job. She asked the pastor of the church to write a letter indicating that he was an outstanding member of the church. She wrote a letter herself, addressed to President Truman, asking him to please return her husband to her and her children, since he was the main source of income for the family and explaining her predicament. She attached the other two letters and sent them to the White House.

Her family and her church prayed that the letter would be well received and answered favorably.

My father spent three months in the Army learning the skills needed to be in the radio communications division. He was a quick learner with a preference for working with electronic equipment, and he enjoyed solving problems. His superiors were pleased with his progress and had plans for him. Although he missed his family, he had resigned himself to staying in the army to fulfill the required time. Meanwhile, my mom's letters were working in the hearts of the officials, and God's hand intervened. Three and a half months after he was called to join the army, he was given an honorable discharge from the US Army to come home and be with his family.

This experience helped my mother confront many seemingly impossible situations in life by claiming God's promises. The promise is there for us too! Do not hesitate. He is just waiting for us to ask so that He can bestow His blessings.

God's Favorite Child

BY ZORAIDA VELEZ-DELGADO

So he got up and went to his father
"But while he was still a long way off,
his father saw him and was filled with compassion for him;
he ran to his son, threw his arms around him and kissed him.

—LUKE 15:20, NIV

My grandmother had seven children. Seven! One day, as the grandkids were playing in the backyard, her sister, who didn't have children of her own, jokingly asked her which child was her favorite. I was about ten, old enough to be curious. Was it my mother? My uncle? The oldest? The youngest? My grandmother replied, "It depends. Usually, it is the one who needs me the most." *The one who needs me the most.* Imagine that!

Throughout the years, I witnessed that love in the way she described it. When my mother was ill, she received all the attention. When my uncle suffered from back pain, she was by his side. When God gave me the blessing of being a mother for the first time, I often wondered if I could ever love another baby the same way I loved my firstborn. Today, both of my kids ask me if they are my favorite, and I always answer that my favorite child is the dog, because it needs me the most.

BLESSINGS

I wonder how the father of the story of the lost son felt when his child came back home. When he saw him in the distance, I can imagine this father's heart sank as he saw how much suffering his son's eyes were showing, how his body was deteriorated by hunger, addiction, and loss. I love how Luke describes that moment in the story Jesus is sharing; the father saw the son while he was still a long way off, and with his heart pounding, he ran out, embraced him, and kissed him. No matter how dirty and smelly he was, his father kissed him.

Luke says that the son started a speech. "Father, I've sinned against God, before you, I don't deserve to be called your son ever again." And this is the best part of the story; the father wasn't listening. The father couldn't listen because, in that moment, all the son needed was love. No judgment, no harsh words, no reminders, no "I told you so." Just love.

We see how the oldest son felt betrayed, excluded, almost invisible. Of course, that did not mean the father didn't love him. It meant that in that moment, the youngest son needed to feel loved, so that is what the father gave.

As you count your blessings today, avoid looking at how God has blessed others versus how He has blessed you. God doesn't have "favorites." He sees the need, He sees our suffering, and He provides according to those needs. Pray today that God gives you not what you want but what your heart needs. It will change how you see His blessings upon you.

Is It Luck, Blessings, or Determination?

BY EVELYN RAQUEL DELGADO MARRERO

*And we know that in all things
God works for the good of those who love him,
who have been called according to his purpose.*

—ROMANS 8:28, NIV

When good things happen to me, am I lucky or blessed? I don't believe in luck to define happy outcomes. Luck has a lot to do with chance. The American Heritage Dictionary defines *luck* as 1. the chance of fortunate or adverse events happening. 2. to gain success or something desirable by chance.

So, if somebody steps on my bad toe, that's bad luck for sure. If I find a twenty-dollar bill on the sidewalk, that's good luck since I am always broke. Those things happened by chance. However, if I run in a marathon and I win first prize, am I lucky, blessed, or determined? You could say lucky if I had not spent the previous year training for the event. You could say blessed because I am healthy and have enough time to train. Nonetheless, that training and determination has to get most of the credit. If I get an A on a test, it has to do more with my preparation than with luck or blessings. It is a result of my determination to excel. God blessed me with the drive, and I prepared myself and dedicated myself to studying.

Blessings have a religious connotation; they are a product of God's interference to make good things happen. God grants us blessings every day. We have life, sunshine, food, health, a house to live in, and much, much more. God blesses us with all the good things we need to have a good life.

The Beatitudes are blessings that Jesus is offering us in order to have a connection with God. Blessed are the poor in spirit, for theirs is the kingdom of heaven. Blessed are those who mourn, for they shall be comforted. Blessed are the meek, for they shall inherit the earth. Blessed are those who hunger and thirst for righteousness, for they shall be satisfied. Jesus offers us blessings so that we can have a good life and the eternal life that He offers.

At the same time, if I want to attain a goal, I need determination in my heart to accomplish it. Anything that is worthwhile to do, God will help us achieve it—though not by luck or blessings, but by effort and determination. I know that without God I can't do anything. I need God to give me strength, to keep me focused, and to guide me if I am to reach my goals.

However, God's greatest blessing to mankind is His forgiveness of our sins. His mercy and forgiveness lead to our salvation and eternal life. We need to be determined to accept that blessing. Aren't we lucky to have such a loving God?

Knowing God

BY ANANDI MOSES

*For this reason, I also suffer these things;
but I am not ashamed, for I know whom I have believed,
and I am convinced that He is able to protect what
I have entrusted to Him until that day.*

—2 TIMOTHY 1:12, NASB

I still remember a conversation I had with my friend years ago. We both had young families and were discussing various topics regarding running our households. My friend had a business and shared with me how she had learned to trust God with her finances. "I never understood," she started. "Every time we made some good money, we always ran into some important expense that ate up our income." She would pray about it and ask God what she was doing wrong that her income was not blessed, and she always lost it to emergencies or other issues that came up. Like clockwork, right after they made a good business deal, they ended up having to shell out the income they made.

"I know the answer now," she continued. "It is not like whenever we made money, we had an emergency." It is that whenever God knew we were going to face something critical, He sent us the money just in time. I stood silently trying to understand the changed perception. The lesson I learned that day proved very important in my understanding of Christian life.

My friend had arrived at the secret of joyful Christian living. The insight she gained is what we call faith. Faith is trusting in the goodness of God. She had come to trust in the goodness of God and interpret her life experiences on that foundation. "Because God is good, and I have committed my finances to Him, I can be assured that everything that happens is in my best interests. Even though it seems like the money I earn is being lost, because God is good, it must be that God is providing to meet my need."

We often judge God based on our experiences. Blessings remind us of God's love, and trials make us wonder if God cares. Our experiences are not a judge of God's character. On the contrary, we should perceive our experiences based on the character of God. Our perceptions are muddled, but God's character is holy and unchanging.

A New Attitude

BY KAREEN WILSON

*Do not be conformed to this world,
but be transformed by the renewal of your mind,
that by testing you may discern what is the will of God,
what is good and acceptable and perfect.*

—ROMANS 12:2, ESV

To heal my body, I had surgery twice—one to remove my breast and the second to remove some of the lymph nodes where the cancer had spread. That second time was scary because I knew if this did not work, the cancer could spread to the rest of my body. I prayed and asked God to guide the surgeon and bless everyone trying to heal me.

When I was on that operating table, I transformed my mind. I had done months of meditation and prayer. I just had an "aha" moment while on the table. It finally clicked. I found the will of God, and I released all the pressure of the world and what it wants from me in terms of perfection. Any spiritual practice will bring you to the realization that you are enough. Through the Spirit, you can do all things and live in the grace of God.

My journey is my perfection. My childhood story, the ups and downs, and all of me, with my bald head, missing kidney, and breast changes. My marriage, children, and career changes make me unique and special. I own them and work them out with the Creator. I learned that for miracles to happen, there has to be an undesirable situation for God to bless. I have been able to see how God works miracles. That in itself is a blessing.

What situation in your life has allowed you to transform and see God in a whole new light?

Bravery

*Have I not commanded you?
Be strong and courageous. Do not be afraid;
do not be discouraged, for the Lord your
God will be with you wherever you go.*

—JOSHUA 1:9, NIV—

Comfort in This Time

BY SANDRA A. SERGEANT

> *[17] The dead do not praise the LORD,*
> *Nor any who go down into silence.*
> *[18] But we will bless the LORD*
> *From this time forth and forevermore.*
> *Praise the LORD!*
>
> —PSALM 115:17–18, NKJV

As a nurse, you are intimately involved in the end-of-life journey of patients and their families. While the work may be emotionally challenging, this verse serves as a reminder to find solace and purpose in caring for the living, providing comfort and support to those who remain. It also underscores the importance of gratitude for the gift of life and the opportunity to serve and make a difference in the lives of others, particularly during times of vulnerability and loss.

The chosen text in Psalms acknowledges that the dead cannot sing praises or actively participate in worship; it reminds us that death is an inevitable part of life and brings about a silence that cannot be reversed. This acknowledgment can serve as a sobering reminder of the finality of death and the importance of cherishing the time we have with loved ones while they are still alive. Indeed, the loss of a loved one is a profoundly challenging and emotional experience for families, regardless of the circumstances or age of the deceased.

While the verse emphasizes the limitations of the deceased in praising God, it also invites the living to continue extolling and worshiping the Lord. It encourages us to find solace and strength in our faith, even amidst the pain of loss, and to appreciate the gift of life we still possess.

Open My Eyes

BY SANDRA A. SERGEANT

When the servant of the man of God got up early the next morning and went outside, there were troops, horses, and chariots everywhere. "Oh, sir, what will we do now?" the young man cried to Elisha. "Don't be afraid!" Elisha told him. "For there are more on our side than on theirs!" Then Elisha prayed, "O Lord, open his eyes and let him see!" The Lord opened the young man's eyes, and when he looked up, he saw that the hillside around Elisha was filled with horses and chariots of fire.

—2 KINGS 6:15–17, NLT

Adversity is defined as a time of difficulty, challenge, or hardship. It represents unfavorable circumstances, obstacles, or setbacks, like the ones Elisha and his servant faced in this passage. To put things into context, the King of Aram sent horses, chariots, and a great army to surround the city where Elisha and his servant were staying.

Like many of us, when faced with adversity, especially one that threatens our security or well-being, our response is the same—fear and trepidation.

I am encouraged that Elisha's first response was, "Don't be afraid." Why? It is because fear is our biggest stumbling block when faced with any adversity. Then, Elisha reminded his servant that there were "more on our side than on theirs."

We often see only the immediate challenges and feel overwhelmed. The miraculous element is that we have a God who promises in Hebrews 13:5-6 (KJV), "I will never leave you nor forsake you." So, we say with confidence, "The Lord is my helper; I will not fear. What can man do to me?" This promise reassures and strengthens our confidence, allowing us to face adversities with faith and courage. It reminds us that we are not alone and that God will always help and guide us.

In times of adversity, I pray that God will open your eyes to see, like Elisha's servant, the entire landscape around filled with chariots of fire. Open my eyes, Lord!

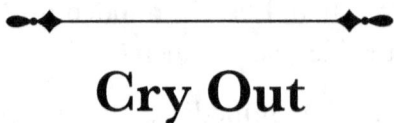

Cry Out

BY SANDRA A. SERGEANT

*I cry out to the Lord, I plead for the Lord's mercy,
I pour out my complaints before him and tell him
all my troubles. For I am overwhelmed,
and you alone know the way I should turn.*

—PSALM 142:1–3A, NLT

This Psalm was written at a time that showcased David's deep despair. He was hiding in a cave, fleeing from King Saul, who sought to kill him. David expresses a deep sense of isolation, distress, and the desperate need for God's intervention in our text. It reminds us that lamenting, deeply despairing, heartfelt expressions are not new emotions; what is essential is David's action plan during this time…he seeks God for deliverance.

I can relate David's emotional state to periods of utter despair, not knowing where to turn, who to talk to, or what to do. Those dark times seemingly have no end. But I am grateful that it is during those times when God carries us. The world offers many fixes when we are faced with daunting situations, but they are only temporary.

In retrospect, those times remind me of growing pains or the labor pains some women experience before holding their precious baby in their arms. During labor, the pain will never end; one minute seems like an hour. Then finally, with a forceful push, new life, birth, and newness happen. Painful episodes in life are similar in nature. The hard times seem never-ending, one event after another; through prayer, faith, and determination, we push through these challenging times and experience growth, renewal, and newness. In retrospect, we are stronger and better because of the experience. We join the Psalmist David to call upon the Lord with grateful hearts because only He knows how we should go.

The last stanza of "Footprints in the Sand" confirms this:

> He whispered, "My precious child,
> I love you and will never leave you.
> Never, ever, during your trials and testings.
> When you saw only one set of footprints,
> It was then that I carried you."

While these words do not appear in the Bible, and their authorship is even highly disputed, they remind us of God's faithfulness that carries us through challenging times. Utter despair? Cry out to the Lord!!

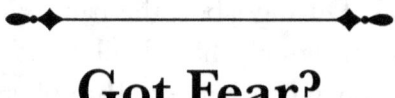

Got Fear?

BY SANDRA A. SERGEANT

*Fear not, for I am with you; Be not dismayed,
for I am your God. I will strengthen you,
Yes, I will help you, I will uphold you
with My righteous right hand.*

—ISAIAH 41:10, NKJV

Though composed of just four letters, its weight is greater than anything that we encounter in life. To deal with this formidable enemy of our lives—fear— someone coined this acronym:

False

Evidence

Appearing

Real

Let's explore to see if it is an accurate representation of the dreaded fear that impedes our path, blocks our progress, and prevents us from attaining all that God has in store for us.

As I review my own personal fears, much trepidation is involved when I have to make bold moves where there is no clear path to the outcome. I have discovered that most of what I worry about actually never occurs. On a deeper level, when I examine the elements that ignited my fear, I find they never really existed. My fear is often triggered by hearsay, lack of critical data, my own personal doubts, and lack of faith. I can attest that my fear was based on false evidence, but because our minds have been created with such precision, thoughts we focus on begin to take on the form of being a reality.

So, what do we do? Understand that fear of the unknown is not new to humanity. But here I rely totally on the promises that God has made to His children, you, and me. In Isaiah 43:1a–2 (NKJV), God gets really explicit in His promise, "Fear not, for I have redeemed you; I have called you by your name; You are Mine. When you pass through the waters, I will be with you; And through the rivers, they shall not overflow you. When you walk through the fire, you shall not be burned, Nor shall the flame scorch you."

I cannot begin to count how many times this text has brought me comfort and courage to move forward. Through it, I felt God's personal touch, for He did not promise I would not go through the floods but that I would not be overwhelmed. And yes, there will be fiery times, but He promises that I will not be burned, and the flames will not consume me.

In addition, our focus text contains an even bolder promise from God and further compounds His love for us. "Do not fear, for I am with you." That seals it for me. How about you? I would like to leave this closing thought that I saw on a postcard which reminds me "I am the daughter of a King who is not moved by the world. For my God is with me and goes before me. I do not fear for I am His."

Do You Believe in Ghosts???

BY EVELYN RAQUEL DELGADO MARRERO

> *But the Spirit explicitly says that in later times some will fall away from the faith, paying attention to deceitful spirits and teachings of demons.*
>
> —1 TIMOTHY 4:1, NASB

For five years before I retired, I worked as an assistant principal at an elementary school in Hartford, Connecticut. This school was built on the grounds of the Hartford Circus fire on July 6, 1944, during an afternoon performance of the Ringling Bros. and Barnum & Bailey Circus. It was attended by 6,000 to 8,000 people and more than 700 people were injured, although some people say that the records are not accurate and that the number of injuries was much higher. More than 167 people died, many being trampled to the ground and asphyxiated beneath piles of people who tripped over each other in their mad rush to escape. The best-known victim of the fire was a little girl known as "Little Miss 1565," so named after the number given to her by the city's makeshift morgue. In 1991, after almost 50 years, she was identified as Eleanor Emily Cook.

A memorial plaque was placed on the elementary school grounds to commemorate this devastating American tragedy. Due to this, many rumors are passed around at the school of ghosts inhabiting the corridors. Custodians of the building got used to strange things happening after school hours; they have even reported that, after cleaning the classrooms and locking the doors, they would return to find the doors unlocked and open on their own. They spoke of times when water would gush out of faucets they had ensured were tightly shut off. And time after time, custodians reported hearing the piano playing music alone in the auditorium.

On one occasion, I was in the cafeteria with the students during lunchtime. A little girl about nine years old was not feeling well and asked me to take her to the nurse. We went to the nurse and, on our way back to the cafeteria, I decided to take a little shortcut through the auditorium instead of going the long way through the hallway to get back to the cafeteria. I held the girl's hand as we walked through the dark auditorium. I had taken this route many times before, but on this occasion, we heard the piano playing in the dark and the whooshing sound of the wind, even though there were no windows in the auditorium. The little girl held my hand tightly and murmured, "Miss, this is scary." I agreed with her; it was a scary moment, even though I am a grown woman with a strong faith in God. I know that Satan desperately seeks to deceive even the most faithful people.

Deceitful spirits are always lurking in the shadows, looking to deceive us and keep us from following God. These spirits try to seduce us from our positions of stability to positions of instability to capture us in their web of lies. We must be alert, realizing that the devil uses deceit to distract us from the truth.

We are reminded in 1 John 4:4, that "He who is in us is greater than he who is in the world." We serve a God who is all-powerful and all-knowing, and who protects His children from the snares of the evil one. Call on His name and He will rescue you.

Breaking My Streak

BY BRYANA WILSON

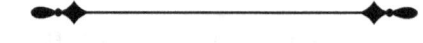

> *"I have told you these things, so that in me you may have peace. In this world, you will have trouble. But take heart! I have overcome the world."*
>
> —JOHN 16:33, NIV

I hadn't cried in school since eighth grade. When the tears came, I sat in chorus class upset over friend issues and drama (nothing unusual for middle school). I sat with my head down as I felt my mascara run. That day, it took over three hours to console me. After that fiasco, I told myself I wouldn't cry in school again. I bragged about that fact. I even boasted proudly that I didn't cry in school. In the spring of my junior year, I only had one year left before officially saying I had never cried on the grounds of my high school. However, on the first day of May, I cried in front of my track coach at 11 a.m. My streak was broken.

The funny thing was that I wasn't expecting to cry that day. But to be honest, who expects to cry at school? May 1st was a sunny spring day. Walking into school, I told my friends, "It's a new month!" and "About a month left of school!" I was overwhelmingly happy, which was weird because the night before, I hadn't been.

I had recently quit track and field with minimal warning to my coaches. I joined my town's team in 5th grade and was running cross country, indoor, and outdoor track. Over the years, I fell out of love with the sport. By my freshman year, I hated the sport, but I wouldn't quit. *"The Wilsons don't quit"* stuck with me. *"Bryana doesn't quit,"* I told myself. I reminded myself that I had only one more season before I never had to step on a track again.

When my friend called and told me that my coach (well, ex-coach) wanted to talk to me, I froze. I knew I hadn't ended my track career on good terms, but I also wanted to avoid the conversation that I knew was coming about *why* I had quit.

When I arrived, he commented, "I have tissues here for a reason." That was all it took to make the tears begin falling.

Something is humbling about crying at eleven in the morning in front of someone, especially in front of someone who has known you since sixth grade. He was my track coach, middle school swim coach, NHS advisor, and algebra and calculus teacher. He knew me and knew how much something must have bothered me for me to cry in front of him.

I believe a false narrative surrounds being upset. Many say to trust in God or just to be happy. But that isn't feasible. Jesus cried. He felt sadness, depression, and anger. So why can't we feel those same things? It is essential to feel your emotions. It is human. Don't push away sadness. Embrace it, find the cause, and learn to grow from it. God knows life isn't easy and peaceful. The important thing is to know that you aren't alone.

For Such a Time as This

BY KAREEN WILSON

> *When Esther's words were reported to Mordecai, he sent back this answer: "Do not think that because you are in the king's house you alone of all the Jews will escape. For if you remain silent at this time, relief and deliverance for the Jews will arise from another place, but you and your father's family will perish. And who knows but that you have come to your royal position for such a time as this?"*
>
> —ESTHER 4:12–14, NIV

Can you think of a time when you were put into a position where you had a significant impact?

The civil rights movement's story of Rosa Parks refusing to give her bus seat to a white person just to comply with racially motivated laws is very well-known and oft-repeated. Rosa Parks, however, was not the first woman to refuse to give up her seat on a bus. In 1944, Irene Morgan Kirkaldy was traveling on a Greyhound bus in Virginia when she was told to give up her seat to a white couple. Then came fifteen-year-old Claudette Colvin in 1955. These individuals stood firm and stayed in their seats. Their defiance created the genesis of a movement. They were placed in those situations "for such a time as this."

Their stories remind me of Esther who was a beautiful woman born in a time when women had few choices. Being chosen as queen to a king who had exiled the former queen because she would not "dance" for his guests must have been difficult. Easter was raised in a blessed Jewish home that upheld values and virtue. She was then thrust into a superficial royal life that was the exact opposite of her past. Through it all, she must have often wondered, *What is my purpose?*

She was positioned to save a whole race of people. The pain of being forced to marry a man who would not value her made her a hero. God has the power to place Esther (you) in a situation that will make a significant impact on God. Her bravery and intelligence (your abilities) can solve any problem. Believe in yourself and your relationship with the Lord. You were created for such a time as this.

Thank God for all the problematic situations in which you find yourself—for they may turn into a way to make a difference for Christ.

In Times of Adversity

BY SANDRA A. SERGEANT

> *David now stayed in the strongholds of the wilderness and in the hill country of Ziph. Saul hunted him day after day, but God didn't let Saul find him.*
>
> —1 SAMUEL 23:14, NLT

This story is a recounting of King Saul's tireless pursuit of David. This is not a case of revenge on Saul's part, for David did no wrong. Saul relentlessly pursued him because he was consumed by jealousy and driven by his desire to harm David. Can you relate to this story when you are hated and attacked for no reason other than someone or some group deciding to make you their target and setting out to destroy you by tarnishing your character?

The story reminds us that God did not allow David to be found despite Saul's best efforts. In the face of adversity, God can make way for us where there seems to be no way. He can shield us from harm, guide our steps, and keep us hidden from those who seek to bring us down.

It is essential to note that David's deliverance did not come instantly. He spent years in the wilderness, facing numerous challenges while hiding from Saul. Yet, through it all, God's timing was perfect. Sometimes, we may grow weary and impatient, wondering when relief will come. But in the waiting, we can trust that God is at work orchestrating His plans for our lives. He is preparing, strengthening, and molding us into the women He wants us to be. Today, let us surrender our timelines to Him and trust that His timing is always perfect.

In the wilderness seasons of our lives—times of isolation, uncertainty, or difficulty—God remains with us. His loving presence surrounds us. He promises to shelter us under His wings and shield us from harm. Today, let us lean on His strength, trust in His timing, and embrace the truth that, just as He preserved David, He will faithfully guide and protect us through every season of life.

Pay It Forward (Part 1)

BY KAREEN WILSON

When you do something for someone else, don't call attention to yourself. You've seen them in action, I'm sure—'playactors' I call them—treating prayer meetings and street corner alike as a stage, acting compassionate as long as someone is watching, playing to the crowds. They get applause, true, but that's all they get. When you help someone out, don't think about how it looks. Just do it—quietly and unobtrusively. That is the way your God, who conceived you in love, working behind the scenes, helps you out.

—MATTHEW 6:3–4, MSG

Pay it forward. It is the name of a Hollywood movie and a common cliché phrase. We have heard it many times, but what does it really mean? "Pay it forward" means performing an act of kindness for someone, hoping the recipient will do something wonderful for someone else. In our world of social media where people are valued by their "friends and likes," we desire to find a way to spread real love. We hope that a small act of goodness will cause ripple effects and that more and more acts of kindness with thrive in the world. Based on a study in the *Journal of Social Psychology*, people who performed one random act of kindness daily for ten days experienced a significant increase in overall happiness than those who did not.

James Fowler, an associate professor of political science at the University of California in San Diego, and *Nicholas Christakis*, a Harvard sociology professor, studied people who played a "public good game." The results showed that when one person gave money to help others, the recipients were likelier to give away money in the future. The domino effect continued as more people were swept up in the tide of kindness and cooperation. In short, Fowler said, "You don't go back to being your old selfish self."

What if you could trace your act of kindness and see how it impacted the world? I once saw how my act of kindness caused a ripple effect of goodness. It is totally true, but it sounds like a fiction novel.

What random act of kindness have you done for someone else?

(To be continued)

Pay It Forward (Part 2)

BY KAREEN WILSON

The generous man will be prosperous,
And he who waters will himself be watered.

—PROVERBS 11:25, NASB

Every year at our practice, we forgive two families of their debt to the practice. One year, we started a wave of goodwill that is magical. Our patient Julie, had a terrible toothache that resulted in a root canal treatment (RCT) and crown being done in our office. She was going through a divorce from a less-than-wonderful man, she was losing her house in West Hartford, she was penniless, and, on top of that, she showed up in our office in pain. We treated her, and after it was all said and done, she owed us $1,147.

Julie came in a few months after treatment for a routine follow-up exam. When she was finished, she pulled out her checkbook and begged for forgiveness, saying she knew she owed us money, that she could only pay $100, and that she would pay us as she could. Our team member pulled up her account and told her that she didn't owe anything. She was adamant that she did owe a bill, so the employee called me.

I approached Julie and asked if she had received my letter. She said no, that she hadn't gone through her mail because she had been busy dealing with the aftermath of her divorce and her ill mother. When I told her that we had forgiven her debt and that we only asked her to "pay it forward," Julie started to cry. She was so grateful, and she said she had a friend who had just lost her daughter, and she was going to put the money towards the funeral expenses. We thought that was that and the end of the story.

Two weeks later, Julie didn't show up for her appointment, and I was upset! I had just forgiven her debt of more than a thousand dollars, and she didn't show up for an appointment. Then, a few weeks later, she came in to apologize for missing her appointment. She told us that the day before her appointment, she received a phone call from the nursing home where her mother lived. Her mother was dying, and she needed to fly to Seattle immediately. She hopped on the next flight, but her mother died while she was on her way to Seattle. I immediately felt bad for getting upset about a missed appointment, but she proceeded to tell me a story that made me feel incredible.

Can you think of a time that you misjudged another's actions?

Pay It Forward, Part 3

BY KAREEN WILSON

*Be kind and compassionate to one another,
forgiving each other, just as in Christ God forgave you.*

—EPHESIANS 4:32, NIV

When Julie arrived in Seattle, she had to settle family affairs. She was an only child, and her father had passed away two years prior. She was a little nervous about what she would find because her family was so frugal; her parents seemed to have no money. She wondered where she was going to find the money to bury her mother.

As she did a little research, she discovered that her parents were very wise with their money. Their apparent frugality was just that they saved money instead of spending everything they made. They had a large investment portfolio, and most of their investments were in a little company (at least back then) named Amazon. Her parents were rich. Julie would never have to worry about money again. In fact, her kids, grandchildren, and many great-grandchildren would never have to worry about money again.

While in Seattle, she went to the local Applebee's to grab dinner with a friend. While there, she became friendly with their waitress and discovered that she was a single mother working two jobs and taking the bus to and from her job because her car had died. Julie said, "I thought of my mother's two-year-old, almost brand-new Subaru sitting in the driveway unused. I told her I had a car for sale that needed a starter, but she could look at it. The waitress said her boyfriend was a mechanic and that she would love to come take a look.

When they met and the waitress said she wanted to buy the car, Julie said to me, "I thought of you, Kareen. I remember you saying to pay it forward. Pay it forward. So, when that waitress asked how much I wanted for the car, I told her ten dollars."

The story seems to end there, but this is actually where it gets really interesting. When Julie was back in Connecticut organizing some paperwork from closing her mother's affairs, she could not believe her eyes. She looked at the sales receipt for the car and the death certificate from the nursing home. Remember how the waitress said that she worked two jobs? Her other job was as a CNA at a nursing home. She was the nursing assistant who was with Julie's mother when she died.

Pay it forward. You never know how that drop of kindness can cause a ripple effect that spreads worldwide. Mother Teresa is documented as saying, "I alone cannot change the world, but I can cast a stone across waters to create many ripples." Go cast your stones.

Hyper Connectivity?

BY KELLEY MATIERIENE

*So continuing daily with one accord in the temple,
and breaking bread from house to house,
they ate their food with gladness and simplicity of heart.*

—ACTS 2:26, NKJV

I woke up with a long to-do list, but I wasn't ready to get out of bed.

I reminded myself that if I didn't get started early, I would never be able to tackle all the things I had to do for the day. Then my phone rang. I could see that the call was from my best friend from college, and for a split second, I considered not answering. Don't get me wrong. I love talking with her. I just knew we hadn't talked in a while, so I was pretty sure the conversation could go on for hours. That was the problem! What about my long to-do list and what I needed to accomplish that day or at least start my week off with a shorter to-do list?

I picked up the phone, and we chatted, caught up, and three hours later let each other go with plans to catch up again. In a society where individualism and productivity are promoted, where

Instagram, Facebook, and TikTok are constantly reminding us of what others are accomplishing or how many friends or followers we have, are we missing the mark?

In a world of hyperconnectivity, my friend and I lamented about feeling disconnected, about not truly investing in relationships with friends at the level we desired as we worked our jobs, started our families, or even decided on where we would live. It's something we realize later in life that we didn't value, and, to our dismay and slight disappointment, maybe it was more important than we realized. In a world that is hyper-connected, so many of us are more unconnected than ever.

In the first few chapters of Acts, we get a sense that the early church was of God and daily connecting with one another. The words *one accord* and *daily* are used, which gives a sense of consistently being together. I realize that my community now may not look like the community in the Book of Acts. People are busy, and who will tackle that to-do list if you don't? But creating a circle of like-minded individuals who pray for you and hold you up in tough times is becoming increasingly more important. Due to our global abilities, being intentional about building community has to be something in which we invest our time and energy. It's not until something happens that we realize just how key it is to be mentally and spiritually grounded.

Today, think about one or two people with whom you want to continue to build community. Then write down three ways you will continue to foster relationships with those individuals.

Dinner with the Enemy

BY SANDRA A. SERGEANT

As the Aramean army advanced toward him, Elisha prayed, "O Lord, please make them blind." So the Lord struck them with blindness as Elisha had asked. Then Elisha went out and told them, "You have come the wrong way! This isn't the right city! Follow me, and I will take you to the man you are looking for." And he led them to the city of Samaria. As soon as they had entered Samaria, Elisha prayed, "O Lord, now open their eyes and let them see." So the Lord opened their eyes, and they discovered that they were in the middle of Samaria. When the king of Israel saw them, he shouted to Elisha, "My father, should I kill them? Should I kill them?" "Of course not!" Elisha replied. "Do we kill prisoners of war? Give them food and drink and send them home again to their master." So the king made a great feast for them and then sent them home to their master. After that, the Aramean raiders stayed away from the land of Israel.

—2 KINGS 6:18–23, NLT

Reflecting on the lessons from 2 Kings 6, I am continually amazed by how God handles challenging situations and their relevance in our everyday lives. Today's passage highlights the story in which Elisha's servant is afraid due to the surrounding army. Elisha prays for his eyes to be opened to see that God is on their side, providing reassurance and dispelling fear.

This sets the stage for the verses mentioned above, which depict how God directs Elisha to handle the threatening enemies whose sole purpose is to destroy them.

God guides Elisha to pray for the enemies to be struck blind. While we may not pray for harm upon our perceived enemies, the crucial lesson here is the power of prayer. God answers Elisha and allows him to lead the blinded enemies into the hands of their opponents in Samaria. Then, Elisha prays again, and their eyes are opened, revealing their location in the enemy camp. This miraculous intervention demonstrates God's sovereignty over their situation.

Instead of responding violently or in retaliation, Elisha instructs the king to prepare a feast for the enemies and send them home. This act of hospitality and kindness towards those who sought harm defies human reasoning but showcases the transformative power of God's love and mercy. It is a reminder that there are situations only God can handle, and His ways often transcend human understanding.

Drawing from the story of Elisha, Proverbs 25:21–22 reinforces the principle of responding to enemies with kindness. It suggests that if our enemies hunger, we should provide them with food; if they are thirsty, offer them water. This strategy of responding to enemies with acts of kindness and love showcases the true character of God, who is merciful and loving.

May we strive to reflect God's character in our interactions with others, responding with love, kindness, and mercy even when faced with adversity or hostility.

Communion with God

*As a deer pants for flowing streams,
so pants my soul for you, O God.*

—PSALM 42:1B, ESV—

Spiritual Heights

BY ZORAIDA VELEZ-DELGADO

> ^{14}*You are the light of the world.*
> *A town built on a hill cannot be hidden.*
> ^{15}*Neither do people light a lamp and put it under a bowl.*
> *Instead, they put it on its stand, and it gives light to*
> *everyone in the house.* ^{16}*In the same way, let your*
> *light shine before others, that they may see your*
> *good deeds and glorify your Father in heaven.*
>
> —MATTHEW 5: 14–16, NIV

Getting ready to work is stressful for me, and the reason might not be what you think. I am a career coach, and a leadership development Jedi, so understanding where people come from is at the center of what I do, and I love it! I tend to be very patient with people, try to be outward when others are inward, and I like to listen to what others have to say. So, I love my job, but I despise traffic. So, all that education, experience, and people-loving skills wash away when I am driving to work.

The problem is not that others are driving recklessly; the problem is the way I react to it and, to be honest, I am not proud of my actions. It is hard for me to understand why people see a construction sign about an upcoming closed lane and don't move to the open lane until the very last minute because they can't wait in line like the rest of us.

I also despise it when drivers honk their horns when the traffic light turns green. I also get annoyed at those who use the emergency lane as a regular lane to pass other cars. I have a whole list of things I despise while driving. It's a hereditary trait. My mother used to fight with other drivers… but with the windows up. One time, someone started honking behind her, and she began opening her window. I was just sure she was going to insult the guy, but she simply placed her hand on top of her car and said, "You can go over me. I dare you." I still laugh when I think of that day.

Recently, I was driving to work when I saw a person driving carelessly behind me. Other drivers started moving to the side of the road to leave space for the car to maneuver around them, so I did the same. I caught a glimpse of the driver showing the magical finger to the other complaining drivers, and then it happened. He hit a car that was waiting to turn left. It was a sad moment for the poor guy who got hit out of nowhere and for the reckless driver, because it was, after all, a sad ending to his stupidity.

When I drove by the accident, I noticed this bumper sticker on the car that caused the accident: "Do you follow Jesus this closely?" A sticker will not speak as loudly as actions. Believers don't need to put Jesus on their t-shirts, key chains, or bumper stickers. Believers need to act like Christ, speak love like Christ, and even drive like Christ.

Miserable Comforters

BY ZORAIDA VELEZ-DELGADO

> "I will teach you about the power of God;
> the ways of the Almighty I will not conceal.
> You have all seen this yourselves.
> Why then this meaningless talk?
>
> —JOB 27:11–12, NIV

For many people, COVID-19 was just a year-long isolation period that ended with a new way of seeing life. For others, COVID-19 decimated their family. Many lost multiple family members: children lost both parents, grandparents, and even siblings. I stopped watching the news because it became unbearable to listen to so many sad stories. Pastors started to preach about the power of God. It is easy to believe in God when everything is going well. But what happens when we lose everything?

The story of Job came to mind during that time. Like many people across the world, Job lost his family, fortune, and health. Three of his friends came to visit him in his misery. His friends had Job's best interests in mind when they arrived. They really wanted to support him, so they sat with him for seven days and seven nights without uttering a word. They just mourned with him.

Then Job's humanity came through; he broke the silence, spoke up, and cursed his fate. This is the man who had spoken words that encouraged those who were about to quit, words that had put stumbling people on their feet and imparted fresh hope to people about to collapse. (Job 4:1–6) But now, Job is on the receiving end, and it is his turn to receive encouraging words. Sadly, that is not what happened. In fact, in chapter 16, Job calls his friends a bunch of "miserable comforters." Ouch!

Have you ever been a "miserable comforter?"

Asking Job if he had done something deserving of his misery was not comforting. These were not asked to judge Job; they were supposed to comfort him. Job responds that, no matter what has happened to him, "as long as I draw breath, and for as long as God breathes life into me, I refuse to say one word that isn't true. I refuse to confess to any charge that's false. There is no way I'll ever agree to your accusations. I'll not deny my integrity even if it costs me my life."

Wow! God's power had not left Job. If death was looking for Job, it was going to find him by God's presence.

I wonder how many Covid patients had to face judgment from their friends for getting sick. How many went to rest in spiritual pain because they were surrounded by miserable comforters? Can we take a moment to reflect on our own comforting style? Are we able to offer hope versus damnation? Are we able to instill peace versus spiritual war? Can we inspire trust, forgiveness, and love? After all, we all serve a Mighty God, one we can trust with all of our hearts, one that whispers in our ears, "Be still and know that I am God."

Needed Or Wanted

BY TANIA FUENTES-DAVITT

> *This is how God showed his love among us:*
> *He sent his one and only Son into the world*
> *that we might live through him.*
> *This is love: not that we loved God,*
> *but that he loved us and sent his Son as*
> *an atoning sacrifice for our sins*

—1 JOHN 4:9–10, NIV

I hate not being productive and feeling useless. If I go a whole day without getting anything done, it makes me feel worthless. I am used to being very active in helping others around me, either in my church family, actual family, or friend circle. In the middle of 2020, I went from being very active in my church preaching and teaching and helping out wherever I could, to doing nothing and being very isolated from those around me. It was very jarring to my sense of identity. I went from feeling like God had a use and a plan for me, to feeling like an island floating out in the middle of nowhere. How could God use me now? Was I even important to God if I couldn't do anything important for Him?

It was around this time that I was reading the book *A Heavenly Man*. This book talks about how God worked in China in the midst of persecution and oppression against Christians. Many of the believers in China were imprisoned for their faith. For me, reading this book, I thought of being in prison as being the worst thing that could happen to a Christian. The author, however, through his experience with God, saw things differently. He liked to call imprisonment "God's training ground." To explain why, he describes his own imprisonment and how God drew near to him and showed His love for him in this environment that was free from other distractions. By having to completely rely on God in the harsh conditions, he developed a faith in and relationship with God that could not be shaken.

Through this man's experiences as well as my own, I was impressed with the thought that God doesn't need us. He doesn't need us to work to meet His requirements. He doesn't need our grand gestures or for us to be getting everything we think we need to get done every day. God wants us. Need and want are very different. God wants an intimate relationship with us more than He wants us to be out working for Him. There are so many great men in the Bible who spent many years in relatively obscure positions with little influence. Moses was a farmer, David tended sheep, and John the Baptist was in the wilderness. Little is written about the long periods of time that these men spent building a relationship with God. Even Jesus spent many hours alone with God in prayer, even though He could have been out preaching and teaching and healing. He saw that this time alone with God was just as necessary and vital.

Remember that God *wants* you…He doesn't *need* you. He wants to have an intimate relationship with you. Are you prioritizing time with God above time working for God? How is God calling you to spend more time with Him in your day-to-day life?

The Power of Stillness: Discerning God's Whisper (Part 1)

BY AVALEY FRANCES MATIERIENE

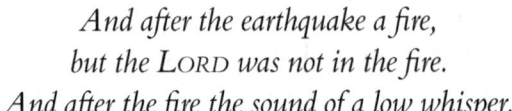

And after the earthquake a fire,
*but the L*ORD *was not in the fire.*
And after the fire the sound of a low whisper.

—1 KINGS 19:12, ESV

In the chaos and busyness of life, it can be challenging to discern the voice of God amidst the noise and distractions that surround us. We long to hear His guidance and receive His messages, but our minds are filled with the clamor of responsibilities, worries, and the constant buzz of the world. However, within the stillness lies the key to unlocking the whispers of God's voice.

Let us reflect upon the encounter of the prophet Elijah on Mount Horeb, where he sought to hear from God. In the midst of powerful natural phenomena—a fierce earthquake and a blazing fire—the Lord was not found. Instead, God chose to reveal Himself in a gentle whisper, a still, small voice that followed the tumultuous events. This serves as a powerful reminder that God's voice often speaks softly, yet profoundly, in moments of tranquility.

To discern God's voice, we must intentionally quiet our hearts and minds, creating space for stillness in our lives. It is within this sacred hush that we position ourselves to hear the gentle whispers of His guidance, encouragement, and instruction. Just as we tune our ears to listen attentively to a faint melody, we must tune our spirits to the whisperings of the Holy Spirit.

Carve out time each day to retreat to a quiet place—a sanctuary where you can be alone with God. In this intimate space, cast aside distractions and busyness. Allow the world's noise to fade into the background as you turn your focus solely toward the presence of God. Embrace the silence and solitude, inviting His Spirit to permeate every corner of your being.

Trust that in the midst of the quietness, God's voice will resonate within your soul, bringing clarity, direction, and comfort. As you seek His guidance, immerse yourself in His Word, the Bible. The Scriptures are a lamp to our feet and a light to our path (Psalm 119:105). They provide a reliable confirmation of God's messages and principles. Align your thoughts and decisions with the eternal truths found within its pages.

(To be continued)

The Power of Stillness: Discerning God's Whisper (Part 2)

BY AVALEY FRANCES MATIERIENE

> *And after the earthquake a fire,*
> *but the LORD was not in the fire.*
> *And after the fire the sound of a low whisper.*
>
> —1 KINGS 19:12, ESV

In the stillness, you may experience various ways in which God confirms His voice. He may bring a sense of peace that surpasses understanding, granting you an assurance that His message aligns with His will. He may provide confirmation through the wise counsel of trusted believers, whose words resonate with what you have heard from God. Additionally, God may use the circumstances and events of your environment to affirm the path He is leading you on.

Yet, discerning God's voice does not always come instantly or without challenges. It requires patience, perseverance, and unwavering faith. Sometimes, it takes time to fully grasp the meaning of the messages we receive. We may question if what we heard was truly from God, especially when circumstances do not align with our expectations.

During these moments of uncertainty, remember the words of Isaiah 55:8-9, "For my thoughts are not your thoughts, neither are your ways my ways, declares the Lord. For as the heavens are higher than the earth, so are my ways higher than your ways and my thoughts than your thoughts." Trust in God's sovereignty and divine wisdom. Even if His response differs from what you anticipated, have faith that His plans are far greater and more intricate than our limited understanding can comprehend.

Embrace the journey of discerning God's voice. As you persistently seek Him, remaining open to His whispers, you will experience a deepened intimacy with the Creator of the universe. Your relationship with Him will flourish as you learn to recognize and obey His voice in the stillness. May you find solace, guidance, and unwavering faith in the gentle whispers of God's voice as you cultivate the discipline of stillness in your life.

Cultivating a Grateful Heart

BY AVALEY FRANCS MATIERIENE

*Do not be anxious about anything,
but in every situation, by prayer and petition,
with thanksgiving, present your requests to God.*

—PHILIPPIANS 4:6, NIV

In the journey of life, I recently embarked on the practice of keeping a gratitude journal. As I intentionally cultivated a grateful heart, something remarkable unfolded within me. I began to experience a profound sense of contentment and peace.

Through the power of gratitude, the grip of depression and anxiety that had weighed me down started to loosen. The act of counting my blessings and expressing thankfulness lifted the heavy burden of negativity from my shoulders.

In Philippians 4:6, we are reminded not to be anxious about anything but to present our requests to God with prayer, petition, and thanksgiving. Gratitude is an essential component of this instruction. It redirects our focus from worry to appreciation, from fear to faith.

When we approach God with gratitude, we acknowledge His goodness and faithfulness in our lives. We recognize His provision and care, even in the midst of challenges. Gratitude opens our hearts to His peace, knowing that He is in control and that He has our best interests at heart.

As we continue to cultivate a grateful heart, let us make it a daily practice to offer our prayers and petitions to God, accompanied by thanksgiving. May gratitude be our companion on the journey, uplifting our spirits, and bringing us closer to the source of true contentment and peace.

Let us be encouraged by the transformation that gratitude can bring. It has the power to lift our spirits, ease our anxieties, and fill our hearts with joy. As we express gratitude to God, may we experience His loving presence and find solace in His promises.

Embracing God's Wake-Up Call

BY *AVALEY FRANCES MATIERIENE*

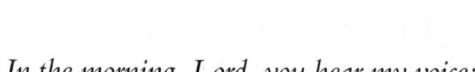

*In the morning, Lord, you hear my voice;
in the morning I lay my requests before
you and wait expectantly.*

—PSALM 5:3, NIV

As I reflect on my journey of faith, I am continually amazed by the ways in which God reveals Himself in the smallest details of my life. One such revelation occurs every morning as I reach for my trusty alarm clock. It's a simple act that holds a profound message: God's presence and guidance extend even to the ringing of an alarm. Over time, as my relationship with God has deepened, I've noticed a beautiful pattern emerge. Whenever I set an intention to rise at a specific time and diligently set my alarm accordingly, a remarkable occurrence takes place—I awaken naturally, often a good ten to fifteen minutes before the alarm is set to go off. In these sacred moments, I can't help but feel as if God Himself is gently nudging me awake, whispering, "I am the one who wakes you up, not the alarm clock." It is a profound reminder that God is intimately involved in the details of my life, even in something as mundane as waking up each morning. This divine wake-up call has taught me a valuable lesson about trust and surrender. It serves as a gentle invitation to lay my requests before the Lord and wait expectantly, just as the psalmist declares in Psalm 5:3. When I surrender my plans and desires to Him, I am met with His perfect timing and guidance. In those quiet moments before dawn, I find solace in knowing that God is faithful to His promises. He hears my voice, listens to my prayers, and aligns my waking moments with His divine purpose. It is a testament to His unfailing love and the depth of His care for His children.

As I continue to cultivate a closer relationship with God, I am reminded of His presence in every aspect of my life. He is not confined to grand gestures or extraordinary moments; rather, He reveals Himself in seemingly ordinary occurrences, reminding me of His constant presence and watchful eye. In a world filled with constant distractions and busyness, let us not overlook the gentle reminders of God's presence in our lives. Pause, reflect, and offer gratitude for His faithfulness and His intimate involvement in even the smallest details. May we find reassurance in the knowledge that our loving Father is always near, ready to guide, protect, and awaken us to the beauty of His plans. As we surrender our desires to Him, may we experience His perfect timing and the peace that passes all understanding.

Scripture assures us that God is not only the keeper of time but also the orchestrator of our lives. So, in each wakeful moment, may we find comfort in His divine presence, knowing that we are held securely in His loving hands.

What Do You Seek?

BY ANANDI MOSES

And Jesus turned and saw them following, and said to them, "What are you seeking?"

—JOHN 1:38A, NASB

We are created to move towards something. We feel satisfied when we know the purpose of our actions. We may not even be aware, but our hearts are fixed on things, and we work towards them. Jesus once asked two men, "What are you seeking?" It is important to God what we are moving towards, what we seek after, and what drives us. The answer to this question can determine our eternal destiny and the quality of our life here on earth. It is worth our time to contemplate this question.

Moses in the Bible was a great leader. God saw him fit to lead a whole nation of people for forty years in a journey to find their freedom and home. Moses had a huge responsibility that he worked to fulfill. On the surface, it may seem like that was his goal desire, and purpose, but if we look closer, we will find where his heart was really fixed.

At the burning bush, Moses asked God, "What is your name?" During his conversation with God in the wilderness, he asked,

COMMUNION WITH GOD

"Please let me know Your ways so that I may know You" (Exodus 33:13, NASB). He said, "If Your presence does not go with us, do not lead us up from here" (Exodus 33:15, NASB). He asked God, "Please, show me Your glory" (Exodus 33:18, NASB). Time and again, we can see through Moses' petitions that his heart was fixed on knowing God. He was seeking God Himself and His presence.

Reading the book of Psalms, we can easily see the center of David's life. He said, "One thing I have asked from the Lord, that I shall seek…To behold the beauty of the Lord" (Psalm 27:4, NASB). His heart was fixed on the person of God. He writes, "Delight yourself in the Lord; And He will give you the desires of your heart" (Psalm 37:4, NASB).

These giants of faith in the Bible had a heart that was seeking and desiring after God Himself and not just what He provides. Jesus said, "But seek first His kingdom and His righteousness, and all these things will be provided to you" (Matthew 6:33, NASB). Like Moses and the Psalmist, pray for a glimpse of God's beauty and glory. God will help you fix your heart on Him. Then, all your other desires will be sanctified. God will reveal Himself to you, and all your desires will be fulfilled.

Auto Subscription

BY KAREEN WILSON

*Be strong and very courageous.
Be careful to obey all the law my servant Moses gave you;
do not turn from it to the right or to the left,
that you may be successful wherever you go.*

—JOSHUA 1:7, NIV

I just canceled a subscription. It was on autopay, and I realized I was not using the service. We are living in a subscription economy. You receive a monthly service or product, and money is automatically taken from your account and put into the hands of the provider. From Netflix and Amazon Prime to vitamins and health products, many things in our lives show up on autopilot.

While subscriptions are a convenient way to live, consider your subscription with God. It doesn't cost anything but your time and commitment to daily education in God's Word.

Think of the benefits! A daily subscription to God's Word provides education on living a whole and blessed life with renewed strength.

In our verse today, God provides a promise. Keep the law always on your lips and meditate on it day and night. The result is that you will be successful wherever you go and whatever you do.

How do we do this? Read God's Word. Keep praying. This will allow you to be like Christ and seek success in things that will bless God and your fellow man. Connecting with God will build wisdom that allows you to discern greatness and not shallow and selfish ideals.

Build your life around a subscription that costs you nothing. A daily, monthly, and yearly connection to the wisdom of God will bring you a life of joy!

The Presence of Jesus Christ

BY KIERRA WILSON

*For where two or three are gathered together in My name,
I am there in the midst of them.*

—MATTHEW 18:20, NKJV

I have been attending Camp Winnekeag, an Adventist summer camp since I was three years old. I have never felt closer to God than when I spent my time at camp. During worship services, we sing song after song, praising the Lord. The created memories are incredible and truly enhance my time at camp. I even remember songs sung years ago and am still able to sing the lyrics word for word. It's like no other feeling in the world when I am singing with my friends at camp, often moving me to tears. The feeling of so many people coming together to worship our Lord is incredible. Matthew 18:20 assures of His presence, and I can sense His presence as we sing praises. From the year I first attended camp by myself at age six, I knew it was where I belonged. I knew that spending time with others and worshiping Christ together was where I felt most at home. Looking at this Bible verse, I've begun to understand why. I feel most at home because Jesus is there with me.

After my tenth year of attending summer camp, I decided to be baptized and gave my life to God. At the end of the two weeks I spent at camp, I felt closer to God than ever. Being baptized was probably one of the best decisions I have ever made, for I have never been happier than I was in that moment. The presence of Jesus Christ is a powerful and wonderful feeling. It's important not only to spend personal time with God but also to worship Him with others.

What experiences in life bring you closer to God?

Divine Connections— Guided by Grace

BY AVALEY FRANCES MATIERIENE

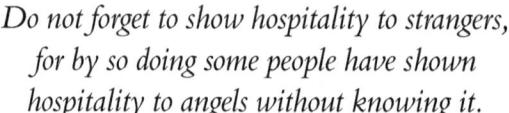

Do not forget to show hospitality to strangers, for by so doing some people have shown hospitality to angels without knowing it.

—HEBREWS 13:2, NIV

As an exchange student in the Philippines, I embarked on a transformative journey to attend a summit in Thailand alongside my fellow exchange companions. Little did I know that, amidst the unfamiliarity of a foreign land, we would encounter a Thai gentleman whose presence would become a profound example of divine connections and the power of hospitality.

This stranger, though not associated with our exchange program, recognized us as foreigners in his homeland and graciously took on the role of our personal tour guide. With open arms, he welcomed us into the heart of Thai culture, offering an insider's perspective and sharing the hidden gems of his country. Through his selflessness and genuine care, he enriched our experience and left an indelible mark on our hearts.

This encounter serves as a powerful reminder of the divine orchestration at play in our lives. God's guiding hand often manifests through unexpected connections, using the kindness and hospitality of others to guide and bless us on our journey. In the midst of our travels, this Thai gentleman became a vessel of God's grace, illuminating the path before us and offering us a glimpse into authentic Thai culture.

In reflecting upon this remarkable experience, I am reminded of the wisdom found in Hebrews 13:2, which encourages us not to forget the importance of showing hospitality to strangers. For in doing so, we may unknowingly encounter angels among us. Through the kindness and generosity of this Thai gentleman, we were reminded of the profound impact we can have on others' lives when we extend a hand of welcome and embrace the divine connections that come our way.

Let us remain open to the unexpected encounters and divine connections that God orchestrates in our lives. May we be vessels of hospitality, extending grace and love to those we meet, knowing that in doing so, we participate in God's work of guiding and blessing others on their journeys.

A Journey to Trust

BY MICHELLE ANDERSON

*Fear not, for I am with you; Be not dismayed,
for I am your God; I will strengthen you,
Yes, I will help you, I will uphold you
with My righteous right hand.*

—ISAIAH 41:10, NKJV

I can still remember my feelings that day in July when my life's "peace" began to unravel. My mother, a single mother of two children, had always been the rock of our family. Being from the West Indies, she possessed a strong, independent will that had always amazed me. I can only remember a few times growing up when I saw her cry or even express helplessness. As a retired nurse, she valued her independence and lived alone in Toronto, Canada, while my sister and I had emigrated to the United States.

She visited often, but despite our many attempts to convince her to relocate closer to us, she would adamantly protest and express her desire to remain alone. This was a constant source of stress, as I knew she was getting older and constantly worried about her getting sick and being alone at home, with no help in an emergency.

Well, on this particular day, my nightmare became a reality. As my sister and I were visiting Maryland one weekend, we called our mother to update her since she couldn't join us.

I still remember how my body reacted to her voice when she answered the phone, as she sounded weak and faint. She told us she was not feeling well, and I could hear the fear in her voice which I had never heard before in all my years growing up. She explained that "something" was not right with her and that she hadn't been able to eat for three days.

My insides tensed as I imagined her at home, helpless and afraid.

After praying with her, worry began to overwhelm me. At that moment, I could only focus on the logistics of her getting to the hospital, and I started frantically making plans to get to her as quickly as possible. The thought that nagged at me all evening was, *how can I even sleep knowing that my mother is in need and I can't help her?*

At some point that night, my then five-year-old son turned and said, "Mommy, don't be afraid; God will take care of Nana; just trust Him." Immediately I recognized this not as my son's words but as God's. I knew I needed to access the biblical emergency line, which are Scriptures that contain the help required. The Scripture that kept me that day and, in the days, to come was the text for today, Isaiah 41:10. Whatever your emergency; God promises to hold you or your loved one in His hand, precisely his right hand, which is a place of strength and authority—a symbol of God's presence, protection, and blessing. This reminds us that He can handle our crises while keeping us safe and secure. You can exchange your fear for faith today.

Anchor of Truth

BY ANANDI MOSES

*Your word is a lamp to my feet
And a light to my path.*

—PSALM 119:105, NASB

In the world of social media, everyone can bring their ideas and opinions to the public. There is no effective gatekeeping system to check the variety of ideas and news that spread so quickly around the world. Artificial intelligence (AI) adds another level of complication to the information we consume. With AI, we do not even know if we are seeing and hearing a real person. Virtual reality is the next thing that is catching on very fast. Navigating this world of make-believe can be very confusing and scary. It is very easy to lose touch with the real world and float around in this stimulating artificial Internet world of media, AI, and virtual reality. But while it is easy, it is neither healthy nor productive to do so. We need to guard ourselves against being sucked into this confusion. We need to hold on instead to what is true and beautiful and unchanging.

God has not left us without protection against this assault on our senses and minds. The Scripture is our anchor in these times. Daily time in the unchanging truth of Scripture is the way to keep us grounded and have the wisdom to separate error from truth. It is our light and our guide to keep our paths straight and to keep us from falling into the deception all around us.

The Word of God is unlike the media created by men. It is true and unchanging. "Your word, Lord, is eternal; it stands firm in the heavens" (Psalm 119:89, NIV). His word endures when the world changes. "The grass withers and the flowers fall, but the word of our God endures forever" (Isaiah 40:8, NIV). His word will never pass away no matter what happens in our world. "Heaven and earth will pass away, but my words will never pass away" (Matthew 24:35, NIV).

The Bible will lead us to the wisdom that we truly need for these times. God's laws and principles will help us to know how to live our lives in a way that is pleasing to God. It will help us steer clear of the confusion of this world if we ground ourselves in it.

Truth and Freedom

BY ANANDI MOSES

*And you will know the truth,
and the truth will set you free.*

—JOHN 8:32, NASB

Jesus was talking to some believers and told them, "You will know the truth, and the truth will set you free." This is a profound statement. It can be applied at many levels to understand how truths about many things set us free.

For anyone to improve themselves and their situation, the first condition is acceptance of reality. You cannot change anything of which you are in denial. Change can only follow acceptance. The sooner we come to know and accept reality, the process of change can begin. The reality here may mean the truth about us, others, or our situations. For example, anyone seeking to break free from an addiction must know the truth about their addictive tendencies, the power of addiction, and their powerlessness over addictive behavior. This is the starting point of healing and freedom.

Apart from personal truths, there are truths that may affect us as a society. Scientific truths can influence whole generations into accepting belief systems. Cultural truths can change the outlook of a whole country.

At any level, acceptance of truth is easier said than done. Truth causes discomfort. It is often unpleasant. It may make us look like fools. People go to great lengths to keep believing in what gives them comfort. If we prefer comfort, we may never find truth or freedom. But if we seek after truth, we will find comfort in the end.

Jesus said, "I am the truth." If we know Jesus, we will find freedom and comfort. Not only will He bring us comfort and freedom here on this earth, but one day in eternity "He will wipe away every tear from their eyes, and there will no longer be any death; there will no longer be any mourning, or crying, or pain; the first things have passed away" (Revelation 21:4, NASB).

Commitment to God

And you shall love the Lord your God with all your heart, with all your soul, with all your mind, and with all your strength. This is the first commandment.

—MARK 12:30, NKJV—

A Moment of Neglect

BY RAQUEL QUINONES

But when he saw that the wind was boisterous, he was afraid; and beginning to sink he cried out, saying, "Lord, save me!"

—MATTHEW 14:30, NIV

At the beginning of the year, I was committed to exercising on my treadmill. After a couple of days, when I felt confident about what I was doing, I decided that I would read a book while I ran so that I could make better use of my time. I felt that I no longer needed to hold on to the handles or attach to my clothing the little emergency cord that allows the machine to shut off in a moment of need.

Wanting to turn the page of my book, my hand struck the knob that increased the speed to something I would never be able to match. I lost my balance and tried to jump on the edge of the machine but to no avail. My dramatic fall on the moving belt caused my husband to run to my aid.

The experience of Peter walking confidently on the water came to my mind. Perhaps proudly, Peter took his eyes off Jesus and looked to his surroundings, maybe even to see if those with him were noticing what he was doing. Of course, he began to sink, and at his desperate call for help, Jesus extended his hand and saved him from what could've been a liquid tomb.

So often we feel so secure about the decisions and plans that we make. We feel supported by our titles, experience, positions, etc. Unknowingly, we remove our eyes from Jesus and then find ourselves confronting gigantic waves (problems) in our paths, and we, like Peter, call out, "Jesus, save me! Jesus, help me!" Only by realizing our own weakness and keeping our eyes fixed on Jesus can we be secure.

Daughters of our Celestial King, take time every day to know and behold Jesus. This experience will allow you to walk steadfastly in this stormy world. If in a moment of neglect, you lose your balance and fall, remember that Jesus is ready to embrace you in His loving arms and tell you, "My daughter, I am here to sustain you and help you; have no fear." Then He will offer you new opportunities. Sometimes we will have scars, like the ones I have on my legs from my fall, but that is the way we learn to put more trust in the Divine and less in ourselves. "Fixing our eyes on Jesus," we will walk until our eyes soon meet the saving gaze of our Lord Jesus Christ, when we will walk secure and redeemed for all eternity.

I Love Silence

BY EVELYN RAQUEL DELGADO MARRERO

¹¹ The LORD said, "Go out and stand on the mountain in the presence of the LORD, for the LORD is about to pass by." Then a great and powerful wind tore the mountains apart and shattered the rocks before the LORD, but the LORD was not in the wind. After the wind, there was an earthquake, but the LORD was not in the earthquake. ¹² After the earthquake came a fire, but the LORD was not in the fire. And after the fire came a gentle whisper.

—1 KING 19:11–12, NIV

This is a very noisy world. I mean the kind of noise measured in decibels as well as the noise that cannot be measured, like confusion and craziness. I have worked as a teacher and administrator for exactly half of my life. Schools are usually very loud places. Having twenty-plus kids in a classroom or five hundred students in a cafeteria at the same time can be very loud, confusing, and very crazy. Students need to express themselves, and it is fun to see them socializing and having fun. But, in all that exerted energy and loudness in the cafeteria, there is not much opportunity to listen. If we want to get our point across in the cafeteria, there must be silence. In the classroom, if we want the students to learn, the atmosphere must be calm and loving. That's the way that they can listen and internalize what is being taught.

At the end of the school day, when I got in my car to drive home, I really enjoyed my twenty minutes of silence. Those twenty minutes afforded me some time to think and reflect on my day. It was during those twenty minutes that I could plan the rest of the day with my family. I wanted to leave the loud, busy day behind and be calm to deal with my three kids and my husband. I didn't even turn on the radio in my car unless it was absolutely necessary. I just love silence. During my twenty-minute ride, I had time to calm down, relax, and quiet my senses so that I could transmit to my family my attention and love for them.

It is during those quiet times that we can think of what God wants from us. If God wants to speak to us, we must find quiet time in which we can listen to His voice. The Bible says that when God talks with you and me, He does not come with a big, powerful wind with an earthquake, or with fire. He comes with a soft whisper. God is a lot calmer when He deals with us than we are when we deal with others. God deals with us with grace and loving kindness. The significance of God appearing to Elijah in a gentle whisper is to reveal the tender nature of God. It is important for us to know that the God of fire and brimstone is not what draws us near to Him. It is His kindness, mercy, compassion, and love that draw us in. That is what God wanted to show Elijah.

In this noisy world, it is sometimes difficult to hear when God speaks to us. When God speaks to your heart, He does not speak with a loud thunder but with the gentle whisper of a still small voice. We must take a few minutes each day to listen to that voice.

When Duty Replaces Devotion

BY ESTHER PELLETIER

> *I know you are enduring patiently and bearing up for my name's sake, and you have not grown weary. But I have this against you, that you have abandoned the love you had at first.*
>
> —REVELATION 2:3–4, ESV

Some people are easy to love…like the baby who is sweet-smelling, rested, and fed, staring intently into your eyes with a big, gummy grin. Or like a friend with a mischievous smile who surprises you with a visit or unexpected gift.

For as long as I can remember, one of those easy-to-love people for me has been my mom. I felt content near her. One of our strong bonds was gardening. Every summer, I'd hold the tomatoes upright while she put on the cutworm collars, pounded in the stakes, and gently tied them with pantyhose supports.

Then came the summer when we were in the garden again. I was digging the holes, and Mom was padding about slowly, very confused. After a while, I asked her when she was going to come help me. She said she wasn't, that she was afraid of falling over, and I'd have to do everything myself. That was the beginning. She had some small strokes, fell, and broke bones. I've moved in. Her mind is slipping; increased dementia keeps her focusing endlessly on worries and anxieties. It is harder and harder to share with her. It feels like Mom is slipping away from me.

And I ask myself, as I silently pray for patience, "Have I lost my first love for Mom?" I can do caring acts and words for her, but my heart hurts and my mind wanders away from the uncomfortable scenes of her decline before me.

The early Christian church at Ephesus was a caring church. Like me with the baby monitor near my bed at night, the Ephesians worked tirelessly to bring the gospel to the then-known world. They were commended by Jesus Himself for their good works, their labor, and their patience without fainting.

But Jesus, knowing their hearts, knew they had lost something precious. This church began with firsthand witnesses to Christ's life and work. The first apostles, as babes in faith, had actually walked, talked, and eaten with Him, but had they learned from Jesus directly? Is there any place of more contentment than face-to-face with Jesus? Now, this group had lost the joy and love of just being with Jesus. They were sweating out in the field, but they weren't connected to the reason why. Jesus' friend, Martha, was busy preparing a meal alone while her sister, Mary, sat at His feet. She was distracted and resentful in her good works because she had not filled up on Jesus first. Jesus reminded Martha to pause and choose, to let her good works wait until she was full of His peace and love.

How can I be full of God's pure love for my mom? Can I slow down and remain present to how God is loving Mom in this moment and take my lead from Him? When we read the Bible and pray together, I am reminded that the Holy Spirit is not held back by a mind that is losing its ability to reason. Our personalities may change with age, but God's love for us and in us, "is the same yesterday, today and forever" (Hebrews 13:8).

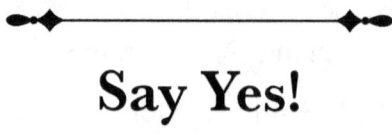

Say Yes!

BY ADRIENNE MCCLAIN

*His mother saith unto the servants,
Whatsoever he saith unto you, do it.*

—JOHN 2:5, KJV

When Jesus turned water into wine at the wedding at Cana, it was the first miracle of Jesus' ministry. This was a pivotal moment in the story of Christ's divinity.

Try to picture this scene. As the guests were enjoying the beautiful wedding celebration, they ran out of wine. I can only imagine how Mary felt a sense of anxiety for the newly wedded couple.

The first thing Mary thought to do when she found out that the wine had run out was to pray. She whispered a prayer to God, who had promised to bless this union and the service celebrating it. She probably whispered a prayer to God because she had asked Him to be with her as she managed this big event.

Although this problem seemed unsolvable, Mary turned to God. I believe the Holy Spirit told Mary to go to Jesus with this problem. But if I were in Mary's situation, it would have been difficult for me to obey the Holy Spirit. Remember, Mary gave birth to Jesus under remarkable circumstances. But since Jesus' birth, nothing else remarkable has happened. Mary only had a slight conception of Jesus' mission here on earth. She believed He was the Son of God, but she, like everyone else, believed the Messiah would defeat the Romans and sit on King Herod's throne. She didn't know that Jesus would open blind eyes and heal leprosy. She had no clear understanding of what Jesus would do and, for the past thirty-three years, Jesus had only been a baby, then a student, and then a carpenter. Jesus had never performed a miracle in thirty-three years. Why did she think He would or could now? It was the Holy Spirit. Mary was used to saying "yes" to the Spirit of God, so she calmly said "yes" now. She told the servants, "Whatsoever he saith unto you, do it" (John 2:5, KJV).

What about you, ladies? Is it easy for you to say "yes" to the Holy Spirit, even when it seems to be counterintuitive? Do you say "yes" even when it seems impossible for God's way to be successful? Do you say "yes" even when you don't want to because you know that God's way is always best? Let's say "yes" to the Holy Spirit today and every day.

Hold Them Tight! (Part 1)

BY ZORAIDA VELEZ-DELGADO

*Meanwhile, God heard the boy crying.
The angel of God called from Heaven to Hagar,
"What's wrong, Hagar? Don't be afraid. God has heard the
boy and knows the fix he's in. Up now; go get the boy.
Hold him tight. I'm going to make of him a great nation."*

—GENESIS 21:17–18, MSG

I woke up this morning feeling burnt out. My knees are tired from praying, my heart aches with heartbreak, and my soul needs hope. I am raising teenagers, and it is exhausting. I have been reading The Message version of the Bible, and today I was looking for hope during this stage of my life when I found something in the story of Hagar that I had not seen before!

Poor Hagar fell into a trap set by her masters' insecurities, lack of trust in God, and self-centeredness. Being loyal was supposed to bring her job security, a sense of belonging, and mental peace. It did the opposite. Looking back, she should have seen the red flags and the possibility that she could end up taking the fault for the consequences of her master's poor decisions. She did try to defend herself, but those who knew her well didn't need an explanation, and those who needed it did not care.

Now, she finds herself in the middle of the desert with no water for herself or her son. Abandoned, betrayed, scared, and alone, I'm sure she cried many times. That is not how the story should have ended. That was not the plan. The perpetrators walked away without any damage to them, and she was left with bits and pieces of what once was her reputation and self-esteem. Life is not fair, working hard didn't pay off, being obedient didn't have the fruits she expected, and now her son was going to pay for it all. Maybe her son had been unkind to his younger brother, but isn't that normal? Nothing could bring her peace as she walked on the hot sand.

"When the water was gone, she left the child [her teenage son] under a shrub and went off, fifty yards or so… 'I can't watch my son die.' As she sat, she broke into sobs."

This moment breaks my heart like no other in the Bible. As a mother, I have seen my children bear the consequences of people's insecurities, prejudice, and selfishness. And it is painful. I can imagine Ishmael's heart and body were hurting, not just due to the lack of water and nutrients, but from disappointment, abandonment, and heartbreak…Hold On!

(To be continued)

Hold Them Tight! (Part 2)

BY ZORAIDA VELEZ-DELGADO

> *Meanwhile, God heard the boy crying. The angel of God called from Heaven to Hagar, "What's wrong, Hagar? Don't be afraid. God has heard the boy and knows the fix he's in. Up now; go get the boy. Hold him tight. I'm going to make of him a great nation."*
>
> —GENESIS 21:17–18, MSG

Hagar sobbed, maybe remembering the day Ishmael was born, his first smiles, first steps, first kisses and hugs, those first words, curious questions, and adventures. He was her life, and now she couldn't witness his death. She may have sobbed loudly, but it was Ishmael's cry that reached God's ears. It was the cry of the destitute teenager that broke God's silence. "The angel of God called from Heaven to Hagar…Don't be afraid. God has heard the boy…." I particularly love the next verse: "Up now; go get the boy. Hold him tight. I am going to make of him a great nation."

Three commands that change the story: Get up, go get your son, hold him tight.

Get up, this is not the end of this story.

Get your son, he needs you!

Hold him tight because the enemy wants to bring him down.

Hold him tight because he needs to overcome his fears in order to do amazing things.

Hold him tight because he needs to feel safe to take risks, and you are his example.

Hold him tight because I have a plan for him.

No matter how tired your knees are, how much your heart aches, or how exhausted your heart is, God is using this story to remind us that we need to get up because we are setting an example for them. We need to get our kids and bring them to the Lord every day, and we must hold them tight because He has a plan, even if all we see is a desert.

Jonah and Giving Mercy

BY KAREEN WILSON

*Today, if you hear his voice,
do not harden your hearts.*

—HEBREW 3:7B–8A, ESV

As I walk up the cobblestone stairs, I disappear into a labyrinth of stone. I turn left and discover galleries, apartments, and monasteries as I climb and wander around. The journey is a wonder as I think of what it must have been like in Ancient Joppa.

Joppa is called Jaffa today, and I ascend into a pretty, hilly park overlooking the Mediterranean Sea and the Israeli port of Jaffa, home to beautiful gardens and a wishing bridge with views over the city. The neighborhood is old but posh and the place to walk where the ancients walked.

Sitting on the hill, I hear a tour guide telling her group the story of Jonah and how he tried to run from God. Jonah's story teaches what happens when you go in the opposite direction from where God is trying to lead you. Jonah had taken a boat from the port of Joppa to run away to Tarshish which is the south of Spain today. Jonah knew that he had tried to run from God but was useless.

COMMITMENT TO GOD

The story of the whale is one of reflection and pain. Three days in the pit of darkness in disgusting partially digested seafood will force one to sit and deal with their foolishness and repent.

This story also highlights a refusal to find mercy for others. Remember the part of the story where Jonah was angry with God for not destroying the people of Nineveh? I wonder how his heart can be so hard until I think of how I judge people and have resentfulness in my heart. I realize that I am no better than Jonah was in his spitefulness. But we must be grateful for God's mercy. I am thankful that God our Father in Heaven has mercies we cannot comprehend.

Has God been clear about what needs to be done, but you ran the other way?

The Perfect Recipe

BY ELINETE RODRIGUES REIS

*Your word is a lamp to my feet
And a light to my path.*

—PSALM 119:105, NKJV

I bake on a regular basis. And as a baker, I know for a fact that accurate measurements are essential. Baking is a very precise science. A lot of chemistry is involved, and a recipe must be followed precisely. There's no room for guessing.

Being so used to making the same recipes over and over, once in a while, I will decide to adapt the recipe. I skip the measurement cups, scale, and portions. I have done this a million times. I talk to myself, trying to convince my brain that the end result will be great. And I mix the ingredients by guessing how much of each item to use. As much as I think I am smart enough to create beautiful desserts and pastries on my own, my decision to walk away from the recipe ends in disaster every time, and I find myself frustrated, tired, and angry because I wasted precious time and ingredients.

When I look at all the instructions God left to us in His Word, I can easily associate them with baking. Everything instructed in the Bible helps us to live a better life and to be safe from dangers and frustrations.

Psalm 119:105 says the Word of God is a lamp for my feet, a light on my path. Everything we need is in the Scriptures, a perfect recipe. All we have to do is follow it to be successful. If you look in the Bible, you see examples of both ways…those who followed God's instructions had a blessed life, and those who decided to follow their own path had to deal with pain and struggles. Look at Absalom, the Israelites in many periods of their history, King Ahab, and many others. I am sure you can come up with a list in your head. Deciding to stay away from God's instructions is setting yourself up for failure.

As you go through your day, take a moment to thank God for the guidance He has provided for your life. In the Bible, you can find guidance to have a successful life. Follow the recipe carefully and enjoy the blessing of a beautiful outcome.

Diet

So whether you eat or drink or whatever you do, do it all for the glory of God.

—1 CORINTHIANS 10:31, NIV—

Do You Want to Be Made Well?

BY MICHELLE ANDERSON

"Do you want to be made well?"...
Jesus said to him, "Rise, take up your bed and walk."
And immediately the man was made well,
took up his bed, and walked.

—JOHN 5:6, 8–9A, NKJV

In the story from John 5, we encounter a man who had been paralyzed for thirty-eight years. Jesus saw him lying by the pool of Bethesda, a place where people sought healing. Jesus asked him a simple yet profound question: "Do you want to be made well?" This question goes beyond physical healing; it probes the depths of our hearts and challenges us to examine our willingness to embrace transformation in every aspect of our lives.

Prior to the birth of my son, I had been living in an unhealthy state but longed to be healthier. I had desired to shed excess weight, improve my overall well-being, and live a more vibrant life. However, I found myself trapped in poor eating habits and a sedentary lifestyle. Despite my desire for change, I had become complacent, resigned to the idea that things would always be the same.

DIET

One day, my husband lovingly challenged me after complaining of not feeling great to commit to one week of dedicated effort in making healthier choices. After all my excuses as to why nothing would work, my husband wagered that if there were no visible results, I could quit. With a mix of skepticism and hope, I reluctantly accepted the challenge. For that one week, I committed to a balanced diet and regular exercise, pushing myself out of my comfort zone.

To my astonishment, after just one week, I stepped on the scale to discover that I had lost five pounds! This small victory ignited a spark within me, fueling my determination to continue on this path of transformation. What was initially a one-week challenge turned into six months of consistent effort, resulting in a weight loss of fifty pounds and a newfound sense of energy and vitality.

Reflecting on my journey, I realized that Jesus often poses the same question to each of us: "Do you want to be made well?" This inquiry reaches deep into the recesses of our hearts, revealing our true desires and intentions. It challenges us to move beyond mere words and embrace a life of intentional action and transformation. When we truly surrender our desires for healing and transformation to Jesus, we open ourselves to His power and presence.

God's Design: The Purpose of Our Diet

BY MICHELLE ANDERSON

> *For we are His workmanship,*
> *created in Christ Jesus for good works,*
> *which God prepared beforehand that we should walk in them.*
>
> —EPHESIANS 2:10, NKJV

In Ephesians 2:10, we are reminded that we are God's workmanship, created in Christ Jesus for good works. God's purpose for our lives encompasses every aspect, including our diet and how we nourish our bodies. In the beginning, God provided clear guidance on the ideal diet for humanity. Genesis 1:29 (NIV) reveals His design: "Then God said, 'I give you every seed-bearing plant on the face of the whole earth and every tree that has fruit with seed in it. They will be yours for food."

This divine instruction emphasizes the consumption of fruits, nuts, grains, and plant-based foods as the foundation of our diet. God's intention was for us to enjoy the abundant variety of plant-based foods He created, aligning our eating habits with His design for optimal health and well-being.

However, in a world filled with dietary trends and fads, it is easy to lose sight of God's original plan. Without awareness of who we are and why we are here, we can find ourselves constantly searching for the next quick fix or the latest diet trend, never truly finding satisfaction or answers.

Yet, God has placed within us a desire to know our purpose and to live according to His plan. I encourage you to embark on a journey towards a healthier lifestyle and pause and reflect on your motivations and goals. It is crucial to align our desires with God's purposes for our lives, including how we nourish our bodies. This means embracing the awareness that God created us for good works, which includes taking care of our physical well-being.

In this process, seek the Lord's guidance and wisdom. Allow Him to reveal His purposes for your life and the role your diet plays in fulfilling them. Let Him reshape your perspective on food and nourishment, viewing it as an opportunity to honor Him and care for the body He has given you.

As you embark on your journey of health, remember that it is not solely about physical transformation but about aligning your entire life with God's purposes. Surrender your eating habits, desires, and struggles to Him, and let Him lead you towards a healthier lifestyle that brings glory to His name.

Nourished by God's Provision

BY MICHELLE ANDERSON

*And the LORD God commanded the man, saying,
"From any tree of the garden you may freely eat."*

—GENESIS 2:16, NASB

In our pursuit of a healthy lifestyle, nutrition plays a vital role. The food we consume has a direct impact on our physical well-being, energy levels, and overall health. God, in His infinite wisdom, designed our bodies to be nourished by the foods He created. Genesis 1:29 (NIV) reminds us of God's provision: "Then God said, 'I give you every seed-bearing plant on the face of the whole earth and every tree that has fruit with seed in it. They will be yours for food.'"

In our journey to make wise nutritional choices, we may find ourselves tempted by foods that bring temporary satisfaction but lack the nourishment our bodies truly need. I can remember every year at Christmas when the office would be filled with cookies, cakes, and many other tempting treats. In my mind, I always believed that I could eat in moderation until one cookie turned into five! Unhealthful foods can be a stumbling block for me and for many people I know. Broccoli rarely tempts me, but sugar-laden baked goods or crunchy chips certainly do.

I personally understand the struggle of giving in to cravings and indulging in unhealthy food choices. While I am not saying you can never eat treats on occasion, a regular serving of daily junk food (which I existed on at one point in my life) robs us of the real food that God offers. It was in love that God carefully provided a bountiful array of foods with varying textures and tastes to provide us pleasure and freedom in enjoyment. After the creation of Adam and Eve, He reminded them of all the wonderful foods to which they had access that were not only beautiful but great tasting.

The food that God gave Adam and Eve provided the physical energy they needed to fulfill their purpose. He continues to provide us with the same foods that nourish and sustain us without limit or guilt. Asking ourselves a few simple questions before reaching for a snack or planning a meal can help us make wiser choices. Is this food truly nourishing? Does it contain elements of God's creation?

In our fast-paced society, it can be tempting to prioritize convenience over nutritional value. However, when we choose wholesome, nourishing foods, we experience the benefits of increased energy, improved focus, and a strengthened ability to carry out the tasks God has entrusted to us.

Nourishment for Body and Soul

BY MICHELLE ANDERSON

*Who satisfies your mouth with good things,
So that your youth is renewed like the eagle's.*

—PSALM 103:5, NKJV

As followers of Christ, we must realize that our bodies are temples of the Holy Spirit (1 Corinthians 6:19). Just as we strive to nurture our spirits through prayer, worship, and the study of God's Word, we are also called to nourish our bodies in a way that honors God. Psalm 103:5 reminds us of God's desire to satisfy our mouths with good things, or good nourishing foods that will create youthful renewing.

In a world obsessed with finding the key to reversing aging, God has already provided the secret—healthy eating. In my younger years, I was trapped in a cycle of unhealthy eating habits. My palate had become accustomed to the flavors of processed foods and junk foods, which made natural and wholesome foods seem bland and unappealing. I did not like the way I looked or felt. I did not understand that my energy levels, mental clarity, and overall well-being were influenced by the foods I consumed. I soon came to realize that as a Christian, I was called to be a good steward of my body, recognizing it is a gift from God.

With much persistence and prayer, I eventually began to experience a transformation in my palate and perspective. I turned to God for strength and guidance, asking Him to help me appreciate and enjoy the foods that He designed for me to consume. As I sought His wisdom, I discovered the beauty and deliciousness of fruits, vegetables, and whole grains. The goodness of God's provisions began to satisfy my mouth and rejuvenate my body.

Choosing to prioritize healthy eating as Christians is not about depriving ourselves or adhering to strict diets. Instead, it is about embracing the abundant variety of nutrient-rich foods that God has placed before us. When we nourish our bodies with whole foods, we equip ourselves to serve God well. Our physical well-being impacts our ability to carry out His purposes with energy, vitality, and clarity of mind.

Let us remember that God's desire is to satisfy us with good things. He provides an array of foods that are not only nourishing but also delightful to our taste buds. When we neglect our physical health by consuming foods that lack nutritional value, we hinder our ability to serve God effectively. As we eat healthfully, we honor God by caring for the bodies He has entrusted to us.

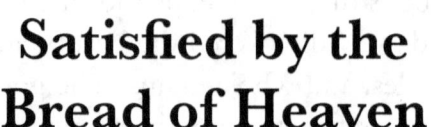

Satisfied by the Bread of Heaven

BY MICHELLE ANDERSON

They asked, and he brought quail and gave them bread from heaven in abundance.

—PSALM 105:40, ESV

In the Psalms, we encounter a beautiful yet sad depiction of God's provision and satisfaction. Psalm 105:40 recounts how God responded to the Israelites' cry for meat in the wilderness. He brought them quail to satisfy their hunger and provided them with the "bread of heaven." Sadly, the Israelites gorged on the quail, neglecting God's provision of heavenly bread, and, as a result, lost their lives.

The Israelites thought that the earthly meat while pleasing to the taste buds, could satisfy their cravings. They soon began to consume more and more, attempting to fill what could only be satisfied by God. Yet, throughout their years in the wilderness, God's bread was given in correct portion sizes and satisfied their needs.

As a dietitian, I often counsel individuals on the importance of nutrition and making wise food choices. One of the recommendations I frequently make is to incorporate more whole grains. Whole grains, such as whole wheat bread, are rich in fiber, vitamins, and nutrients that are vital for our well-being. However, making the switch from refined white bread to whole wheat can be challenging for many.

Refined white flour, commonly used in white bread, is stripped of its fiber and valuable nutrients during processing. These refined grains quickly convert to sugar in our bodies, leading to spikes in blood sugar levels and subsequent cravings for more food. This can create a cycle of overeating and feeling unsatisfied, which is not God's ideal. When we eat the foods God provides in the right state, such as whole grains, we can enjoy food the way it was designed and not be tempted to overeat to the point of sickness or death.

In a culture that often encourages us to seek satisfaction in temporary pleasures, Jesus offers something far greater. Unlike the refined flour in physical bread or other unhealthy foods that leave us longing for more, Jesus' bread is the ultimate comfort food for our souls. Let us remember that God's provision includes both spiritual and physical sustenance. He desires to satisfy the hunger of our souls and bodies with His provisions, which bring lasting contentment, peace, and fulfillment.

Discipline for Wholeness

BY MICHELLE ANDERSON

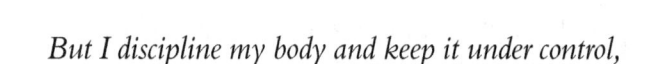

*But I discipline my body and keep it under control,
lest after preaching to others I myself should be disqualified.*

—1 CORINTHIANS 9:27, ESV

In our journey through life, it is not uncommon to find that the paths we choose hold the potential for personal healing and growth. Often, God uses our own struggles as a catalyst for the work we are called to do. This rings true in my own life as a dietitian.

Since childhood, I have wrestled with my relationship with food. Growing up in a single-parent household, I had the freedom to make my own food choices. Unfortunately, those choices often consisted of unhealthy options like chocolate bars, chips, cookies, and cakes. It wasn't until my adult years that I began to grasp the significance of nutrition for overall well-being.

Experiencing the transformative power of a plant-based diet on my own health ignited a passion within me to learn more and help others experience similar results. Thus, I embarked on the path of becoming a dietitian, aiming to assist not only myself but also those around me in making healthier choices.

However, as I journeyed on this path, I realized that healthy eating was not always easy for me. Despite my knowledge and passion, I found myself struggling at times. The temptation to veer off course and indulge in unhealthy options would arise. It was in these moments that the words of 1 Corinthians 9:27 resonated deeply within me: "But I discipline my body and keep it under control, lest after preaching to others I myself should be disqualified."

This verse serves as a powerful reminder that our lives, professions, and actions are a sermon to those we encounter. Even if we do not actively preach or teach, our lives speak volumes. We are living examples of the principles we profess. This applies not only to our spiritual lives but also to our physical well-being.

In striving to live a life that exemplifies discipline and self-control, we honor God's call to stewardship over our bodies. Just as we are called to nourish our souls through prayer and the study of God's Word, we are also called to nourish our bodies with healthy choices. By practicing self-discipline and making conscious efforts to prioritize our physical well-being, we create a consistent sermon that extends to ourselves and others.

The journey towards wholeness, both spiritually and physically, requires grace and discipline. It is a continuous process that demands our attention and commitment. As we discipline our bodies and keep them under control, we cultivate habits that align with God's design for our lives. By doing so, we ensure that our words and actions match, allowing us to effectively minister to others through the consistency of our own lives.

Eating for God's Glory

BY MICHELLE ANDERSON

*So, whether you eat or drink,
or whatever you do, do it all for the glory of God.*

—1 CORINTHIANS 10:31, NLT

In the hustle and bustle of life, it's easy to overlook the significance of our daily activities, including eating and drinking. However, the Word of God reminds us that even in these seemingly mundane actions, we have the opportunity to glorify the Lord.

1 Corinthians 10:31 declares, "So, whether you eat or drink, or whatever you do, do it all for the glory of God." These words challenge us to approach our eating habits and choices with a fresh perspective. It encourages us to recognize food as a gift from God and to honor Him by taking care of our bodies through healthy eating practices.

Gluttony, the excessive indulgence in food and drink, can lead us astray and distract us from our relationship with the Lord. It can become a stumbling block, hindering our spiritual growth and diminishing our capacity to serve Him effectively. However, when we acknowledge food as a gift and approach it with gratitude and self-control, we open the door to drawing closer to God and bringing Him more glory.

By making conscious choices to nourish our bodies with wholesome foods, we demonstrate our stewardship over the temples God has entrusted to us. Choosing nutritious foods not only benefits our physical health but also impacts our spiritual well-being. When we fuel our bodies with the right nutrients, we experience increased energy, mental clarity, and overall vitality. These physical benefits can enhance our ability to serve God and fulfill the purposes He has for us. Furthermore, when we approach our meals with gratitude and mindfulness, we invite God into our daily routines. We cultivate a spirit of thankfulness, recognizing that every morsel of food is a provision from our Heavenly Father. In this mindset, even a simple meal becomes an act of worship, an opportunity to acknowledge God's goodness and provision in our lives.

As we strive to glorify God in our eating and drinking, let us also remember to extend grace to ourselves and others. We live in a world filled with diverse food choices, and maintaining a balanced approach can be challenging. However, by seeking wisdom and guidance from the Holy Spirit, we can navigate this aspect of our lives with discernment and self-control.

Guarded Appetites

BY MICHELLE ANDERSON

*A person without self-control is like a
city with broken-down walls.*

—PROVERBS 25:28, NLT

The issue of gluttony is addressed multiple times in Scripture, and it is not portrayed in a flattering light. God's concern is not to deprive us of pleasure or good things but to guide us towards something better. He wants us to experience the fullness of life and enjoy the benefits of optimal health.

Indulging in unhealthy eating habits, particularly overeating, can never deliver true health. The excessive consumption of processed foods can leave us feeling sluggish, irritable, and disconnected from God's purpose for our lives. Recognizing that food is a gift from God and caring for our bodies by making wise dietary choices can help us draw closer to Him and bring Him greater glory.

Self-control is a godly character trait that Scripture consistently encourages us to cultivate. The book of Proverbs warns that a lack of self-control leaves us vulnerable, like a city without walls. In contrast, the apostle Paul speaks of athletes exercising self-control in all things, aiming for an imperishable prize (1 Corinthians 9:25).

When we exhibit self-control in our eating habits, choosing foods that God has designated as nourishing and consuming them as close to their natural state as possible, we bring glory to God. By not allowing any food to become an idol in our lives, we demonstrate that our ultimate satisfaction and fulfillment come from our relationship with Him.

Our commitment to living set apart from the world, seeking to bring praise to the Lord in every area of our lives, including our eating, is an act of worship. When we find joy in the foods God has given us and use them in ways that honor Him, we reflect His goodness and faithfulness to those around us.

Let us remember that He has given us everything we need, and we can use every aspect of our lives, including our diets, to love, serve, and honor Him. May our eating habits be no exception as we seek to glorify Him through self-control, gratitude, and wise choices that promote health and well-being.

Breaking Free from Emotional Eating (Part 1)

BY MICHELLE ANDERSON

> *From now on, think of it this way: Sin speaks a dead language that means nothing to you; God speaks your mother tongue, and you hang on to every word. You are dead to sin and alive to God. That's what Jesus did.*
>
> —ROMANS 6:11, MSG

The object of my affection was always there, three times a day, every day. Unlike the ability to throw out the last unhealthy DVD or CD, there was always another meal coming. So many times, I found not only was I consuming food, but I was consumed WITH food. My struggle with emotional eating didn't happen overnight. I got into the habit of rewarding myself with food for happy and sad times. At the time, this practice seemed harmless; however, I slowly came to realize that instead of God being my comforter, food was.

Food had become my best friend. While there's no doubt that food is good and God created it for our nourishment and enjoyment, a problem occurs when we take pleasure in food more than we delight in Him. God is the only one who can truly satisfy our hearts. He is the provider and sustainer of our emotional well-being, so when we seek to satisfy ourselves with something other than Him, we inevitably end up with a bigger mess on our hands. When we seek satisfaction in anything other than God, we will inevitably endure the afflictions of the world instead of enjoying the affections of God. Just like for the fish about to be caught by a fisherman, the bait is enticing, but it will lead to destruction.

Overcoming emotional eating requires surrendering our desires and cravings to God. It involves seeking His comfort and finding satisfaction in His presence rather than turning to food for solace. It may not be easy, but with God's strength, we can overcome it. When we fully grasp that God's love and provision are greater than any temporary satisfaction we derive from food, we open ourselves up to His healing and transformation.

As we surrender our struggles to Him and trust in His guidance, we can experience the freedom, joy, and abundant life that He has promised us. Let us hold on to the truth that we are dead to sin and alive in Christ, and through His power, we can overcome and live victoriously.

(To be continued)

Breaking Free from Emotional Eating (Part 2)

BY MICHELLE ANDERSON

> *The temptation to give in to evil comes from us and only us. We have no one to blame but the leering, seducing flare-up of our own lust.*
>
> —JAMES 1:14, MSG

Why is it so hard to overcome emotional eating? There were times when I thought I would never conquer my battle with it. The cravings were so intense at times I could hardly think straight. Particularly after a stressful event, I found myself reaching into a bag of something and completely losing track until the bag was empty. For those of you who are struggling, trust me, I understand the stronghold of this issue. My biggest struggle in overcoming emotional eating was the fear of not being able to stop. The thought of conquering this entire battle seemed daunting and impossible. But here's what I learned: we don't have to be overwhelmed with the task of overcoming all at once. Instead, we can focus on allowing God to help us defeat each individual temptation that comes our way.

The key to overcoming this is to focus on one meal at a time. The first meal will be the hardest. The next will be a little easier, and so forth. Before you know it, a few meals will become a hundred. With every temptation, we have a choice: Will we succumb, allowing it to strengthen the stronghold it already has over our lives? Or will we allow God to do amazing work in us as a result of this temptation?

In order to gain willpower over food, we must also clothe ourselves with the presence of the Lord Jesus Christ (Romans 13:14). By immersing ourselves in His Word and cultivating a deep and intimate relationship with Him, we guard our hearts and minds against the allure of indulging in our desires. It is through His strength and guidance that we can resist temptation and overcome the stronghold of emotional eating.

Finally, deciding to not indulge our desires, but rather focus on aligning our desires with God's will is critical to overcoming emotional eating. When we seek His presence, wisdom, and power, we gain the strength and willpower to make choices that honor Him and bring us closer to the abundant life He has for us.

Remember, the battle against emotional eating is not one that we fight alone. God is with us every step of the way, and as we surrender our struggles to Him, we can experience victory. Trust in His transformative work in your life and be encouraged that, with God, you have the power to overcome.

Encouragement

*I can do all things through Christ
who strengthens me*

—PHILLIPIANS 4:13, NKJV—

Best. Day. Ever

BY KAREEN WILSON

Here is what I have seen to be good and fitting: to eat, to drink, and enjoy oneself in all one's labor in which he labors under the sun during the few years of his life which God has given him; for this is his reward.

—ECCLESIASTES 5:18, NASB

"And God saw all that He had made, and behold, it was very good. And there was evening and there was morning, the sixth day" (Genesis 1:31).

Have you thought about what your perfect day would look like? The word *perfect* is used to describe what you think would happen for there to be joy in all aspects of each moment of that day.

My ideal day started as I woke to the sun shining through my windows, and I knew it would be a blessed day. My husband and I were staying at our house in Vermont and decided to ski our favorite mountain. We jumped in the car and drove slowly down the winding road through farms and wide-open spaces. When we arrived, the sun was high in the sky, and there were few people since it was late in the season. We headed to the mountain, and the snow was smooth without ice and moguls. The air was crisp and clean. At the top of the mountain, we looked out over the vastness of the green trees covering the hillside.

After skiing, we drove back to the house and waited for my good friends to arrive for the weekend. We had plans to visit the spa, hike, snowshoe, dine out, and have a great time with each other. We did all that, and to make it even better, we had light snow one evening and sun the next day, just in time for us to enjoy a beautiful hike. We laughed and joked and uplifted each other during each activity. Those are precious memories that I want to remember forever.

As I reflect, I know the highlights were the experiences and the people with whom I experienced those moments. Human interaction will feed the soul. Experiencing the enjoyment of sitting in a soft lounge chair and looking out large floor-to-ceiling windows to see snowflakes fall ever so gently to the ground was so peaceful, and I knew that God had created that moment for me.

Think of the great moments of your life. Cherish them. Especially the moments that included friends and family. Our God wants us to have pleasant moments that take our breath away.

Can you remember moments that took your breath away? Plan fun times with family and build special moments.

Believe in His Word

BY KAREEN WILSON

⁸ For my thoughts are not your thoughts, neither are your ways my ways, saith the LORD. ⁹ For as the heavens are higher than the earth, so are my ways higher than your ways, and my thoughts than your thoughts. ¹⁰ For as the rain cometh down, and the snow from heaven, and returneth not thither, but watereth the earth, and maketh it bring forth and bud, that it may give seed to the sower, and bread to the eater:
¹¹ So shall my word be that goeth forth out of my mouth: it shall not return unto me void, but it shall accomplish that which I please, and it shall prosper in the thing whereto I sent it.
¹² For ye shall go out with joy, and be led forth with peace: the mountains and the hills shall break forth before you into singing, and all the trees of the field shall clap their hands.

—ISAIAH 55:8–12, KJV

Sometimes, what God says does not seem genuine or relevant. We doubt His Word when we cannot see what is before us. We turn to Scripture to guide us, but the words on the page seem cluttered and have no strength in our lives. When our souls are in distress, nothing God says matters.

ENCOURAGEMENT

There were days when I thought God had deserted me, and I could not stand on His promises because I felt everything was a lie. Picking up the Bible was painful, and I felt no joy in leaning into His grace.

In these dark times, we need to remember when we plant seeds for our gardens. I love flowers, and, in Canada, where I grew up, lush botanical gardens were in everyone's backyard. Canadians inherited the love of manicured lawns and gardens from the English.

We would plant seeds in the greenhouse in early spring because of the short growing season. We would put a tiny seed in the soil and wait. It took great faith to know that the seed you planted today would grow into a beautiful flower that would bring joy in the future.

So, it is with God's Word. The words we read and put faith in take time to grow in our hearts. We are planting seeds for the future, and the words we see today may not bring us immediate joy. We must believe that the tiny seed planted in our hearts will one day develop into that tree or plant that will give us hope in our dark days.

In today's verse, we read how heaven's rain comes down and makes things grow. The Word of God makes things perfect, and every word that proceeds from God has a purpose, and those words will be completed and fulfilled. The metaphor of rain and growth helps us understand that God's Word has a growing season. It is planted as a seed, and God sends the rain to help that seed grow. It will grow, and every word has purpose and intention.

Read God's promises and plant the seeds in your heart. On those dark days, take the flowers that have been growing daily on your walk with God and use them to brighten your day when you need them.

What words for God have helped you through your life? Can you list ideas and thoughts that make you grateful?

Conformity Is Too Easy

BY BRYANA WILSON

*Do not conform to the pattern of this world,
but be transformed by the renewing of your mind.
Then you will be able to test and approve what God's
will is—his good, pleasing, and perfect will.*

—ROMANS 12:2, NIV

While my friends spent their Saturdays at movie theaters and amusement parks, eleven-year-old me often sat restlessly in church wearing puffy dresses and singing hymns. As I got older, I missed out on more events because of my religion. Volleyball tournaments were missed, SATs were rescheduled, and party invitations were declined.

However, as I grew up, so did my perspective. When homework piled up and deadlines approached, I looked forward to Sabbath breaks. Friday evenings were filled with family dinners (which seldom happened during the week because of conflicting schedules) and deep talks surrounding religion, politics, and philosophy. These conversations with my parents allowed me to form my spiritual and moral beliefs.

Then, as the Bible said, I would rest. Throughout my life, I have never done homework on the Sabbath. I never wanted to and never feared falling behind academically. I savored my weekly breaks from rhetorical analysis, integrals, and Avogadro's number.

When I think back to fifth-grade-me holding that invitation, I vividly remember the excitement at knowing what was inside. Then, I remember the disappointment and embarrassment when I declined the invitation. But seventeen-year-old me knows something that eleven-year-old me did not. By rejecting that pink, glittery invitation, I acquired something better: the value of non-conformity.

History is never made by people who try to blend in. Progress never comes from those who discard who they are. C.J. Walker, Sadie Alexander, and Rosa Parks all left their mark on society by keeping their beliefs close to them. As I continue to grow in my values, I celebrate the importance of being unique and accepting my differences. I aspire to maintain my originality to empower myself and contribute towards a better world.

How can teenagers learn to be strong in their faith in God?

A Journey of Loss and Hope

BY MICHELLE ANDERSON

> ²⁰ You who have made me see many troubles
> and calamities
> will revive me again;
> from the depths of the earth
> you will bring me up again.
> ²¹ You will increase my greatness
> and comfort me again.
>
> —PSALM 71:20–21, ESV

Life's journey can lead us through seasons of great sorrow and loss. We may face numerous bitter trials, leaving our hearts broken and our spirits weary. In those moments, the faithful God provides sustaining grace and comfort, reminding us of the hope we have in Him.

In a previous reading, I shared about the beginning of my mother's cancer journey. God walked alongside her, providing strength, comfort, and grace throughout her battle. Despite fervent prayers and a deep longing for healing, on January 10, 2020, my mother's journey on this earth ended. The void left by her departure was immeasurable, and my grief was overwhelming.

In the midst of my sorrow, I clung to the promises of God found in Psalm 71:20–21. I found solace in the understanding that, although my mother's body was laid to rest on the earth, it was only temporary. God's promise of restoration and resurrection brought comfort to my grieving heart.

The pain of losing my mother was intensified because she passed away just five days after her birthday. However, in God's providence, her passing occurred just before the onset of the COVID-19 pandemic in March 2020. As I reflected on this, I realized that God allowed us to have a proper funeral in Canada, which she considered home, and gather with loved ones to mourn and celebrate her life—a privilege denied to many who lost loved ones in the following months.

Through the pain of loss, I clung to the sustaining grace of God. Mom found solace in the understanding that death does not have the final say. As a believer in Christ, I know that my mother's spirit is in the presence of God, free from pain and suffering. The truth of the resurrection brought both of us hope and assurance that one day we will be reunited either when I go to heaven or at the second coming of Christ.

A Journey of Contentment and Gratitude

BY MICHELLE ANDERSON

*^{16}Rejoice always, ^{17}pray constantly,
^{18}give thanks in everything;
for this is God's will for you in Christ Jesus.*

—1 THESSALONIANS 5:16–18, CSB

In our faith journey, we encounter situations where we must learn to rejoice and give thanks in everything, even when circumstances do not align with our expectations. The words of 1 Thessalonians 5:16–18 remind us that always rejoicing, praying constantly, and giving thanks in everything is God's will for us in Christ Jesus.

In the first year of my marriage, my husband and I discussed the possibility of purchasing our first home. We dreamed of a place to call our own, filled with warmth and love. However, after extensive real estate searches, we quickly realized how our limited budget severely restricted our options. We had to face the reality that the homes we saw on HGTV with granite countertops, walk-in closets, and kitchen islands probably would not be something we could afford. Once we accepted this reality, we soon settled on a pre-foreclosed home with great "bones" but a less-than-stellar interior. The day we moved in, we could see that our work was cut out for us with significant construction we would have to complete alone and possibly with little help from friends.

Through prayer and reflection, I recognized that our home, while in need of renovation, was a blessing. I realized God was teaching me a valuable lesson in perseverance, faith, and reliance on Him. I discovered that true joy comes not from possessing the perfect home but from embracing the journey and finding contentment in God's provision.

As we worked tirelessly on our home, we experienced God's faithfulness. We witnessed His provision and guidance in every step of the renovation process. Our house became a symbol of His love and grace, a tangible reminder of His faithfulness in our lives.

Rejoicing and giving thanks for everything does not mean denying the challenges or pretending everything is perfect. It means finding gratitude amid imperfection and trusting that God's plan is always greater than our own. It means acknowledging that God's will for our lives may look different from what we anticipated but choosing to trust His guidance and provision.

Grow Up! (Part 1)

BY ZORAIDA VELEZ-DELGADO

> *You have heard that it was said, "Eye for eye, and tooth for tooth." [39] But I tell you, do not resist an evil person. If anyone slaps you on the right cheek, turn to them the other cheek also. [40] And if anyone wants to sue you and take your shirt, hand over your coat as well. [41] If anyone forces you to go one mile, go with them two miles. [42] Give to the one who asks you, and do not turn away from the one who wants to borrow from you.*
>
> —MATTHEW 5:38–42, NIV

I recently found myself in a dispute with a colleague. I was asked to mentor him at work, and he made it clear that I was not the person by whom he wanted to be mentored. So, I recommended another colleague for the task and moved on to another responsibility. Months later, I received an email from his supervisor asking me how he was doing in our mentor/mentee relationship. I was surprised to find out he had chosen not to mention what had happened to his leader, so I responded with a short truth. "We haven't spoken since he made it clear that I was not a good fit for him as a mentor. He is now being mentored by another colleague." The email was clear and to the point. No need for further conversation. But his supervisor wanted to know more. She replied with a list of questions. We have worked together so I went to her office to talk about it. I learned then that my ex-mentee had been complaining about my lack of time, understanding, and relatability as an excuse for the decision to be mentored by someone else. Faced with those accusations, I thought about giving my own side of the story, but I knew his leader didn't need that; she knew me well. She wanted a reason to confront him. I kept my statement short and walked away. Months later, my former mentee applied for a promotion, and, guess who was invited to be part of the interviewing team? Yep, this girl!

(To be continued)

Grow Up! (Part 2)

BY ZORAIDA VELEZ-DELGADO

> *You have heard that it was said, "Eye for eye, and tooth for tooth."* [39] *But I tell you, do not resist an evil person. If anyone slaps you on the right cheek, turn to them the other cheek also.* [40] *And if anyone wants to sue you and take your shirt, hand over your coat as well.* [41] *If anyone forces you to go one mile, go with them two miles.* [42] *Give to the one who asks you, and do not turn away from the one who wants to borrow from you.*
>
> —MATTHEW 5:38–42, NIV

When Jesus came to this world, he took time to remind us of the behaviors that would identify us as His believers. He climbed a hillside with His apprentices and started sharing His expectations with those who claimed to be committed to Him. One expectation that resonates with me is the way He expects us to love those who have hurt us. He called it an old saying that deserved a second look, "an eye for an eye." He said, "If anyone slaps you on the right cheek, turn to them the other cheek also." The fact that He uses different analogies for the same concept tells us what He really meant: People! How can an eye for an eye get us anywhere? Then

He continues, Jesus was saying in essence, "Don't hit back...at all. If someone strikes you, stand there and take it."

Here Is what I have learned about the deeper meaning of this verse. It is not just to turn the other cheek so we can get hit and make our enemies happy. The point is to remove their power to oppress, humiliate, and damage you...to turn that action into a growth experience. Loving those who love you is not challenging; we learn nothing from that experience. What Jesus is saying here is, let your enemies bring out the best in you, not the worst. When someone treats you with evil intent, respond with prayer.

I recused myself from that interview as I knew I was not going to be a neutral opinion. But I did offer him support if he needed it. We are now working together. It is safe to say we both learned a valuable lesson.

Fitness

Dear friend, I pray that you may enjoy good health and that all may go well with you, even as your soul is getting along well.

—3 JOHN 1:2, NIV—

Exercise and Traditions

BY KAREEN WILSON

Dear friend, I pray that you may enjoy good health and that all may go well with you, even as your soul is getting along well.

—3 JOHN 1:2, NIV

Every year (except for one year during COVID), our family rides together in the New York Five Borough Bike Race. When our girls were young, we would ride with them in tow in a seat on the back of our bikes. I remember the first year our oldest daughter Bryana, at nine, rode all forty miles by herself on her bike. As we crossed the finish line, I was proud. A few years later, our other daughter, Kierra, accomplished the same thing all on her own on her terms. We rode in the rain and sunshine. We invited other family members and friends to join us. Everyone knew us as that family who loved to ride together.

Something magical happens when 30,000 people join together to have fun. This race was like a party/ride with frequent stops, free food, and live music. We did it every year except in 2020, due to the COVID Pandemic.

FITNESS

When we exercise, hormones are released in our bodies that make us come alive. You take it to a new level when you add socializing with family and friends and the fresh air of being outside. Then add that it is something you accomplish together, and the moments become priceless.

God created our bodies for movement and experiencing the life-giving creation of traditions that mend the soul and bless the heart. Jesus and His disciples walked from town to town, sharing the good news. Walking is excellent exercise, and they must have bonded and supported each other during their travels.

Find a daily exercise plan that will allow you to develop close ties with your family and friends. Make it a habit that everyone looks forward to and a fun activity that will bring you together and create lasting memories.

Think of a tradition that can include exercise and fun. Make plans to keep the new tradition in all your friends' and families' schedules.

Exercise at Any Age

BY KAREEN WILSON

*She dresses herself with strength
and makes her arms strong.*

—PROVERBS 31:17, ESV

*"Once you exercise regularly,
the hardest thing to do is stop it."*

—ERIN GRAY

Wille Murphy heard a heavy knock at the front door. At the door stood a man doubled over, asking for help. Wille ran to the phone to call 911, and the man followed and tried to attack her. Willie lifted the table and hit the burglar until he fell to the floor, then jumped on him and hit him with a broom. When the police officers came and took the burglar to the hospital, the burglar was thankful just to have the beating stopped.

What if I told you that Willie is 82 years old? What if I told you Willie is a woman? Yes, Willie Murphy is an 82-year-old bodybuilder from Rochester, New York. She started lifting at the ripe old age of 65 to help increase her lung strength after quitting smoking. She started running and lifting at 5 pounds, and after a few years, it turned into her being able to deadlift 225 pounds and win awards for the 50, 100, and 1500 meters in the 55 and over senior Olympics.

Remember Willie when you think you are too old to exercise or too old for anything. She started small, and it turned into a lifelong commitment.

Willie spends her free time at the senior centers teaching others about the value of exercise. She is giving back to her community and helping others learn that "I can't" shouldn't be in their vocabulary.

How will you start your exercise journey? Start small—a couple of light weights and a daily commitment to walking. Introduce biking and stretching for low-impact strength. Move forward with swimming or a sport like tennis or pickleball that includes others for building relationships. God has given you a body to move and keep healthy. Exercise is a part of the equation for better health. Remember exercise knows no age.

God Uses Everyone and Everything

BY KAREEN WILSON

> *Now in a great house, there are not only vessels of gold and silver but also of wood and clay, some for honorable use, some for dishonorable. Therefore, if anyone cleanses himself from what is dishonorable, he will be a vessel for honorable use, set apart as holy, useful to the master of the house, and ready for every good work.*
>
> —2 TIMOTHY 2:20–21, ESV

My mom can cook. I know everyone thinks their mama is the best cook, but my mom loves to cook. She loves to cook for large groups and knows how to feed people's souls with good food. I have tried to follow in her steps. I will call and ask for guidance on how she makes everything taste so good.

I remember when I was growing up, she would try to teach me, but I think she blessed her food with extra love and joy that I would never be able to match. She used the best ingredients, prepared, and gave extra touches. One legendary dish that she would make only a couple of times a year was her gluten steaks, and they were legendary.

She would make big batches because everyone wanted some, plus it was time-consuming. People would try to recreate her magic, but after a while, they just stopped trying and would ask her to make it.

One holiday when I was home, I was determined to learn how to make Mom's gluten steaks. I had tried before, with Mom on Facetime showing me the ingredients and the steps, but the finished product was never quite right.

In Mom's kitchen, we laid out the ingredients and prepped and prepared. When it came time to fry the steaks, I reached for a pan in her closet that was the largest, newest, shiniest pan I could find. I brought it over to where she stood, and she just laughed at me before saying, " I fry only in this pan." She never washed that old, black cast iron skillet in the hot sudsy dishwater in the sink. She just rinsed it out with hot water when she was done. I remember it sitting out on the stove throughout my childhood. I questioned her decision, but she assured me, "It is exactly what we need for this situation. It may be old, but it makes the dish perfect."

That was the missing ingredient. I would never have used some old pan, thinking it could do the job. Plus, I wanted a big pan so we could be more efficient and cook more at once. My mom told me that you couldn't rush good food. All of the elements create the flavor of the meal. Of course, she was right. Those steaks were fried to perfection and tasted like love. I hope someday she will pass down that skill to me.

Next time you feel like you are not worthy, think of that old cast iron skillet. When you consider the old, dark times in your past that make you feel unqualified, or you believe that you are tainted and not fit to fulfill the path God has for you, remember that skill. The most beautiful heroes come out of scandal and dirt. Moses led the people of Israel. Saul hid from man and God when he was to become king. David has some dirt, but God said he was a man after His own heart.

Despite your past, what will you do to make this world a better place? How will you feed the world love, joy, and peace?

Good Thing? Bad Thing? Who Knows?

BY KAREEN WILSON

> *For everything created by God is good, and nothing is to be rejected if it is received with gratitude.*
>
> —1 TIMOTHY 4:4, ESV

The ancient tale of an old farmer is a potent parable of how perspective plays a role in dealing with the world.

Once upon a time, an old farmer lived in a valley with his son, a handsome and dutiful youth. They lived a peaceful life despite a lack of material possessions, and they were very happy.

One day, the old man borrowed money from the neighbors to buy a beautiful young horse. The very same day he bought it, there was a massive storm. The frightened horse jumped the fence and escaped into the hills, and the neighbors came to express their concern.

"Oh, that's too bad. How are you going to work the fields now? And how are you going to repay us?"

The farmer shrugged his shoulders and replied, "Good thing? Bad thing? Who knows?"

A few days later, while walking in the forest to gather new ideas, he bumped into his horse peacefully grazing the grass with another eight fine horses. The farmer took them all, brought them back to the stable, and built a taller fence so the horses couldn't escape. The neighbors again gathered around.

"Oh, how lucky! We thought you were destitute but look at you now. You can do much more work than ever before!" they said.

The farmer shrugged his shoulders and replied, "Good thing? Bad thing? Who knows?"

The next day, the farmer's son fell off one of the new horses and broke his leg.

"Such misfortune," said the neighbors. The leg healed crookedly and left the son with a permanent limp. The neighbors were concerned again, "Now that he is incapacitated, he can't help you around the farm, and he'll never find a fine wife. That's too bad."

The farmer shrugged his shoulders and replied, "Good thing? Bad thing? Who knows?"

Soon, the news came that war had broken out, and all the young men were required to join the army. The villagers were sad because they knew many young men would not return. The farmer's son could not be drafted because of his crippled leg. So, the neighbors gathered around again.

"How lucky! You get to keep your only son."

The farmer shrugged his shoulders and replied, "Good thing? Bad thing? Who knows?" And the story goes on forever.

When we know that all things from God are good and that he knows everything about us, can we rest and not judge the situations that come into our lives? In life, when faced with disappointments or illness, change your perspective; look to the one Who knows it all. Look at your situation through God's eyes.

Jesus Calls Us Out

BY KAREEN WILSON

When he had entered Capernaum, a centurion came forward to him, appealing to him, "Lord, my servant is lying paralyzed at home, suffering terribly." And he said to him, "I will come and heal him." But the centurion replied, "Lord, I am not worthy to have you come under my roof, but only say the word, and my servant will be healed. For I too am a man under authority, with soldiers under me. And I say to one, 'Go,' and he goes, and to another, 'Come,' and he comes, and to my servant, 'Do this,' and he does it." When Jesus heard this, he marveled and said to those who followed him, "Truly, I tell you, with no one in Israel have I found such faith."

—MATTHEW 8:5–10, ESV

My girlfriend wanted a child desperately. After five years of doctors, therapists, naturopaths, and specialists, she was still childless. Each time she did conceive, she would call me a few weeks later to tell me about the miscarriage that left physical and emotional scars. She would take special hormones; she would insert needles into her stomach and hip. She ate, breathed, and slept the notion of holding a baby in her arms. After a particularly devastating miscarriage, I said to her, "Enough! This is tearing you apart, and you are enough without a child. Stop trying."

She looked at me with energy and a courageous smile and said, "I know I was meant to be a mother. I will have a baby. I just know. I believe." My friend was not religious and definitely not a Christian. I could not rebut her unwavering faith. Four years later, she gave birth to a beautiful, healthy baby girl.

As a Christian, I should have been the one to have the crazy faith. I have shared my faith and helped people through many difficult times. Because I am a believer, I know that God can take the impossible and make it possible. But my friend put me to shame. Even though she dealt with the pain and the emotional roller coaster, she had faith that she could move mountains. This reminds me of the story of the Roman centurion.

This centurion was humble enough to approach Jesus and ask for healing for a servant. Consider the fact that he was a Gentile and a top leader asking for something for his slave. He acknowledges that Jesus is a holy man because he says that Jesus is too holy to step foot in his house. Then he says something that leaves Jesus, the Son of God, amazed. The centurion's faith is so strong that he believes Jesus just needs to say the words, and it shall be done. Then Jesus calls out the Jews. He says He has not found anyone with such strong faith among the very people that He has come to save—who should know about undying faith. Wow! The followers must have felt such shame.

Sadly, Christians can be the followers who are put to shame. Jesus calls us out. People who are not religious or don't know God sometimes have stronger faith and conviction than we have. My friend knew that God would bless her with a child someday. Who am I to crush her dreams? I pray that God does not call me out for lacking faith. I wish to believe in God's amazing power.

How can you show your strong faith?

Let's Play

BY KAREEN WILSON

The city streets will be filled with boys and girls playing there.

—ZECHARIAH 8:5, NIV

At that time, the disciples came to Jesus and asked, "Who, then, is the greatest in the kingdom of heaven?" He called a little child to him and placed the child among them. And he said: "Truly I tell you, unless you change and become like little children, you will never enter the kingdom of heaven."

—MATTHEW 18:1–3, NIV

Imagine a child sliding down a large, winding slide. Or a group of children trying to find each other in a game of hide-and-seek in the park. Imagine a dog and its owner engaged in a game of catch in the yard. These images bring joy to the soul and show us at play.

One of my favorite activities is skiing. I learned how to ski later in life, and it has been an activity to which I now look forward every winter. When I fly down the mountain and feel the adrenaline of the speed and air all around me, it brings me back to the feeling of the simple pleasure of play.

We humans tend to think that play is only for children, and we even think that play is for the lazy. When we become adults, we put aside the playful and creative things we used to do.

As our lives get busier and stress takes over, play should become an art form. Actively seeking ways to release, play, and create can be a way for us to deal with life. When we dance to music, paint a picture, or play a board game with family, it brings internal joy and a smile to our faces.

Have you ever considered that play is a part of God's plan? When you see colorful fish and beautiful landscapes, think of how God must have felt delight as He created. Exodus mentions that the children of Israel worshiped, and then they rose up to play. We serve a God that is playful and creative.

As a child, I made mud and rhubarb pies in the yard. Now I create recipes that are fun and healthy. In the winter, we would toboggan down the steepest and fastest hill we could find. Now I ski and enjoy the crispness of the air and the beauty of the snow. I loved running and playing in the woods behind my house as a young girl. Today I enjoy hiking and discovering new areas where I can experience God's nature. When it was raining outside, our family would build forts with cushions from the sofa. These days I enjoy decorating my rooms with paint colors and furniture that make the space bright, peaceful, and fun.

Find time to just let go and have fun! Smile and laugh more. Find something that brings you joy. I challenge you to play a little today.

Little Sparkles of Hope

BY KAREEN WILSON

In the same way, let your light shine before men so they may see your good works and glorify your Father in heaven.

—MATTHEW 5:16, TLV

As I looked out my window one late July, I saw a beautiful display of nature at its finest. The yard flickered with tiny lights moving through the trees, grass, and sky. Our yard is vast and dark, so the lights were bright and intense.

When my girls were small, they would run outside with glass jars to catch those little lights. Once they caught some bugs, they would bring the jar inside and wonder why the bug decided not to shine anymore.

Fireflies aren't actually flying. They are beetles, and they are nocturnal. Fireflies create light in various organs in the stomach by mixing a chemical called luciferin, enzymes called luciferases, oxygen, and the fuel for cells called ATP. Fireflies can regulate how much oxygen gets to the chemicals to create light. Fireflies live for only a few months, hence the show from June to August in my backyard. These beautiful creatures attract each other by displaying their own light show as a form of communication.

Watching the show, I was in awe of how beautifully they all shined together, and it occurred to me that *for me to see their shining light, it must be dark. Their beauty is displayed in the darkness of night.*

I smiled and thought of my life. I was going through a difficult time—a dark time. I had asked God to help me, yet I still felt alone. I was up late because the stress and hurt weighed on me so much that I couldn't sleep. But as I watched that light show, I knew that, even in the dark, God sends little sparks of hope to get me through difficult times. For me to appreciate the fireflies, it had to be really dark. In order for me to see miracles, I have to experience pain.

God will be by your side always. The darkness just means you must trust God's guidance even more. The little burst of light can be the small spark of hope that you need in your life.

Look for fireflies in your yard. How does this display of nature inspire you?

Living Water

BY KAREEN WILSON

Jesus answered, "Everyone who drinks this water will be thirsty again, but whoever drinks the water I give them will never thirst. Indeed, the water I give them will become in them a spring of water welling up to eternal life."

—JOHN 4:13–14, NIV

Have you ever been thirsty? The feeling of thirst and dehydration can lead to some terrifying feelings. The mouth can feel cottony and the tongue enlarged—the lack of water causes headaches and even delusion and confusion.

Fluid intake is crucial for the proper function of organs like the heart, liver, kidneys, and lungs. Water is essential to the function of the body; the brain is 75% water, and the adult body is at least 60% water. Drinking at least 64 ounces of water daily can help keep you healthy.

Studies show that drinking water in the morning can boost your mood, help with clearer skin, and fight toxins. Adding freshly squeezed lemon juice to the water purifies the kidneys and strengthens the immune system by providing vitamin C. We'd be wise to drink twenty-four ounces of warm lemon water every morning. Water is beneficial without a doubt.

Jesus says that the water He gives will give so much more. It is an excellent comparison of Jesus' gifts to water, as water is essential to life. One cannot live without it. Can you imagine never being thirsty? Jesus wants to provide us with living water so good that it gives us life forever with Him.

Living water is the Holy Spirit that flows through us and brings us closer to God. As we drink of the Spirit, we reflect Jesus' character in the world.

Let God's living water fill you and bless your life.

Are you grateful for God's Holy Spirit? How can you share this living water with the world?

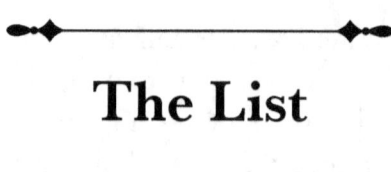

The List

BY BRYANA WILSON

*A joyful heart is good medicine,
but a crushed spirit dries up the bones.*

—PROVERBS 17:22, ESV

I am one of the busiest teenagers I know. There always seems to be a deadline, a project, or an upcoming test. Last year, as Christmas break was approaching, I was swamped with work. My AP classes seemed to have thousands of assignments, and I played two sports while managing club projects. It seemed like I couldn't catch a break. While everyone was enjoying the Christmas spirit, I spent all of my free time studying. I decided that the only way I could keep up the pace was to look forward to something. So, I set my sights on an upcoming Christmas party.

When my friends and I plan parties, we make them extravagant. They're never just a few people. Often, it's tons of teenagers, tons of food, and tons of games and activities. Unfortunately, this meant that whoever was hosting the party had a lot of work to do. And, of course, I was in charge of this Christmas Party.

In the upcoming weeks, my mom bugged me about preparing for the party. Already busy, I didn't want to spend extra time decorating or cleaning. In fact, I debated canceling it altogether. Although my mom could sense my tiredness, she wouldn't let me cancel. So, the party happened.

The hard work paid off: I had the time of my life. Something about being surrounded by people you love always brightens my spirit. Then one of my closest friends sat down next to me.

"Having fun?" I asked. We watched as some other people played ping pong.

"Of course," she said, "I'm glad I got to come." Often, because she lived over an hour's drive away, she couldn't make it to events. We sat in silence for a while before I looked over at her. She was typing away on her phone.

"What are you doing?" I asked.

"When I was in middle school, I started making a list of things that made me happy. Whenever something bad happened, or I was upset, I would look at the list." She looked around at the party, "I'm adding this to the list."

Throughout the following week, I kept thinking about what she had said. It inspired me to create my own list. I sat down for a few minutes and listed what makes me happy, ranging from my family to mozzarella sticks to puzzles. The list had no direction, and when something made me smile, I wrote it down.

Now, over six months later, my list has grown tenfold. I include everything: feelings, experiences, objects, and people. Reading through that list always makes me smile. No matter what life is like, it is important to step back and recognize the joys of being human. Be grateful for the little things, and soon the stress and worry will seem less daunting. Create your list today.

Unwanted News

BY KAREEN WILSON

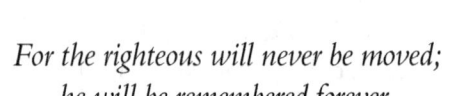

*For the righteous will never be moved;
he will be remembered forever.
He is not afraid of bad news;
her heart is firm, trusting in the* Lord.

—PSALM 112:6–7, ESV

Our family was driving to the Berkshires for a quick family vacation when my cell phone rang. The results of the ultrasound confirmed that I needed to see a urologist. There was a tumor in my right kidney. The urologist my doctor referred me to did not have an appointment for three weeks, but my PCP requested that I be seen the next day. That Wednesday, a week from walking into the urgent care with that debilitating pain, I was sitting in the urologist's office.

This urologist was young, barely out of school. As he showed me the pictures, he said, "You have a stage three cancer tumor on your right kidney."

On the phone, they had said a tumor. They had mentioned nothing about cancer. I am thirty-seven years old with two little girls.

Young black females are not normally diagnosed with getting kidney cancer. I shut down.

The doctor went on about surgery and deciding whether to take the whole kidney or do a partial nephrectomy. I heard none of it. For the next two weeks, I cried. I begged. I poured out my soul to any God who would hear me. Then one day I woke up, and I decided. I just decided. I had made my choice. I was going into surgery, and I was going to be just fine. I am healthy. I am strong. I will survive. Take the whole kidney. I will live with one.

The urologist who happened to be my surgeon was amazing. Remember how I was supposed to see a different urologist? God knows what He is doing. I was in the right hands. Six weeks after my surgery, I was up and running long distances. Three months after surgery, I was on a mission trip to a developing country. I lived my life. I praised God for my healing.

At my five-year check-up, I sat in my car and cried. I was healthy. No complications. I was free. The shed tears were of both gratitude and praise for the body that is fearfully and wonderfully made.

Gratitude showed itself to me.

Watch Your Giants Fall

BY KAREEN WILSON

> *The Lord who delivered me out of the paw of the lion, and out of the paw of the bear, he will deliver me out of the hand of this Philistine. And Saul said unto David, Go, and the Lord be with thee.*
>
> —1 SAMUEL 17:37, KJV

Lawsuits, bankruptcy, divorce, cancer, and the loss of a loved one can all be characterized as the "Philistines" in our lives. Just as the Israelites hid from Goliath and were certain of defeat if they faced him, we, too, feel like the big giants will crush us.

Faith and fear. Pick one. With faith, you are like David and know that God is with you and can defeat and win over anything. With fear, you crawl into the corner and try to avoid the issue or, worse yet, claim defeat. Notice that with fear, the issue does not go away.

Could you look at your issue through a different lens? What if your giants were not that scary? In the story of David, Goliath was extremely large, but he was all brawn and no brain. He also asked David to come closer so that he could see him, and he obviously didn't see the stone coming toward him to duck out of the way so that it would not hit him directly in the forehead. Perhaps the giant was visually impaired. Goliath was somewhat of an anomaly, and people may have treated him as a person with all brawn and no brain. Because of his size, I can imagine it was difficult to move around. He may have been big, but not swift. Goliath was not that big of a deal in the first place.

The same is true of your problems. At first, when you are in the middle of the situation, it overshadows you. But you can find a way to outsmart, heal, and power through because of your faith in the Lord. Victory is yours!

You just need a new perspective—a faith that overcomes fear. Goliath and all your giants will fall.

What giants do you need to overcome in your life? Faith over fear!

Trusting God's Design in Every Detail

BY AVALEY FRANCES MATIERIENE

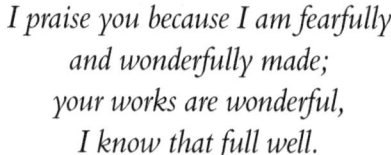

*I praise you because I am fearfully
and wonderfully made;
your works are wonderful,
I know that full well.*

—PSALM 139:14, NIV

Pregnancy is a transformative and emotional journey that unfolds with a myriad of hopes, dreams, and concerns. I was no exception during my first pregnancy. As my belly swelled with life, my heart overflowed with anticipation and questions about my unborn child. Curiosity led me to delve deeper into my ancestry and the family history of my son's father. Little did I know that these inquiries would stir a mix of worries and fears within me.

As I discovered details about my heritage, I learned that my paternal great-grandmother belonged to a native tribe known for their short stature. Additionally, my son's paternal grandmother and aunts suffered from strabismus, a condition affecting the alignment of the eyes. To top it all off, my son's father shared an unusual family trait—his father had three nipples. These revelations weighed heavily on me, intensifying the anxieties and concerns that naturally accompany pregnancy.

In the midst of these worries, I turned to prayer, seeking comfort and divine intervention. I prayed not only for the overall health of my unborn child but specifically for his eyes, longing for them to be healthy and free from any visual impairments. I entrusted my concerns to God, knowing that He alone could shape and mold every aspect of my baby's being.

When my little one finally entered the world, my heart brimmed with joy and gratitude. Not only did he possess perfect vision and healthy eyes, but he also bore a stunning pair of hazel eyes—a true testament to God's marvelous design. As the years passed, my son grew into a remarkable young man, consistently receiving compliments for his captivating eyes.

This experience serves as a profound reminder of Psalm 139:14, which declares that we are fearfully and wonderfully made by our Creator. From the intricate details of our physical appearances to the unique traits inherited from our lineage, God's handiwork is undeniably marvelous. He lovingly crafts each individual, weaving together a tapestry of beauty and purpose.

He Makes Beautiful Things

BY TANIA FUENTES-DAVITT

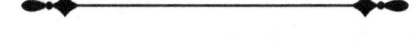

Remember that you molded me like clay.
Will you now turn me to dust again?

—JOB 10:9, NIV

Four days. Four days of excitement and joy before my world came crashing down. It had been months of trying, the anxiety of waiting two whole weeks to see if we could have a baby, and then the disappointment when Aunt Flo came knocking on my door again. I would try not to get my hopes up every time, but inevitably I would psych myself out. Finally, one morning it happened. My husband was on the phone with his mom, and I waved at him excitedly, mouthing "Hang up the phone." I will never forget his clueless face as he just stared at me uncomprehendingly and I mouthed "Hang it up RIGHT NOW."

We were so excited! New life! I felt suddenly so womanly and beautiful. We decided to revel in the moment, keeping it private just between the two of us for a few days before we told our families. Little did I know that the phone call to my mom would not go as planned. Instead of excitement, it was a panicked, "I'm pregnant, but I'm losing the baby." Then, doctors and tests to confirm what my body already knew; the life once growing was gone. How I struggled with God after this. The depression of this moment was a grief that is not logical. I studied the science and knew that, logically, it was just a few cells at that point; but my body was mourning something more.

The months that followed were even harder. Could God not want this for me? Was my inability to carry a child a punishment of some kind? As the months dragged on without success, I wrestled with God. In my mind, I had decided that this was what was going to make me happy and fulfilled. God wanted more for me. Through this time of waiting, this time of the unknown, I had to face the possibility of being barren. I had to discover who I really was and what could make me fulfilled if I never did have a child.

The time I spent getting to know myself better and finding out more about who I am is time that I would not give away even if I had the choice. Wrestling with God in our struggles brings an invaluable intimacy and rawness to the relationship. Just as Jacob wrestled with God in the night, begging God to bless him (Genesis 32), I wrestled with God as I asked for a blessing. Although God never wants us to suffer or go through struggles, the reality of living on a sinful planet is that things happen, painful things. The blessing is that God can make something beautiful out of the struggles we go through. For me, he didn't magically change my situation overnight, but He changed my heart; and I am eternally grateful.

What are you struggling with? Have you brought your struggle to God? Have you had the courage to wrestle with God and ask for Him to bless you in the midst of your hard times?

The Climb (Part 1)

BY KELLEY MATIERIENE

Do you not know that those who run in a race all run, but one receives the prize? Run in such a way that you may obtain it. And everyone who competes for the prize is temperate in all things. Now they do it to obtain a perishable crown, but we for an imperishable crown.

—1 CORINTHIANS 9:24–25, NKJV

The pandemic (2020) left many of us with more time than we knew what to do with. Since I had started trail running the fall before, a portion of my time was used to explore nature and help provide a way to stave off cabin fever.

I didn't have a core group of running friends, but I also didn't want to run in the woods alone. I would invite other runners to explore with me or go whenever someone was looking for a running buddy. One of the first ladies I met was Sarah. Oddly enough, Sarah and I grew up in the same vicinity, just twenty minutes apart, and had never met.

By June, Sara had planned to run the Shut-In Ridge Trail for fun. If you're not familiar with it, the Shut-In Ridge trail follows the 17.8-mile route that business tycoon George Vanderbilt used to take while going from his Asheville mansion, known as the Biltmore Estate, to his hunting lodge in the mountain. Over the course of 17.8 miles, you climb *3,000 feet*. Never one to back down from a challenge, I agreed to join.

Sara planned to run/hike the same path as the Shut-In Ridge trail race but just to the parking lot on Mt. Pisgah and not the lookout. This unofficial race is just under seventeen miles, and we were excited.

Of course, you don't just decide to climb up the side of a mountain. We had to switch up our training to prepare for the climbs ahead. We spent the next six weeks running various parts of the trail to get a feel for what was ahead of us. Sara planned two aid stations along the way; we would need to refuel, but we didn't want to carry supplies as we ran. Our undertaking required serious preparation and even a little sacrifice.

The same is true for the Christian race. It requires preparation and a desire to explore new avenues with God. We can't just hope to draw closer to the master; we must be intentional. We have to train our minds and bodies by living spiritually healthy lives. Today, consider where you are investing your energy; are those investments helping you persevere in your Christian race? Are you building your spiritual muscles?

(To be continued)

The Climb (Part 2)

BY KELLEY MATIERIENE

You search the Scriptures, for in them you think you have eternal life; and these are they which testify of Me.

—JOHN 5:39, NKJV

The date was set for us to run the race on a Saturday morning in August. We planned to start early to avoid the hottest part of the day. Due to the foliage and trees on the trail, the path was pretty well-shaded; still, August is a warm month. We knew the warmer it was, the more water we would need. By now Sarah had invited others to join, and a decent-sized group had committed to do the unofficial race. Our group would meet at various lookouts along the trail and run seven to ten miles to get a feel for the terrain and figure out how to pace ourselves when it was time to complete the entire distance. Also, running portions and finishing it gave us the confidence we would later need when the actual run grew hard.

The trail runs would later become crucial to our success. So often in life, we shy away from the repetition or monotony of doing what we think we already know. We read the Bible and think, *I know the Word. I have read it.* Or we read a book for spiritual enlightenment and feel like we have grown, then never pick it up again.

But what if you did reread it? Look at the same book of the Bible, the exact text from a different angle. The same stories you think you know have many additional lessons the Lord wants us to learn. I always am a little envious when I hear a sermon on a verse I know by heart, but with a twist I never considered. I think, *How did the preacher see that or glean that?* He keeps searching the Scripture. He challenges what he thought he knew and asks God to give him a new heart and a changed perspective on a story that, before his study, had seemed so "been there done that."

The Bible implores us to search the Scriptures to know Jesus. Today I challenge you to tackle your favorite Bible story again. Read it and ask God to show you how to find Jesus anew through your search.

His Love, Your Weight

BY EVELYN RAQUEL DELGADO MARRERO

*But the eyes of the Lord are on those who fear him,
on those whose hope is in his unfailing love*

—PSALM 33:18, NIV

God loves us just the way we are! He loves us with 10, 20, or 100 extra pounds. He loves us if we eat donuts for breakfast if we eat a healthy, very nutritious breakfast, or even if we skip breakfast altogether. He loves us if we have high cholesterol if we have high blood pressure, or if we are fit as a fiddle. God loves us and sent His Son Jesus to rescue us from all our imperfections. We, too, need to accept ourselves with all our imperfections. The main focus when we diet and exercise is to be healthy so that we can focus on what is important. True, we like to look good and sometimes having those extra pounds interferes with our confidence and wellbeing. But, once we realize that the focus is to have healthy bodies, then we start making the changes that are required to become healthy.

My problem is that I don't like having others tell me what to do. When I sit down to eat, I do not need a police person to point out that I'm making the wrong choice. I do not believe in fear-mongering, guilt trips, or shaming. Those are not from God, and the devil uses that to paralyze us into doing nothing.

God has a plan for us. Obviously, if we are unhealthy, we cannot easily do what God wants us to do; so we must take care of ourselves. We cannot let food be our boss. We must take control and choose the foods that will make us healthy. I love to drink a nice tall glass of Coca-Cola after a very stressful day. I rationalize by saying, "Soda isn't as bad as alcohol, and I don't drink that!" But even my seven-year-old granddaughter tells me how bad that is for me.

In reality, I do know that soda has tons of sugar as well as caffeine, which are both harmful and addictive. But instead of giving my stressors to God, I solve the problem in a way that is harmful to me. I realized that I was letting that soda be a boss over me. Without me even realizing it, that soda had become my idol. I was putting it before my health and before God. My de-stressor needs to be God.

Let's take time in prayer today to ask God to be our source of comfort and strength, to rid us of any possible addictions we may have to food. Losing weight is a journey, and God through prayer will help us all the way.

Race Day

BY KELLEY MATIERIENE

> *Therefore, we also, since we are surrounded by so great*
> *a cloud of witnesses, let us lay aside every weight,*
> *and the sin which so easily ensnares us, and let us*
> *run with endurance the race that is set before us.*
>
> —HEBREWS 12:1, NKJV

The morning of the "race" was foggy, and I was running late. We had agreed to meet at the endpoint and carpool back to the starting point. Wrongfully, I assumed I knew how to get to the meetup point, and by the time I decided to tap into GPS, I had no signal. I was on the verge of going home but then decided just to meet the other ladies at the start point. I kept praying that they hadn't started without me.

I connected with them just in time for our pre-race photos. Since we had practiced the first twelve miles numerous times, we knew we needed to start slow. The initial climbs make that an easy choice in the middle, but a few flat spots make you feel like you can run forever. By the time we got to the first aid station, we had separated into groups of two or three. I had taken off running alone but decided at aid station one to wait for Sarah and Ashley.

FITNESS

At mile twelve, my calves started to cramp. I wasn't expecting any cramping because I never had any in the practice runs. For more than a few moments, I considered taking the ride at aid station 2. I mean I had run 12 miles and climbed over 1,000 feet. I had done more than most people would do for the whole day. *Then again,* I told myself, *I am over halfway there. I can walk out of a cramp. I didn't come this far to give up now.* The next mile was slow, but I did it.

So often in life, we become disheartened when faced with insurmountable obstacles. We often hear stories of people who give up when things get tough. While I can't fully understand the depth of everyone's emotional struggles, I want to emphasize that if you persevere through difficult times, there is hope and a brighter future ahead. Taking one step at a time, you can emerge from the darkness and find your way to the other side. Taking one step at a time, you can emerge from the darkness and find your way to the other side.

The Bible reminds us in multiple places, God is with us and we are not alone in this journey. We must hold onto our faith and trust that God's plan is far more significant than the pain, fear, and emotional wounds we may be experiencing. He will lead us to victory.

Today, I encourage you to pray for someone you know who is going through a challenging period. Offer support to the grocery store, the worker at the drive-thru window, or maybe yourself. We often don't realize the burdens others carry until we extend a helping hand

The Finish Line

BY KELLEY MATIERIENE

*But those who wait on the LORD shall renew their strength;
they shall mount up with wings like eagles,
they shall run and not be weary, they shall walk and not faint.*

—ISAIAH 40:31, NKJV

The mountain terrain changes significantly Around mile fourteen or fifteen. Instead of the familiar dirt path with switchbacks that make climbing more manageable, you must now navigate large slabs that look like granite. It is no longer possible to simply shuffle along; you must lift your legs to make progress, or you risk stumbling and falling flat on your face. I hadn't anticipated this part of the climb. Despite others warning me about the toughness of the final two miles, I was unprepared. So far, the climbs have been manageable and relatively short. Somewhere along the trail, we had lost Sarah; and it was just Ashley and me. I was leading, but I was exhausted. I knew the climb was coming, but I had no idea what I would face.

I remember thinking, *If I stop, I'm not sure I'll be able to get back up. Ashley is way too small to carry me out. I don't want to get stuck in the woods. I wonder if I can get airlifted out. Just keep moving, Kelley; this will be all over an hour from now.* I have learned two things over the course of running long distances:

1. I made mini goals instead of thinking about the overall miles left. I would pick a rock, a tree, or anything before me and just get to that point. Then I'd convince myself that I could go to the next milestone if I had come that far.

2. I also learned the power of using imagery to keep me from focusing on the pain. I imagined I was climbing Jacob's ladder to heaven and an angel was in front of me, coaxing me to keep climbing, telling me I could do it. Later, Ashley would tell me she didn't stop because I didn't stop, that she imagined a belt on my waist connected to her, pulling her up.

The climb was incredibly tough, but we persevered and reached the top. From there, all that remained was the descent back to the parking lot, which was challenging because our legs were exhausted. However, with God by my side and Ashley as my companion, I successfully completed the race.

I imagine the sensation of reaching heaven one day will be even more profound. Life has its ups and downs. If we can learn to find the little joys to envision ourselves on the other side, it can make all the difference.

Today, take a moment to write down something you look forward to doing when you reach heaven. Remember that we are assured of victory if we keep walking with Christ.

Knowledge Is Truly Power

BY KELLEY MATIERIENE

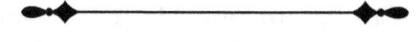

My people are destroyed for lack of knowledge.
Because you have rejected knowledge…

—HOSEA 4:6A, NKJV

The first baby I ever fell in love with was my nephew, Darius. It's not because I had not been around babies before. I am just not a baby person. I don't offer to hold newborns at church or social gatherings. I don't mind entertaining kids, but I was not the girl offering babysitting services growing up. Babies were not my thing, as cute and cuddly as they could be.

When I became a mom, I was terrified. Don't get me wrong; I didn't think I couldn't be a mom. It was just that the responsibility of caring for another life was a bit overwhelming to me. I remember praying during the first year, "Dear Lord, please let my baby live until he's one." It sounds silly now, but during those first few weeks, I was terrified he would die of SIDS, or I would roll over on him in my sleep or forget him somewhere. These things did not happen, of course, as I now have a teenager. And I, of course, did not share these fears with anyone but God.

One particular day, I took my son to see his pediatrician. I was asking her about laying the baby on his back or his tummy because I had heard conflicting advice, and I was worried about SIDS. She then provided statics about SIDS in a pamphlet I could read and let me know that by breastfeeding, I was helping to reduce the chances of SIDS. I had no idea. I was terrified about something about which I wasn't fully educated because I had heard horror stories.

We worry about some things because we have not fully taken the time to learn the truth about the topic. Sometimes, it's people we don't take the time to get to know. Sometimes, it's things or places we don't invest the time to research. Sometimes, that fear keeps us trapped in a life not fully enjoyed because we haven't taken the time to pray about it and ask God to provide direction. Sometimes, the information is in a book a friend provided or one sitting on our bookshelves that we have not taken the time to read. We often suffer because we have not sought the knowledge to advance in power. We lose sleep and fret because we have not searched for the necessary information. With knowledge comes power, power to move forward, power to decide once and for all whether something is worth our time or even something to be feared.

I challenge you today to learn more about something you have been wondering about. Take a deeper dive and get informed; The saying "Knowledge is Power" is confirmed in Proverbs 3:13-14 (NIV) *"Blessed are those who finds wisdom, those who gain understanding for she is more profitable than silver and yields better returns than gold"*

My Psalm 23

BY SARA E. BAYRÓN

Cast all your anxiety on him because he cares for you.

—1 PETER 5:7, NIV

Everyone knows Psalm 23. It is a very powerful psalm that shows how God protects us, guides us, and blesses us. We are His sheep, and He is our shepherd. As the shepherd, He protects us with His unfailing love. I have made this psalm my own to remind me that God is there every step through my struggles and triumphs. He tells us repeatedly to cast all our cares on Him, and He will give us peace. Our anxiety, our burdens, our cares—anything that causes us to worry. We aren't going through anything we cannot cast on the Lord. I always struggle with my weight, so I cast that upon Him. As a reminder, I like to write my own psalms.

My Trainer

My God is my trainer;
That is all I need.
He teaches me to enjoy the greenery of the countryside,

FITNESS

And the stillness of the lakes while I walk the roads.

He comforts my soul.

He guides me to set my goals high and to accomplish them.

Because His name is at stake.

For I love His name.

Although sometimes I feel achy and discouraged,

And the discipline seems harsh,

I will not back out because He walks with me.

His constant care and guidance give me hope.

He makes sure that my nutrition habits

follow the guidelines set up for me.

He anoints me with words of encouragement

So that I feel satisfied and joyful during all my training.

His love and mercy I will remember all the days of my life,

And I know that I will be in shape because I will follow His teachings

for many, many days.

My Psalm 23—In My Words

BY SARA E. BAYRÓN

Cast all your anxiety on him because he cares for you.

—1 PETER 5:7, NIV

He could be my trainer, my healer, my supporter, and my friend and walk with me on this very tough road. You, too, can take Him up on His offer as well. To write your own psalm, answer the following questions. What is the Lord to you? What will make you rest and have peace? Where do you need guidance? In what area of life do you need strength, vengeance, or anointing? What do you need to feel complete? What will you offer Him to live in the house of the Lord forever?

My Healer

The Lord is my healer, I will always be healthy.

His fruits, vegetables, and pure, healthy water will keep me satisfied and content.

He will comfort my mind, soul, and spirit.

He will guide me and discipline me, for His name's sake.

FITNESS

He assures me of His presence when I go through hard times
And strengthens me.
He will destroy my oppressors before me, those who tempt me with food.
He anoints me with so much energy that I feel like a conqueror.
My life feels so full of goodness and mercy,
And I will live in His presence for the rest of my life.

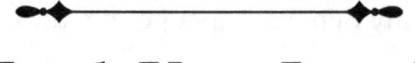

Look Unto Jesus!

BY ANANDI MOSES

*And I, if I am lifted up from the earth,
will draw all people to Myself.*

—JOHN 12:32, NASB

Our world has a lot of self-help messaging around us, which can be important in improving our lives. God has granted us the gift of will. In using our will, we make decisions and take responsibility for our actions. God expects us to take ownership of our lives. Some self-help skills are important in exercising the gift of free will.

But we need to be careful about the belief that is behind a lot of the self-help messages that we hear. The philosophy of looking into oneself to fulfill our spiritual needs is not a biblical one. When the children of Israel faced the plague of serpents in the wilderness, Moses made a bronze serpent and lifted it up. Everyone that looked up at the serpent lived. It was a lesson for the Israelites and us to look outside of ourselves for our deliverance. The more our focus turns away from ourselves, the easier it is to do the right thing. It seems counterintuitive, but the Bible teaches us this principle.

In the New Testament, we are given much clearer instructions about where to turn for our power and redemption. Jesus said that when He is lifted up, He will draw all men to Himself. Instead of looking into ourselves for the answers, we should look up to Jesus. The reference to being lifted up is connected to Jesus being lifted up on the cross for our sins. This particular picture of Jesus on the cross holds excellent promise for bettering our lives. Self-help can give us practical skills to make changes in our lives, but the change of heart and intention has to come from outside of us. Paul catches this truth even more clearly when he invites us to run our race "looking unto Jesus, the author and finisher of our faith" (Hebrews 12:2, NKJV).

The next time you are inspired to work on yourself, look outside of yourself—look at Jesus for strength wisdom, and a change of heart. When your focus is on the right person, self-help will find its proper place in your life.

Embracing Our Unique Design

BY MICHELLE ANDERSON

*For we are his workmanship,
created in Christ Jesus for good works,
which God prepared beforehand,
that we should walk in them.*

—EPHESIANS 2:10, ESV

In a world consumed with comparisons and the pursuit of perfection, it is easy to find ourselves trapped in the snare of comparing our lives, talents, and accomplishments to those around us. I vividly remember a time when I, too, fell into this destructive pattern. Growing up in the shadow of my older sister, who seemed to excel in everything she pursued, I constantly felt inadequate and struggled to measure up to her achievements. However, through a transformative journey of self-discovery and faith, I learned the invaluable lesson of embracing God's unique purpose for my life. Imagine a rose and a violet engaged in a conversation, arguing about who is prettier. The rose boasts of its vibrant colors and enchanting fragrance, while the violet admires its own delicate petals and subtle beauty. Yet, in the eyes of an impartial observer, both the rose and the violet possess a unique and incomparable beauty. Similarly, in the eyes of our Creator, each of us is fearfully and wonderfully made, designed with distinct qualities and purposes.

It was through the lens of Ephesians 2:10 that I began to grasp the truth of my own worth and purpose. I realized that comparing myself to others was not only futile but also a disservice to the extraordinary workmanship God had crafted in me. I discovered that I was created in Christ Jesus, not to replicate the path or achievements of another, but for a purpose uniquely tailored to my own gifts, passions, and calling.

As I embarked on embracing my individuality, I learned to walk confidently in the good works that God had prepared for me beforehand. I understood that my worth was not determined by how I measured up to others but by how faithfully I pursued the purposes God had laid before me. Each step I took in alignment with His will allowed me to discover the joy and fulfillment that come from living out His unique plan for my life.

I encourage you to free yourself from the chains of comparison and embrace the truth that we are God's handcrafted masterpieces. Each of us has been intricately designed with purpose and intention. As we seek God's guidance and align our hearts with His will, we can confidently walk in the good works He has prepared for us.

Embracing Your Authentic Identity in Christ

BY MICHELLE ANDERSON

> *For those whom he foreknew he also predestined to be conformed to the image of his Son in order that he might be the firstborn among many brothers.*
>
> —ROMANS 8:29, ESV

In a world that constantly bombards us with images and expectations, it can be easy to lose sight of our true identity. We often find ourselves striving to fit into molds that others have created for us, seeking their approval and acceptance. However, as children of God, our true identity lies not in conforming to the expectations of others, but in embracing who we are in Christ.

In my younger teenage years, I was quite the opposite of confident. However, I had come to embrace my natural long but curly hair. Yet upon entering high school, something began to change. The voices of the "it" girls began to influence me as they suggested that I would look better with straightened hair. Longing for their acceptance and not understanding who I was, decided to give it a try despite the great lengths it would take to accomplish this task.

As the compliments poured in, I continued to try to change myself, seeking validation and fitting into the mold that others created for me despite the expense and pain it caused. Soon, straightening my hair was not enough. I was also encouraged to try first a little eyeliner and then eventually lipstick. Each inch I gave turned into a painful mile, as I continued to seek validation and approval from others. Before long, I had become so out of touch with who I really was that I did not even recognize myself. My desire to conform to the image others wanted for me became such a driving force in my life that it overshadowed my authentic identity.

When I look back at this time in my life through pictures, I am thankful that I eventually found the courage to break away from the never-ending quest to reflect the image of those around me. However, as an adult, I still find myself wrestling with the pressure to conform to a variety of "images." You see, society constantly presents us with a variety of messages calling us to conform to what others believe we should be or have, whether it be a car, home, or even career path.

In Romans 8:29, we are reminded that God foreknewed us and predestined us to be conformed to the image of His Son, Jesus Christ. Our identity should be found in aligning ourselves with His character and reflecting His love for the world. It is not about conforming to the fads and trends that fade away but about embracing the truth of who we are in Christ.

May You See Yourself as the Lord Sees You

BY SARA TABTABAI

Do you not know that you are God's temple and that God's Spirit dwells in you?

—1 CORINTHIANS 3:16, ESV

"You look like you've lost weight." This common phrase is often said with good intentions and praise, but when said to my daughter, it triggered many ill feelings. Even if said in jest, I shudder at the thought of her being brought to focus on her body as something that must change or shrink from being praised and accepted. Growing up, I focused on my outward appearance and weight. I struggled with a poor body image and disordered eating. I exercised to the extreme and risked my health to pursue a physical beauty standard that was neither attainable nor necessary. Now that I have a daughter, I see myself in her and pray she will avoid that self-inflicted torment. I instead wish for her to focus on self-love, knowing that the Lord created her in His image and that she is perfect.

I have worked hard as an adult to reframe my self-image into a more positive one. In addition to therapy, looking towards the

Scriptures has helped me to understand that my body is a temple that must be cared for rather than punished for not meeting an arbitrary and worldly image. As in 1 Samuel 16:7b (ESV), "For the Lord sees not as man sees: man looks on the outward appearance, but the Lord looks on the heart." God loves what is in our souls and is not deterred by perceived imperfections of the body.

The Bible teaches us to care for ourselves and treat our bodies well; "After all, no one ever hated their own body, but they feed and care for their body, just as Christ does the church" (Ephesians 5:29, NIV). We must care for our own bodies by respecting our physical form and sustaining it with healthy foods and healthy activity. Going to the extreme is not beneficial and interrupts our relationship with ourselves and God.

This journey to self-acceptance has been more critical since I became a mother. I can clearly see in my children that God created each of us in His image and as perfect creatures. Especially as a mother to a young girl, I want to do all I can to guide her toward a positive self-image and to respect and care for her body. She will undoubtedly face societal influences that contradict the Lord's teachings. Still, regarding how she views herself and her physical form, I will teach her that she is divinely made, as described in Psalm 139:13–14a (ESV), "For you formed my inward parts; you knitted me together in my mother's womb. I praise you, for I am fearfully and wonderfully made."

God's Love

*So we have come to know and
to believe the love that God has for us.
God is love, and whoever abides in love
abides in God, and God abides in him.*

—1 JOHN 4:16, ESV—

Grace Under Fire

BY KAREEN WILSON

*The LORD is compassionate and gracious,
slow to anger, abounding in love.*

—PSALM 103:8, NIV

I see the weeping girl standing under a tree. As I walk by, I feel sorry for her and want to stop and ask if I can help. I walk on by and go to the restaurant to pick up my husband's lunch. I walk back to my car and see the girl still standing there. My hand reaches to open the car door, and I hear a voice over my shoulder.

"Ma'am, I am so sorry, I just hit your car." I turned to look at the girl standing under the tree. I looked at my car and saw the damage on the right side. I held my breath to suppress the disbelief and pain I felt as I looked at the dent on the front bumper of my new car.

She is still crying. I swallow the lump in my throat and think of how I can get through this. She is now frantic and full of apologies and regret. I hold my tongue and wait until I can get it together. Finally, I asked for her insurance information, and she told me that she didn't know where to find such documents, she handed me her phone so I could speak to her dad. I continue to stay calm and discuss how we will handle this.

After gathering the information, she calms down, and I offer her some peace. I told her it was okay and that we would figure it out. She looks a little calmer but still shocked.

It takes every prayer to God and patience in my soul to extend some peace to the girl. I think of how irresponsible she was and how these Generation Z kids do not know how to drive, let alone park. But then grace comes into my mind. She did not have to wait for me to return. She apologized over and over. She seems genuinely sorry. Looking at her driver's license, I realize she is a week younger than my daughter. I think of how I would want someone to treat her compassionately. I think of everything I have done and how someone has forgiven me. Grace is for everyone.

We can think of the ways God has extended grace to us. The mercy and love of God is all around us. We don't deserve it, but it is always there. If God can do that for us, then we can do it for our fellow man.

How can you extend grace to those around you?

Heal Me Again

BY KAREEN WILSON

Heal me, Lord, that I may be healed; save me, that I may be saved, for you are my praise.

—JEREMIAH 17:14, NABRE

Nine years after my episode with cancer, I never thought I would deal with it again. It was January, and I was relaxing, reading a book in bed. As I stretched my hand across my chest, I felt something extra beneath my right breast. It felt like a bony growth close to the chest cavity, hard and out of place. I was due for my annual physical, so I decided to complete my yearly ultrasound for breast examination.

When the radiologist entered the room during the ultrasound, I became concerned. She prescribed a biopsy. That is when it all came tumbling down. Cancer cells. Cancer again. My heart plummeted into deep despair. I looked for hope.

It had not spread anywhere. It was in the early stages, and it was curable.

The biopsy indicated I would need chemotherapy to heal. That is when I lost it. I cried. I begged. I prayed to any God that would hear me. But I had been here before. God had heard my cry years ago. I was going to survive, and I was going to thrive. I decided that I was going to come through stronger. This time I was going to heal not only physically but mentally.

It was a difficult process as my team of doctors created a plan to help me survive. I had to look for a blessing in every aspect of my treatment and care. I prayed for God to remove the pain from me, but if I had to go through it, then be by my side. I prayed for God to guide my mind to focus on the positive. At the beginning of my treatment, God had to guide me each and every step of the way, because if God was not there, I knew I would slip into a depression that I might not be able to crawl out of. I stood strong and believed. God's grace has brought me this far.

What blessings are upon me today!

His Mercies Are New Today

BY KAREEN WILSON

It is of the LORD's mercies that we are not consumed, because his compassions fail not. They are new every morning: great is thy faithfulness.

—LAMENTATIONS 3:22–23, KJV

Every day as I climb into my car, I say a quiet prayer, and I thank God for the fact that I have transportation. I also have my radio programmed to play my favorite song as I pull out of the garage. As I drive, "His Mercies Are New Today" rings in my ears, reminding me that today is a new day and God is with me. Micah Tyler's music blesses the ears with lyrics that connect with the soul. He writes, "I have been hard on myself lately, every morning I feel the weight when it's hard to just get out of bed, tell my heart, 'cause sometimes I forget that Your mercies are new today.... I can rest on Your shoulders, there is grace to start over, Your mercies are new today."

We can all relate. There are days when I am paralyzed by all that needs to get done and all the issues coming at me all at once. It is easy to dread getting out of bed and dealing with the mess that we sometimes call life. We must remind ourselves that today is a new day and that we are full of God's grace and find rest and peace in Him. Today we get to start over. It is a new day.

Many people face lives that seem to be cloudy. For them, there is no joy in anything, and they feel there's nothing they can do about it. It is also overwhelming and can lead to thoughts that life is not worth living.

With much prayer and medical attention, these symptoms of depression can be managed. Knowing God's mercies is the cherry on top of it all. God's love and grace can cover all and give us hope for the moment and the future.

How will God bless you today? Are you looking for God's mercies today?

My Grace Is Sufficient

BY PATRICIA REED

*And he said unto me, My grace is sufficient for thee:
for my strength is made perfect in weakness.
Most gladly therefore will I rather glory in my infirmities,
that the power of Christ may rest upon me.*

—2 CORINTHIANS 12:9, KJV

In the English dictionary, two words are spelled alike but pronounced differently, and each pronunciation has a different meaning; that word is *perfect*. The first definition means to be completely free from faults and defects. The second definition means to bring to final form, to improve and refine. When I think of the word *perfect,* I am reminded that no one is perfect, but God. It does not matter how hard I try; I will always be flawed and feel a sense of inadequacy.

In today's text, I am reminded that God's grace is sufficient for me, and His power is made perfect in my weakness. What a powerful and comforting truth! God's grace is sufficient for me. In other words, it is enough! His grace is sufficient for you. Can you shout "Amen"? His grace is sufficient for all of us who "labor and are heavy laden" (Matthew 11:28, KJV).

As women, we tend to feel that we must do everything perfectly. But the Bible says that God glories in our infirmities. When we are constantly in a state of trying to be perfect, we become overwhelmed and neglect ourselves to the point of illness. We must find a balance in our daily walk. He works out our affairs for our good and His glory. We must remember that every area of our life is in a state of development. So do not be discouraged when things do not go your way. The Lord is bringing us along by His timetable. Our faith is growing, and our understanding of God's purpose is unfolding. Make no mistake, the Lord is perfecting or improving and refining us so that He can bring us to our final form.

We will not always be imperfect. When Christ comes to take us home with Him, we will be perfected in Him. Remember in Philippians 1:6 (KJV), God says, "He which hath begun a good work in you will perform it until the day of Jesus Christ." He will complete it not just because He is God, but because He began this work in you. His grace is sufficient for you.

The Art of Complaining

BY KAREEN WILSON

*I cry aloud to the L*ORD*;*
*I lift up my voice to the L*ORD *for mercy.*
I pour out before him my complaint;
before him, I tell my trouble.
When my spirit grows faint within me,
it is you who watch over my way.
In the path where I walk people have hidden a snare for me.

—PSALM 142:1–3, NIV

No one likes a whiner. We all know that one person we dread calling on the phone or inviting to lunch because we know it will be a "Woe is me!" fest. They wear their suffering as a badge of honor.

People can complain about almost anything. While at the Dead Sea on vacation, someone said, "This water is too salty. It is stinging my eyes and burning my skin." It's the Dead Sea. Don't go in!

Sometimes we need to be honest about our feelings. David cried out to God many times in the Psalms and told Him exactly how he felt.

GOD'S LOVE

What if complaining can be good? Sometimes we need to complain without murmuring or grumbling. The difference is that complaining can be an act of faith; grumbling is a lack of faith.

David complains in Psalms saying, "All day long they twist my words; all their schemes are for my ruin…Record my misery; list my tears on your scroll" (Psalm 56:5, 8, NIV). But he backs it up with, "In God, I trust and am not afraid" (Psalm 56:4b, NIV).

Murmuring is complaining just to hear your own voice, and it says you have no faith that God is powerful, loving, and wise to guide and help you.

But faithful complaining is our honest expression of reaching out to the Savior for help.

Be real before God. Come with your hurt and sorrow because He can help you. True lamenting can help process suffering. It is a real and deep conversation with God and building your faith in Him. God knows your heart.

When injustice happens, when you struggle with relationships, when your finances are not where they need to be, talk to God about it. Tell God honestly how you feel.

You don't have to pretend that everything is okay. In the song "God Only Knows" performed by For King and Country, the lyrics are, "God only knows what you've been through. God only knows what they say about you. God only knows how it's killing you. But there is a love that God only knows."

What do you need to complain about to God today?

God's Intimate Knowledge of Our Lives

BY AVALEY FRANCES MATIERIENE

You have searched me, LORD, and you know me.
You know when I sit and when I rise;
you perceive my thoughts from afar.
You discern my going out and my lying down;
you are familiar with all my ways.
Before a word is on my tongue you,
LORD, know it completely.

—PSALM 139:1–4, NIV

As I stroll along the shores of the ocean, I find myself captivated by the sheer abundance of the grains of sand on the beach. In this serene setting, I am reminded of the profound truth that God's knowledge extends far beyond what our finite minds can comprehend. Just as He knows the number of sand grains on the shores, He intimately knows every detail of our lives, our deepest desires, and our heartfelt longings.

Our Heavenly Father, in His infinite wisdom and understanding, has searched us and knows us intimately. He perceives our every thought, even from a distance. Every step we take, every decision we make, He discerns with perfect clarity. No aspect of our lives escapes His notice, for He is acquainted with all our ways.

In the midst of our daily struggles and aspirations, let us find comfort in the fact that God knows us completely. He is intimately aware of our needs, hopes, and dreams. Just as He counts and treasures each grain of sand, He counts us as His beloved children, worthy of His unwavering attention and care.

In moments of doubt or uncertainty, let us turn to our Heavenly Father, knowing that He understands us in ways that no human ever could. He is not distant or detached but intimately acquainted with the intricacies of our hearts. May we find solace and confidence in His all-encompassing knowledge, entrusting our lives to His loving guidance.

As we stand on the shores of life, let us remember that we are known and loved by the Creator of the universe. Just as He knows the countless grains of sand, He knows us intimately and walks alongside us in every step of our journey. May we embrace His deep knowledge of us and find comfort in His everlasting presence.

Vulnerability with God

BY TANIA FUENTES-DAVITT

> *Can a mother forget the baby at her breast and have no compassion on the child she has borne? Though she may forget, I will not forget you!*
>
> —ISAIAH 49:15, NIV

Becoming a mother is such a culture shock. The life you once knew is gone in an instant. For me, it was especially jarring as my baby was born six weeks early. I had a vague timeline and thought I knew what to expect and how things would be. And then one night of blood, pain, and fear, and everything is different. Suddenly, your needs and your pain do not matter. You live from one cry to the next, dropping everything at a moment's notice to tend to this little being under your care.

The sleep-deprived haze of new motherhood is not for the faint of heart. I remember feeling like I was propelled forward from the deepest of sleep, my arms finding my child before I even consciously knew where I was or what I was doing. Personal hygiene was an afterthought, while pain and discomfort after going through labor and birth were all put into perspective.

GOD'S LOVE

My baby was colicky, he was diagnosed with acid reflux, and breastfeeding was not the easy experience that I expected. I remember waking up in the middle of the night with my baby crying and the milk just spilling down the front of my shirt. My body had exactly what he needed, but because he didn't know how to connect with me, he couldn't latch on and eat, so I couldn't easily give it to him. I felt so helpless. How I longed to be able to easily latch my baby and give him what he needed—that comfort and closeness and connection.

Through those dark nights, sitting alone with an infant, I thought about how God longs to connect with us...how God has exactly what we need if we will just let Him draw near to us. I thought about how we are made to be in constant connection with Him, just like a baby is made to connect with its mother. He is not intimidated by our cries.

When newborn babies don't know what they need, they just cry out that something is wrong. We can cry out to God when we don't know what we need to do. The love we feel on earth is just a pale shadow of the love God feels for us. We can't out love God. No mother on earth loves her child more than God loves us.

In what ways is God calling you to come into a deeper connection with Him? Have you cried out to God and trusted Him with your struggles?

God Sees Your Needs

BY TANIA FUENTES-DAVITT

Elijah was afraid and ran for his life. When he came to Beersheba in Judah, he left his servant there, while he himself went a day's journey into the wilderness. He came to a broom bush, sat down under it, and prayed that he might die. "I have had enough, LORD," he said. "Take my life; I am no better than my ancestors." Then he lay down under the bush and fell asleep. All at once an angel touched him and said, "Get up and eat." He looked around, and there by his head was some bread baked over hot coals and a jar of water. He ate and drank and then lay down again. The angel of the LORD came back a second time and touched him and said, "Get up and eat, for the journey is too much for you."

—1 KINGS 19:3–7, NIV

I curled up in a ball and pulled the covers tightly over my head. *I can't do this, God,* I thought. *It's too much.* The negative thoughts swirled like angry hornets.

If only you were a better Christian, you could stay positive through this. If God really loved you, this wouldn't be happening. The "ifs" haunted me, and made me feel not good enough, not Christian enough, not holy enough. When the storms of life come, sometimes the inner storm is just as strong as the events that plague us. Not only are we struggling with what is happening, but we struggle with feeling like we are not good enough in how we handle the situation.

In times like these, I like to think of the prophet Elijah. This was a man of God; he literally called down fire from heaven, a miraculous sign from God. But right after this, we find him running for his life and lying under a tree feeling as though he isn't good enough and asking God to end his life. What does God do in response? Does God reprimand him and agree that he is not good enough? No! God has compassion for him and provides for his needs. He sends an angel who provides him with food and water and allows Elijah to rest and recover.

God doesn't just care about what we do for Him; He cares about providing for us and taking care of us along the way.

If you feel low, burned out, and like you can't continue, know you are in good company. Many prophets and heroes in the Bible often felt this way. Know that it doesn't mean something is wrong with you; it just means that it may be a good time to rest and recover and recharge with God. God says, "Come to me, all you who are weary and burdened, and I will give you rest" (Matthew 11:28, NIV).

Take time to recharge with God today. Spend some time resting in the knowledge that God still loves and cares for you despite how low you feel on any given day.

Forgetful but Not Faithless

BY TANIA FUENTES-DAVITT

Who shall separate us from the love of Christ?
shall tribulation, or distress, or persecution,
or famine, or nakedness, or peril, or sword?

—ROMANS 8:35, KJV

Alzheimer's is a terrible disease. My grandmother, who was a force of nature and someone who could not be trifled with, could feel her mind slowly slipping away. She would joke with me all the time that one day she would not remember my name and would hobble over to me. Of course, I would ask her not to talk like that, assuring her it would never happen. Looking back now, I think she knew. Consciously or unconsciously, she was trying to prepare me for what was coming. It was a slow fade; she started repeating her stories, and then she would get lost in a house she knew well. Conversations with her would go in circles.

For her eightieth birthday, we flew her to our home and had a birthday party for her with everyone around. I love listening to the wisdom of others, and every year I ask people what their birthday wisdom is for that year. It is fun to see the different pieces of wisdom people acquire as they age. We'd had several conversations on repeat that day, but I asked her what her birthday wisdom was. I don't remember her exact words, but I do remember that it was the most coherent thing she said all day. She talked about how God is faithful and that He is to be trusted. In all that Alzheimer's had taken away, it had not taken away her faith and trust in God and His love for her.

The global pandemic in 2020 was not kind to the elderly. My dad and uncle made the very difficult decision to put her in a nursing home in Puerto Rico, and, with the status of the world, we could not visit. Communication was nonexistent. The thought of her being isolated in a nursing home had me restless and even sleepless. I remember sobbing one night, missing her, and worrying for her. I called out to God in my tears. At that moment, I felt that God saw me, and I was assured that God loved my grandmother more than I ever could. I knew He was with me in this moment of pain and despair, and I knew He was with my grandmother regardless of whether I could be with her or not. Although God did not miraculously heal her so that she could be released from the nursing home, she had something more precious than physical healing: she had her relationship with God and, even in her disease, the conviction of His love and care.

Whose Fault Is It?

BY EVELYN RAQUEL DELGADO MARRERO

*No temptation has overtaken you except
what is common to mankind. And God is faithful;
he will not let you be tempted beyond what you can bear.*

—1 CORINTHIANS 10:13A, NIV

My granddaughter is three years old. When you ask her, "Who made this mess?" She blames one of her daycare friends or one of her cousins, even though they are not present. It is amazing that, even at that age she assumes that maybe she might get away with something.

It is always easier to blame someone or something else for what we do. We hear excuses like, "I'm stuck in a bad marriage," "I don't have a job," or "I was an unwanted child." All this could be absolutely true, and such circumstances cause a lot of pain and suffering, but we cannot blame others for how we choose to react to those circumstances. We cannot use them to stay in that bad situation because there is a way out. Christ has offered to liberate us.

All of mankind has temptations. They might be different for each one of us, but God gives us a way out. God is faithful; He will not let us be tempted beyond what we can bear.

GOD'S LOVE

When I was in college, a group of us went on a hike. The hike included climbing a mountain. On one side of the mountain, we needed to climb using the roots of some trees to get to the top. The climb was about thirty feet high. Everyone was climbing one at a time. When it was my turn, I started off very brave, but when I was about twenty-five feet up, I looked down and panicked. I hung there shaking. I couldn't climb up, and I couldn't go down either. My friends were trying to encourage me to go up the rest of the way. I was almost at the top, but I couldn't move. I was afraid. I just stood there grabbing onto that root in panic. Finally, one of my friends climbed up behind me and told me to sit on his head; then he propelled me the rest of the way up.

This, many times, is what happens with God's people. We know what is right, but we are paralyzed by fear. We blame others or ourselves for being unable to move. We say, "I am not strong enough, or smart enough, or brave enough." That weakness is what the devil uses to control us. When we sin, he makes us believe it's our fault. The devil uses those thoughts to convince us our excuses are valid. If we let the devil win by making us believe we are lost, he has won.

When we give in to our weaknesses, we are telling God that He is not powerful enough to help us to be strong. We might even be tempted to blame God for not making us strong enough to resist temptations. But God wants to remind us that He will always be our strength and that He is there even when we fail. He is there to propel us to move forward. Remember that He will not let us be tempted beyond what we can bear.

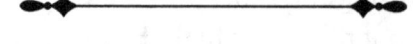

The Golden Rule

BY EVELYN RAQUEL DELGADO MARRERO

*So in everything,
do to others what you would have them do to you.*

—MATTHEW 7:12A, NIV

I am sure that you all know and practice the Golden Rule which states that we should treat others the same way we would like to be treated. In our everyday lives, we teach it to our kids and our students. We treat others well, expecting them to do the same to us. When Jesus was talking to His disciples, He emphasized that this was the Christian's duty to his neighbor, a fundamental ethical principle.

Do other religions practice the Golden Rule?

Aristotle, an ancient Greek philosopher, and scientist, promoted the Golden Rule about 2,400 years ago. He said that it would bring peace to the world. Confucius had a teaching called Jen that Westerners have labeled The Silver Rule: "Do not do to others what you do not want others to do unto you." Buddhism says, "Hurt not others in ways that you yourself would find hurtful." And Hinduism says, "Do not do to others what would cause pain if done to you."

The Silver Rule states that negative behavior will happen because of bad things you do to others. In other words, bad behaviors have consequences. "If you do something to hurt someone, that hurt is going to come back to you." Much like the Karma in Hinduism, it's the cause and effect of your behaviors. "If you don't want pain, don't inflict pain."

That is pretty clear-cut, and it seems that all these rules are very similar, but the Golden Rule focuses on the positive. The Golden Rule has a proactive spin to it. "Do good, and good will happen to you."

Regardless of what others do to you, Jesus wants us to treat others with respect, love, and positivity. In Leviticus 19:18b (KJV), God says, "Thou shalt love thy neighbor as thyself." I think this was introduced in the Old Testament, so the principles of the Golden Rule were given to God's people way before Jesus gave the Sermon on the Mount where He elevates the laws of the Old Testament to a higher level.

Love is the difference between the Golden Rule and all the other rules. Jesus wants us to go as far as loving our enemies (Matthew 5:44). That is what a true Christian should do. The Golden Rule of the Old Testament now rises to the height of the love that Jesus showed us when He died on the cross.

Grandma's Calling

BY EVELYN RAQUEL DELGADO MARRERO

But seek first his kingdom and his righteousness, and all these things will be given to you as well.

—MATTHEW 6:33, NIV

My grandmother's conversion to Adventism is remarkable. She married young to a man who was fourteen years her senior. He was not only older, but he was street-wise as well. He had been raised on the streets by himself since his mother died young and his dad was an absent father. He worked as a street vendor, so he spent many hours on the streets. Sometimes, he didn't go home for days. In those days, to be able to make a living as a street vendor, you had to travel to different towns. He had a pushcart to carry his merchandise, so wherever the night caught him, that's where he stayed. That arrangement is not always conducive to a happy marriage.

Grandma soon had a baby boy and was pregnant with her second child. Her living conditions were less than desirable. She felt lonely, impoverished, sad, and miserable. On top of all that, she found out that her husband had another woman in one of the places where he stayed. That other woman also had a child with him and was pregnant again. My grandmother felt hopeless.

GOD'S LOVE

Without letting anyone know, she devised a plan. She was going to tie a heavy rock to her clothing and to her son's clothing and jump into the bay. She wanted to end her life, but God had other plans for her.

She loved music and, on her way to the bay she leaned against a building. She heard some music coming from the building and stopped long enough for a lady to come out of the building and invite her in. I see the Holy Spirit in action here. The lady was the sister of a missionary who was in Puerto Rico doing evangelistic work. Mr. Prince was the evangelist's name. He introduced my grandma to Jesus. Jesus gave my grandma peace, security, and literally salvation. His family became very friendly with my grandma and her family and as she learned more about Jesus, she learned about love, health, order, and structure that helped her with bringing up her family. Eventually, her family consisted of five boys and three girls who loved and feared God. The story is told that she gave Bible studies to her husband and taught him to read using the Bible as her teaching tool. Eventually, he was also converted to Seventh-Day Adventism.

She shared the gospel with her parents and her siblings, and they all converted and became colporteurs, teachers, and health professionals in Puerto Rico. She shared it with her neighbors and every one she found on the street. She embraced the gospel with such enthusiasm and sincerity that she brought hundreds of people to Jesus' feet.

Because of Grandma's witness, her relatives down to the third and fourth generations have accepted Jesus as their personal Savior.

Follow the Instructions

BY MICHELLE ANDERSON

*Therefore, confess your sins to each other
and pray for each other so that you may be healed.
The prayer of a righteous person is powerful and effective.*

—JAMES 5:16 , NIV

Have you ever attempted to build a piece of furniture following directions but missed a step and, as a result, could not get the results promised? Well, the same thing can happen to us spiritually. If we are honest, at some point in our Christian journey, there are times when things just don't seem to be working according to plan, and the results can be devastating. During these times, I have found it is essential to revisit the instruction manual, "the Bible," asking God to reveal where I may have gone off track.

I've shared the story of my mother who had fallen ill and was not able to eat for three days; she was utterly alone. The next day, she went to the emergency room for lab work and a slew of tests. Unfortunately, she received no answers about what was wrong other than a diagnosis of anemia from "unknown causes," but no source of bleeding was found. Over the next several days, my sister and I arrived to be with her at home while spending many days in prayer. One day after reading our Scripture text for today, we decided to call for an anointing service at her home.

As we prepared for this anointing service, we read James 5, which contained instructions on what to do if anyone was sick. In addition to asking for the anointing, several other steps were given as a prerequisite to her healing, but these steps are frequently overlooked. In my mother's case, after revisiting Scripture and through prayer, the Lord had impressed her with the need to confess or make things right with others. In the following days, I saw my mother humble herself and apologize to many individuals, including me, admitting wrongs she felt she may have committed. Witnessing the peace, freedom, and healing my mother obtained from following God's healing instructions was a powerful reminder of our need for confession for spiritual and physical health.

After her confessions, my mother received healing just as James 5:16 promised. She immediately began to revive and, within two short weeks, could eat and resume her normal life activities. I will always appreciate this experience as I saw firsthand that God's promises are sure. Still, it is up to us to follow the directions entirely for the best results.

Sufficient Grace

BY MICHELLE ANDERSON

Therefore, I will boast all the more gladly of my weaknesses, so that the power of Christ may rest upon me.

—2 CORINTHIANS 12:9B, ESV

Life can sometimes present us with challenges that leave us feeling weak and helpless. We may plead with the Lord for deliverance, longing for our circumstances to change. In those moments of desperation, God's response to us may not always be what we expect. However, His sustaining grace remains ever-present, providing strength and comfort even in our greatest weakness.

After riding high from the apparent miraculous healing of my mother from her unknown health crisis, our faith would soon be tested again. Approximately three months after enjoying a time of remission, my mother, in Michigan visiting my sister for the holidays, began complaining of shortness of breath and weakness. Once again, we found ourselves in the emergency room where, this time, she was admitted. We would soon learn that she was battling non-Hodgkin's lymphoma, cancer with which I was unacquainted but would soon come to know all too well.

As my sister and I pleaded with God for miraculous intervention, we instead witnessed my mother endure countless hospitalizations, treatments, and setbacks, yet her cancer remained relentless. It seemed our prayers went unanswered, and hope began to fade.

Amidst the physical and emotional turmoil, however, my mother clung to 2 Corinthians 12:9. She found solace in the words of the apostle Paul, who had also pleaded with the Lord three times for relief from his affliction. Paul also received an unexpected response from God—a reminder that His grace was sufficient, and His power was made perfect in weakness.

Amid my mother's terminal illness, we witnessed God's sustaining grace unfold remarkably. Financial burdens that seemed insurmountable were miraculously lifted through unexpected provisions. Friends and family rallied around, offering comfort, love, and practical support.

Mom realized that God's sustaining grace was not merely about physical healing but His presence and provision in every aspect of her journey. In her weakness, she experienced the power of Christ resting upon her. His grace infused her with the strength to face each day, cherish moments of joy amidst the trials, and find peace in uncertainty.

Today, if you find yourself in a place of weakness, take heart. God's sustaining grace is available to you.

Forgive to Live: Embracing the Power of Love

BY MICHELLE ANDERSON

*Love is patient, love is kind. It does not envy,
it does not boast, it is not proud.
It does not dishonor others, it is not self-seeking,
it is not easily angered, it keeps no record of wrongs.*

—1 CORINTHIANS 13:4–5, NIV

In a world that often portrays love as a fairy tale with perfect endings, it can be easy to develop unrealistic expectations about relationships. Many of us have grown up reading romance novels and watching movies where love always feels good, and conflicts are quickly resolved. However, when the reality of marriage sets in, we may find ourselves confronted with challenges and disagreements that can strain our relationships.

As a young wife, I was heavily influenced by the idealized notions of love as a result of countless hours spent reading and watching fictional love stories. As a result, I believed that my relationship would always be filled with joy and happiness. Yet, as the early years of marriage unfolded, I quickly discovered that conflicts and misunderstandings were inevitable. In these moments, I would often rehash a list of wrongs my husband had committed, increasing the length of the list with each argument.

As time passed, I noticed that this habit of holding onto grudges and keeping a record of his wrongs was taking a toll on my well-being. Not only did it strain our relationship, but it also affected my physical and mental health. In my moments of prayer and reflection, I felt convicted by the truth revealed in 1 Corinthians 13:4–5.

The Scripture reminds us of the characteristics of true love—love that is patient, and kind and does not keep a record of wrongs. It challenges us to let go of our pride, anger, and the need for self-justification and instead embrace forgiveness and kindness. In doing so, we unlock the transformative power of love, not just in our relationships but also within ourselves.

I quickly realized that harboring resentment and continually bringing up past wrongs hindered my ability to experience true love and healing. I understood that forgiveness is not just an act of kindness towards my husband, but also a crucial step toward my own well-being. By relinquishing the habit of keeping score and choosing forgiveness, I witnessed the restoration of my physical health, mental peace, and relationship.

As we embrace forgiveness in our relationships, we open ourselves to the transformative power of God's love.

The God Who Sees: Comfort in His Presence

BY MICHELLE ANDERSON

So Hagar gave this name to the LORD Who spoke to her, "You are a God Who sees."

—GENESIS 16:13A, NLV

There are moments in our lives when we feel invisible, overlooked, and unseen. In those moments, we long to be acknowledged, understood, and recognized for our efforts and struggles. We desire to be seen, to have someone notice and validate our experiences.

In the midst of such seasons, it is essential to remember the story of Hagar. She found herself in a desperate situation, feeling abandoned and alone. Pregnant and cast out by Sarah, her mistress, she wandered in the wilderness with no one to turn to. It was in this place of isolation and despair that God revealed Himself to her. God spoke to Hagar, assuring her that He saw her, heard her cries, and understood her pain. Overwhelmed by this encounter, Hagar gave a name to the Lord who saw her: "You are a God Who sees." In that moment, Hagar discovered the truth that we all need to remember—God sees us even when we feel invisible.

There have been times in my life when I have felt unseen, yet I have come to realize that this happens when my focus has shifted away from God. As the youngest sibling, I often existed in my sister's shadow. Going to a new grade where she had previously been meant dealing with many people who did not see me but saw my sister instead. To combat this, I often found myself trying to be different or seeking recognition, praise, and validation from others. In doing this, I found that I lost sight of the One who truly sees me.

In my moments of feeling invisible, I realized the importance of redirecting my gaze back to Christ. Instead of seeking recognition from others, I must choose to seek God's presence. His love and acceptance are unwavering, and His eyes are always upon us. In His sight, we are seen, known, and cherished individually.

May you, too, find comfort in knowing that our Heavenly Father sees you in every circumstance. He sees the work you do behind closed doors, the sacrifices you make, and the challenges you face. He sees your heart and is intimately acquainted with your every need. As you shift your focus from yourself to God, we discover that His recognition and approval are far more valuable than any human accolade. He lifts us higher, not to a podium or a stage, but to a place of deep intimacy and relationship with Him. In His presence, we find true fulfillment, purpose, and peace.

God's Will Be Done

BY SYLVIA GOBEL

*And this is what God has testified:
He has given us eternal life, and this life is in his Son.*

—1 JOHN 5:11, NLT

My husband had to have an ablation procedure to open his sinuses. It was a simple outpatient procedure, and when it was over, the doctor told me he had done well and would be out in about an hour. However, just five minutes later, the doctor and a female chaplain came out and told me that my husband's heart had stopped. He didn't respond after two cardiac electrical shocks. They were continuing CPR, but he was still not responding. They asked me to contact any family, so I called my daughters. Then they wanted me to go be with my unresponsive husband. Since I was sobbing, the doctor left me with the chaplain.

I started to pray out loud with my arms up in the air saying, "Lord, You have promised that in times like this, You will help us. Please bring Terry back to life!" Then I thought, *Who am I to tell God what to do?* So then I said, "Lord, if it is not your will for my husband to live, then please give my daughters and me the supernatural strength to face this." The doctors and nurses did CPR over an hour and, miraculously, his heart began to beat again. Everything was normal, and he had no heart or brain damage.

"God is our refuge and strength, always ready to help in times of trouble. So, we will not fear when earthquakes come and the mountains crumble into the sea" (Psalm 46:1–2, NLT).

"And it is impossible to please God without faith. Anyone who wants to come to Him must believe that God exists and that he rewards those who sincerely seek Him" (Hebrews 11:6, NLT).

"And we are confident that he hears us whenever we ask for anything that pleases him" (1 John 5:14, NLT).

I am so grateful and honored that our loving Savior saw best to bring my husband back to life. I know God answers differently sometimes, but He never leaves us alone and is always ready to give us His love through people, His peace, and His supernatural strength to face whatever may come our way in life. Keep on trusting Him. He is trustworthy.

He Loves Me, He Loves Me Not

BY ANANDI MOSES

*But God demonstrates His own love toward us,
in that while we were still sinners,
Christ died for us.*

—ROMANS 5:8, NASB

It was an overcast winter morning. My heart matched the gloom outside as I was coming home from a grocery trip. I was getting ready to open the car to get out when I noticed the snowflake on the window. I have never seen a perfectly shaped snowflake except in pictures. I didn't even know that snowflakes could grow symmetrically to the size visible to the naked eye. This one was perfectly symmetrical and beautiful! It felt like a little gift from God to cheer me up. I realized that I was on God's mind. My spirit lifted immediately, and an assurance of God's goodness and care settled in my mind. It was a beautiful moment that has stayed with me.

God sometimes sends these special gifts of love to cheer us along the way, but sometimes there are no snowflakes to find. God appears to have become silent. Our hearts are so burdened that our senses are dulled to the blessings around us. We can't seem to find assurance or sense God's presence. Ironically, this is the time when we need it the most. What can we do at these times?

Of all the reminders of God's love, nothing compares to the cross of Jesus. This is an enduring reminder of God's love that is grounded in all other assurances that we may seek. In times of need, the cross is sufficient to lift us up. In order for the cross of Jesus to give us assurance, we must personalize the cross in terms of our salvation. We should seek to understand the enormous price paid for our redemption. Then, when we cannot find tangible evidence of God's love, we can rest in the love of God that shines through the cross of Christ. It will tell us how much He loves us and what He is willing to do for us.

We need not play games like children plucking away at the petals wondering, "He loves me, He loves me not." With every good thing that happens to us, our hearts are filled with the assurance of God's love. When times are rough, we need not fear that He has abandoned us. We can be sure of His love not only from what happens to us in our lives but also through our realization of the love of God at the cross. It gives us comfort and peace in times of need.

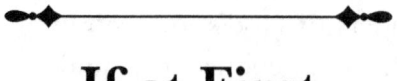

If at First

BY KELLEY MATIERIENE

*How priceless is your unfailing love, O God!
People take refuge in the shadow of your wings.*

—PSALM 36:7, NKJV

The first time I took my son to the beach, he was about nine months old, and I was so excited! My dad wanted me to pick up a bike for him in New Jersey, and I decided to stop by the New Jersey shore and introduce my son to the beach now that he was old enough to enjoy it.

I love the beach—the smell of the sea and the sound of the crashing waves is exhilarating. I love the feel of the sand between my toes and the way the ocean seems to go on endlessly, blue and beautiful. That day, we drove three hours up the coast; my son fell asleep in the car and woke up on the beach…only he was not excited.

As we got out of the car and put him in his stroller, he was pouty. Then I sat him down in the sand, and the look on his face said it all. He was not happy to be at the beach. He was not impressed by the sand, the people, the sounds, or the smells. To this day,

I still look at those pictures and chuckle. We didn't stay by the water long. Now, of course, my son loves the beach; he wants to go every summer, and he is in love with surfing and riding the waves; but his first go at it wasn't at all what I was hoping for it to be. Now, I didn't stop taking him to the beach or introducing him to this place that I loved because I knew he would love it too once he just found his own way to embrace it.

Having kids has opened my eyes to the way God loves me. He doesn't force me to love what He loves. What God does in a way that's all His own is introduce me to His cares and desires. He gives me the opportunity to taste and see. He isn't put off if I am hesitant on the first encounter. He gives me another opportunity when I am older and maybe a little more mature, when He knows I may be more able to handle what He has for me. His love is slow and kind; it doesn't cause Him to become angry. Instead, He just keeps on loving.

Today, I am so grateful that God meets me where I am…that He sees me, knows my needs, and caters to the manifestations of His love to meet me where I am. He does this not because He has to but because He loves me. And He loves you. How have you seen God meeting you at the point of your need this week?

Keepsake

BY SANDRA A. SERGEANT

The LORD is my shepherd; I shall not want. He makes me lie down in green pastures, he leads me beside still waters, he restores my soul. He leads me in the right path for his name's sake. Even though I walk through the darkest valley, I fear no evil; for you are with me; your rod and staff—they comfort me. You prepare a table before me in the presence of my enemies; you anoint my head with oil; my cup overflows. Surely goodness and mercy shall follow me all the days of my life, and I shall dwell in the house of the LORD my whole life long.

—PSALM 23:1–6, NRSV

When I was a little girl, my mother taught me this Psalm, and we memorized it. We said it every night as our "prayer" before going to bed as far back as I can remember. Long after I married and left home, I found solace in those sacred words; I would say them whenever I felt afraid, unsure, or just as a prayer at night. Verse 4 was especially meaningful to me; it speaks of walking through the valley of the shadow of death without fear because of God's presence. It is particularly comforting and has brought me immeasurable comfort in times of fear and uncertainty. When I feel persecuted, verse 5 comes to mind, where He promises to prepare a table in the presence of my enemies and confirms His anointing. Here the psalmist reminds me of God's abundant provision and blessings, even in the presence of adversaries. And what comfort and trust the last verse promises! Indeed, without a doubt, goodness and mercy will follow me all the days of my life, and I will dwell in the house of the Lord forever.

I recognize Psalm 23 as my security blanket because it brings me a deep sense of peace and reassurance. This psalm is a powerful reminder of God's presence, protection, and provision, even amid challenging circumstances.

May these words also be a source of comfort, encouragement, and assurance for you, reminding you that you can trust in God's unwavering love and care in every season of your life.

Mistakes as Examples of Grace

BY MEGAN BLACKMORE

> *But for that very reason I was shown mercy so that in me,*
> *the worst of sinners, Christ Jesus might display*
> *His immense patience as an example for those who*
> *would believe in him and receive eternal life.*
>
> —1 TIMOTHY 1:16, NIV

In my lifetime, I am ashamed of some of the choices I have made. I am not proud of some of my decisions. Sometimes, I wish I could go back in time and undo them.

But we all know time travel is a work of fiction, and we are left with the inability to take back actions and words.

Still, a part of me wouldn't go back in time and have a do-over if given the opportunity. The reason is that this life is full of sin, and if I hadn't made the particular wrong choices I did make, I would have just made others. I would just have a different mistake to try to fix.

Although I am not proud in the least bit of some choices I have made, especially during my teenage years before I met Christ, and even a few I made after I was baptized, I have realized that those decisions taught me lessons that are now examples of the Lord's grace to others who have perhaps made choices similar to mine or even choices they deem worse than the ones I made.

When we wrong someone, it feels good to know that they forgive us. It's like a weight has been lifted; we feel better both physically and mentally. That is especially true when we have hurt someone we love deeply who offers us forgiveness we feel we don't deserve.

We should have that same feeling, knowing that despite all the wrong choices we have made of which we are now ashamed, it is through these decisions that we truly see the magnitude of the forgiveness and mercy the Lord offers to us, and the undeserved love and grace He extends to us.

When we make mistakes, we tend to hide them, sweep them under the rug, and make sure they don't see the light of day; we don't want anyone to even catch a glimpse of them. That's natural. We're embarrassed, ashamed, fearful of how someone might look at us. But being vulnerable and sharing testimonies of wrong choices can help others see the grace of the Lord; our sinful decisions can be used as an example of the Lord's forgiveness to us.

It can sometimes be a challenge to fully grasp and understand the Lord's loving forgiveness. Seeing how much the Lord has forgiven others gives us hope that He will forgive us, too. Being vulnerable is often not a way we want to be, but being vulnerable before others is something of more value than we can fathom to our fellow sinful humans. Others are struggling, and we have the ability to help by using our lives as examples of overcoming sin through the Lord's forgiveness and grace.

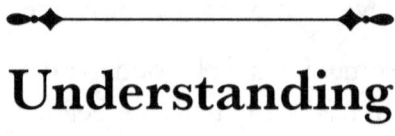

Understanding

BY MEGAN BLACKMORE

*Do you not know? Have you not heard?
The Lord is the everlasting God, the Creator of the
ends of the earth. He will not grow tired or weary,
and his understanding no one can fathom.*

—ISAIAH 40:28, NIV

It brings me great comfort to know that the God I have chosen to serve never grows tired or weary.

Something as simple as this is hard to understand or fathom, especially for me as I am currently more than eight months pregnant. I am always tired. To think that God, the Creator of all we see, do, and think never grows tired nor even weary is just unimaginable.

Think of everything the Lord does for us in just the twelve to sixteen hours we are awake every day. He hears and answers all of our prayers, and He keeps us from so many dangers. Imagine what would happen if, every single day, every employee who works in your building lined up at your door, or better yet, standing in your office, talking to you all at the same time. Imagine that most of them with big issues, and even bigger problems. Your brain would explode.

But, for God, this is all in a day's work, and He loves it. It doesn't bother, annoy, or burden Him. In fact, it's probably like music to His ears, being in communication with His children whom He loves more than we can understand or fathom.

With our limited understanding as mere human beings, we can't wrap our heads around many things pertaining to God. But I believe this is a good thing. If we had the same understanding as our Creator, why would we need a Creator? If a student knows everything the teacher knows, why take the class?

As Christians, we know that we need our Savior, our Creator. So, to be made with limited understanding is a humbling and reassuring asset. It means I will always need to lean on God for all my understanding and not on my own knowledge which has been tainted by this sinful world.

When we recognize our need for God—something I am still learning every day to do—we realize that it's good to have a God who knows it all, in ways more than we can ever even learn. We serve a God who can do it all; His knowledge and wisdom are something only He will ever hold. Who better to trust with your life than a God like that?

Our need for God and our understanding of His infinite power is never a weakness, but a great strength we can hold onto throughout our lives in this crazy world until His glorious return.

Authorship of God

BY ANANDI MOSES

For it is God who is at work in you,
both to desire and to work for His good pleasure.

—PHILIPPIANS 2:13, NASB

Writing is creative work. Authors who write novels and stories have the unique power to create people, places, and plots as they desire. They can take their characters wherever they want them to go and invent situations as they please. A very interesting work to do!

Can you imagine what kind of stories God would write if He were an author?

We need not wonder. The Bible has lots of examples. His authorship is unique in that His characters are not imaginary. He seeks the cooperation of the characters to move the story forward.

Under the magic of His pen, the mundane becomes extraordinary, the regular turns into the unexpected, the usual becomes special, averages become excellent, and the run-of-the-mill becomes a passion. God's stories are not always about great people. They are sometimes about common people who became special because of

His authorship. That makes each of us an excellent candidate to be part of His work.

We can see a semblance of ourselves in many characters in the Bible.

The temper of Moses, the lust of David, doubts of Thomas…

Pride, arrogance, greed, foolishness, obstinacy, unfaithfulness…

Weakness, fear, failure…

Thankfully, the stories don't end that way.

Moses went to heaven without waiting in his grave, and David became a man after God's own heart. Paul ended up changing the world forever for the sake of the gospel, and Peter was given the courage to be crucified upside down for the cause of Christ.

Unholy thoughts, unholy deeds, unholy traits, unholy people. Everything goes under the pen of the Master Author. What comes out is the holy book! He is willing to do that same work in your life too, if you will allow Him to use you.

Giving

*A generous person will prosper;
whoever refreshes others will be refreshed.*

—PROVERBS 11:25, NIV—

Giving 2.0

BY KAREEN WILSON

Each of you should give what you have decided in your heart to give, not reluctantly or under compulsion, for God loves a cheerful giver. And God is able to bless you abundantly, so that in all things at all times, having all that you need, you will abound in every good work

—2 CORINTHIANS 9:7–8, NIV

As I write the donation check, I feel a sense of honor for being able to give. The next day I forget that I have given; there is no emotional attachment to my gift. Many times, when I give to various charities and return my tithe, it can feel like giving out of a sense of obligation. Even if it is not an obligation, I have no idea why I am giving. I simply feel nothing. Of course, we should give our money to those in need, but we should consider how we give and step it up to giving 2.0.

I was listening to a podcast on happiness, and a social psychologist relayed how she encourages others to donate to charity as it creates joy and long-lasting pleasure. However, when it came time to review her taxes, her accountant told her to follow her own advice. Her charitable giving did not reflect her words, so she set out to fix that. She realized that when she gave, it was one-time gifts in small amounts that were not truly sacrificial. She researched and found the solution to her giving.

In Canada, you can give to a charity called the "Group of Five" Refugee Sponsor Agreement. The eligibility to donate has a few stipulations that raise the bar; Giving has to be a group effort. The group of friends, coworkers, or family who make up a group must work together to raise $40,000 to sponsor a family from Syria as they immigrate to Canada. The group learns about the family and finds a home, school (if the family has children), and social services from the day they enter the country. The groups typically find it easy to raise the money, but the commitment to finding shelter, work, and schooling proves to be a physical commitment. By the time the group meets the family at the airport, they have already formed a tight bond. As they watch a strong father cry tears of joy over what this group has done for his family, each one realizes their impact on this family's existence, creating more compassion and joy than just writing a check. The group continues to support the family for at least a year, or as long as is needed.

The good Samaritan exemplifies compassionate giving. He not only provided care but also arranged for the wounded man's recovery and future stability. Despite being strangers from different ethnic backgrounds, the Samaritan went out of his way to support the injured man by the highway. This demonstrates love for one another, which God encourages us to embrace.

Look around. Can you find ways to bless someone else through your giving?

Money! Who Needs It?

BY SANDRA A. SERGEANT

Honor the LORD with your possessions and with the first produce of your entire harvest.

—PROVERBS 3:9, CSB

And you shall remember the LORD your God, for it is He who gives you power to get wealth, that He may establish His covenant which He swore to your fathers, as it is this day.

—DEUTERONOMY 8:18, NKJV

In today's reflection on the biblical aspect of money, it is essential to recognize its significance in our lives. Money is a subject that permeates our daily transactions and conversations, and the Bible has much to say about it. In fact, approximately 2,350 verses in the Bible address money, which is almost twice as many as those about prayer and faith. Jesus had a lot to say about money. Nearly fifteen percent of everything Jesus spoke about related to money and possessions. Sixteen out of his thirty-eight parables dealt with the topic of money. However, it is essential to note that the kingdom of God takes precedence over money in His teachings.

For believers and humanitarians, money has great value because it can do great good. It can provide food for the hungry, drink for the thirsty, clothing for the naked, defense for the oppressed, and help for the sick. As one writer aptly puts it, "Money is more valuable than sand, only as it is put to use in providing for the necessities of life, blessing others, and advancing the cause of Christ." (Christ Object Lessons–351.3)

We are entrusted with resources and gifts from God. It is our responsibility to seek wisdom in managing them. By doing so, we have the privilege to participate in the Great Commission. We must recognize that our possessions are not our own; they belong to God and should be used for His glory and the well-being of others. In essence, God blesses us for the sole purpose of allowing us to bless others.

This prayer by King Solomon in Chronicles 29:11–12 (ESV) beautifully encapsulates our perspective on money and possessions:

"Yours, O Lord, is the greatness and the power and the glory and the victory and the majesty, for all that is in the heavens and the earth is yours. Yours is the kingdom, O Lord, and you are exalted as head above all. Both riches and honor come from you, and you rule over all. In your hand are power and might, and in your hand, it is to make great and to give strength to all."

May we approach money and possessions with a mindset rooted in the understanding that they are gifts from God to be used wisely and selflessly for His purposes and the betterment of humanity?

The Wealth Gap

BY KAREEN WILSON

> *And a ruler asked him, "Good Teacher, what must I do to inherit eternal life?" And Jesus said to him, "Why do you call me good? No one is good except God alone. You know the commandments: 'Do not commit adultery, Do not murder, Do not steal, Do not bear false witness, Honor your father and mother.'" And he said, "All these I have kept from my youth." When Jesus heard this, he said to him, "One thing you still lack. Sell all that you have and distribute to the poor, and you will have treasure in heaven; and come, follow me."*
>
> —LUKE 18:18–22, ESV

Can you imagine walking away from God…seeing God stretch out His hand, then turning to move away with sorrow in your heart? This is the story of the rich young ruler in Matthew 17. This wealthy man approaches Jesus and wants to know how he can enter the kingdom of heaven. He knows that he has kept all of the commandments since childhood, and he thinks it will be easy. The ruler thinks that it is a simple transaction like all of his investments in life. Being a religious man, he thinks he must do something or earn his way to inherit love from God. When Jesus tells him what he should do, he turns away and, in sorrow, gives up on God.

For most people, this story is about how hard it is for rich people to get into heaven. Jesus states that it is easier for a camel to go through the eye of the needle than for a rich man to enter the kingdom of heaven (Mark 10:25). I challenge you to look at this passage with an open mind and through a different lens.

Jesus had many other interactions with wealthy men. Zacchaeus was the short but wealthy tax collector who followed Jesus as soon as He said, "Make haste, and come down; for today I must abide at thy house!" (Luke 19: 5 KJV

Matthew was also wealthy and dropped everything and everyone to follow Jesus. Nicodemus, a prominent Pharisee, and wealthy individual, took a bold step by jeopardizing his social status and reputation to align himself with Jesus' cause.

The story of the rich young ruler was not about how being wealthy makes it impossible to enter God's kingdom. It was about rejecting God. We all have something that stands in the way of our relationship with God. It could be money, time, the sabbath, materialism, family, drugs, food…practically anything that separates us from God.

You just need to decide what is more important. Is anything keeping you from God today?

When Jesus commanded, "Sell all you have and follow Me," the rich young ruler felt it was just too high a price to pay for time with the Savior. His faith stopped at an investment of time and talents devoted to God. The Bible says that he walked away sorrowfully, meaning that he wanted to serve God, but he was unwilling to do what it took to make that happen. By walking away, he broke the first commandment: "You shall have no other gods [things] before me" (Exodus 20:3).

Is anything separating you from God today?

God's Pruning Process

BY BRYNA QUIRING WALKER

I am the true vine, and My Father is the vinedresser.
Every branch in Me that does not bear fruit He takes away;
and every branch that bears fruit He prunes,
that it may bear more fruit.

—JOHN 15:1–2, NKJV

"Lord, if there's ever anything in my life You want me to give up, please make it clear and help me to be obedient, no matter how difficult it is." I had prayed this many times and increasingly felt that God might call me to sacrifice something I cherished.

Soon after my last prayer of that nature, God directed my husband and me in exactly what He wanted us to do. He clearly called us to begin giving away our possessions to prepare to follow where He would lead. I was amazed that God miraculously made His will known to us after years of praying for direct guidance. It was an immense blessing, but it also came with a struggle.

Years earlier, I had realized my passion for working with preschoolers when I served as a missionary teacher overseas. After returning home, I continued my childcare career. I collected many children's materials that I used extensively in my work, along with special items I'd saved from my childhood.

I had a dream to have my own Christian preschool where I could use my passion for children while teaching them about God. I thought God might bring my dream to fruition, but He hadn't yet. Now He was telling me to give away my treasured children's materials and possibly lead me away from childcare. I went through a period of intense struggle. I had been using my items to bless the children with whom I'd worked. Why would God want me to let them go?

Over time, I began to surrender. I started giving away items, asking God to guide me to give to the right people, especially to those in need. He connected me with people who greatly appreciated what they received and who were touched when I shared how God was leading me. The process became easier as I continued to give. God blessed me with joy in following Him, and I began to want His plan for my life over my own desires.

God often calls His followers to let go of what they cherish, just as He called Abraham to sacrifice Isaac, even though he was a promised son. God may return the sacrifice to us after we surrender it, as He did with Abraham. However, it's most important to obey Him no matter what the immediate outcome is. God wants us to place Him as the highest priority and ultimate authority in our lives. When we do, He blesses us with peace from living by His will.

God always works His pruning process in our lives for good. It results in us producing more fruit for His kingdom and experiencing more of His spiritual blessings. It results in deeper relationships and the flourishing of our faith.

Hope

*May the God of hope fill you with
all joy and peace as you trust in him,
so that you may overflow with hope
by the power of the Holy Spirit.*

—ROMANS: 15:13, NIV—

The Promised Land

BY KAREEN WILSON

> *So the people shouted when the priests blew the trumpets. And it happened when the people heard the sound of the trumpet, and the people shouted with a great shout, that the wall fell down flat. Then the people went up into the city, every man straight before him, and they took the city.*
>
> —JOSHUA 6:20, NKJV

When you pray, God can make the walls about your situation fall. Miracles happen. The impossible becomes possible.

After years of slavery, traveling the road to the promised land, seeing their leader die without seeing the promised land, and then waiting to step into the promised land, Joshua is commanded to take the city of Jericho. Not only was Jericho one of the oldest cities known to civilization but it was also fortified. It sat upon a hill with walls thirteen feet high and six feet wide at the base, encircling the city (Britannica, 2023). Back in the day, Jericho was a military fortress. This wall and the fact no one had defeated Jericho was a strong deterrent to Joshua and the Israelites.

Can you imagine Joshua's reaction when God says He will give him Jericho? Joshua imagines the battle plans and how they will fight and crush their enemies with skill and might. But then God came up with an unusual way to conquer the military Goliath. March around it a few times, and the walls will come tumbling down on the seventh day. What? Even though he was a man of faith, Joshua still must have thought this plan to be crazy. I'm sure he thought, *I don't see how this can take the city. Plus, my people will laugh at me when I tell them this is the plan, and our enemies will laugh and do even worse than laugh when they see us.*

Faith is the only way to believe such a plan. With faith, they did move forward. And by faith, the walls came tumbling down.

We can learn so many lessons from this story—patience, timing, and faith all wrapped up in one. We must wait for God to work His miracles when they are needed to fulfill the promises that have been made, promises that will always come to pass.

The Walls of Jericho Come Tumbling Down

BY KAREEN WILSON

After they defeated Jericho, Joshua sent some men to Ai. Ai was near Beth Aven, east of Bethel. He told them, "Go to Ai and look for weaknesses in that area." So the men went to spy on that land. Later, the men came back to Joshua. They said, "Ai is a weak area. We will not need all of our people to defeat them. Send 2000 or 3000 men to fight there. There is no need to use the whole army. There are only a few men there to fight against us." So about 3000 men went to Ai, but the people of Ai killed about 36 men of Israel. And the Israelites ran away. The people of Ai chased them from the city gates all the way to the quarries. The people of Ai beat them badly.

—JOSHUA 7:2–5, ERV

Yesterday we learned of Jericho and its mighty walls. We saw how God helped the Israelites conquer Jericho in a way you know was all by God's power and not man's might.

But did you know what happened to the Israelites after that great victory?

HOPE

They got crushed by a tiny town called Ai, just five miles from Jericho—a city with no walls or history, and one that should have been a walk in the park to defeat. What happened?

When the Israelites were chased out of Ai and sent back defeated, they decided to pray. And pray and pray and pray some more. Like fasting, ashes, and sackcloth praying. Then God told Joshua, "Enough praying; get up and fix the issue holding you back from conquering your enemies. I want to help you but can't help in your mess." Of course, I paraphrased, but please read Joshua 7 to understand the scenario.

When you have a big victory in your life, do you become complacent with the little things, get cocky, and believe everything is under control? Is it faith or pride that guides you to your next victory? If we apply this concept to yesterday's example, we can see where we have made huge victories but remain losers in small battles. Some of us are still fighting for equality. We have disagreements among ourselves. We pray, pray, and pray and have no action behind our prayers. I purchased a sweatshirt at a Christian café that says, "Love Is Action." When we get up from our prayers, are we the answer to that prayer? As you fight for social justice, give back to your communities for education, and volunteer your time to make the world a better place. May your words not return to you void but fulfill every prayer that proceeds out of your mouth (Isaiah 55:11).

What gratitude will bring action?

Remember Me

BY PATRICIA REED

*And Samson called unto the Lord and said,
O Lord God, remember me.*

—JUDGES 16:28A, KJV

The story of Samson and Delilah is a familiar one. We know that God had ordained Samson to be a judge of Israel. God anointed him to be a Nazarite, which meant he would be consecrated, and set apart for God's glory. Because of the anointing in his life, he had restrictions placed on him; he could not touch a dead body, drink anything that contained alcohol, or even cut his hair. We also know that Delilah deceived Samson into telling her the source of his strength. Because Samson loved women, mingled with idolaters, and was bent on self-pleasing, he was distracted from his divine assignment.

Have you been so distracted lately that you walked away from God and His principles? Do you find yourself in compromising positions? Are you no longer set apart? Even though Samson stepped away from God, God never left him. When the Philistines began to make a mockery of him, Samson prayed to God: "And Samson called unto the Lord and said, Oh Lord God, remember me."

This is a lesson for us all. When we walk away from God, when we stop doing what we know is right, when we no longer feel the need to pray, God is still there, waiting with open arms for us to remember Him.

As with Samson, God never forgets us! The Bible says in Jeremiah 1:5 (KJV), *"Before I formed thee in the belly, I knew thee: and before thou comest forth out of the womb I sanctified thee, and I ordained thee a prophet unto the nations."* God does not forget us. We are the ones who forget. May we remember God today.

Imago Dei (Part 1)

BY ZORAIDA VELEZ-DELGADO

Jesus answered: "Don't you know me, Philip, even after I have been among you such a long time? Anyone who has seen me has seen the Father. How can you say, 'Show us the Father'?"

—JOHN 14:9, NIV

He was born very early on a hot, humid morning on the 4th of July in the beautiful state of Michigan. He had big eyes, chubby cheeks, and long arms and legs. He took a few seconds to cry, so when he did, everyone in the room stopped to hear him. It was a sweet cry as if he were shy about letting out his fear of being in a cold, new place. My first thought was a prayer: *Just like Hannah, I prayed for this child; My boy, my sweet boy.*

Raising him was such a joy. He was curious, funny, loving, and sweet. At church, he was known for his ability to memorize Bible verses, and his willingness to participate in children's stories and sing in the kids' choir. One day, he came back from school and, as usual, sat down to do homework with his father and started talking about his day. To our surprise, he started asking us why people would say that he was "brown and bad."

HOPE

My husband and I are from Puerto Rico; we have an accent and brown complexions. We had not forgotten we were different from our Caucasian brothers and sisters, but it was not a common topic of conversation. In the wake of so many public confrontations between the police and people of color, I knew a conversation was necessary at some point, but I was not expecting to have it with my ten-year-old son!

(To be continued)

Imago Dei (Part 2)

BY ZORAIDA VELEZ-DELGADO

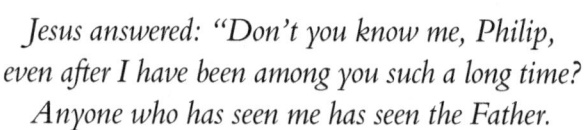

*Jesus answered: "Don't you know me, Philip,
even after I have been among you such a long time?
Anyone who has seen me has seen the Father.
How can you say, 'Show us the Father'?"*

—JOHN 14:9, NIV

That night, we discovered that my sweet boy had been exposed to hatred and bullying because of who he was. He had been quiet about it because he didn't understand why it was happening to him. He thought he was meant to be bad because he was brown. Have you ever prayed in the middle of a conversation? Yep, that was me, praying and praying for my son's heart. He was hurt, and we were hurting for him.

I found a picture of what Jesus probably looked like—a painting of a brown man with long hair, big brown eyes, and a kind smile. My son rejected the idea that this could be Jesus.

"That is not Him. Jesus is white!" he said.

We took the opportunity to teach him a history and geography lesson, and then we landed on Genesis 1:27 where Moses describes the moment of creation; our three-in-one God touched the dirt he had created, to form a man with His hands, in His image.

"So, God is not white?" he asked.

"All we know is that He chose to come to this earth in a brown suit." He smiled. Although those words came out of my mouth embedded in deep sadness, his response filled my heart with joy because it reminded me that we were all created in the image of our Heavenly Father. What a gift!

That night, I fell on my knees in tears. What kind of society have we created where a child does not feel safe among his classmates and community? Who's teaching their children to hate others based on race? In a world where we face so much hatred towards those who look different than us, one thing we ought to remember is that God created us in His image, and by doing so He claimed us as His own.

We have had many conversations since then in an effort to prepare our son to be a confident man of God so that, when you encounter him, you'll benefit from the love, respect, and dignity you deserve as a child of God, created in His image.

Dear Lord, help us to raise children who can respect Your image in themselves…and in others. Amen.

Easily Discouraged

BY MEGAN BLACKMORE

May the God of hope fill you with all joy and peace as you trust in him, so that you may overflow with hope by the power of the Holy Spirit.

—ROMANS 15:13, NIV

Being pregnant, I desire my baby to come early. I don't mean scary early, but maybe two weeks early. I am so eager to meet our daughter that thinking of her coming early is so exciting!

Sadly, our midwife told me that, for the most part, first-time moms don't usually deliver early, and, in fact, usually deliver later than their due date.

I remember leaving this thirty-seven-week appointment and crying in the passenger seat while my poor, confused husband drove us home. I was in the last few weeks of my pregnancy, but thinking I might possibly have to wait even longer than my due date crushed my heart. I mean, I truly could not stop crying. Yes, I blame the hormones, but I also know that I am an easily discouraged person to begin with.

I ultimately realized during that final stretch that when anyone told me that my baby was more than likely to come late, I immediately got upset and even annoyed at them for saying this. Especially when I felt as though they were laughing at my hopeful desire for my daughter to come early…which actually ended up happening!

My excitement and emotions during those last few weeks of gestation made me unstable. I placed so much focus on my desires and emotions that I left very little room, if any at all, for the timing and will of the Lord. I let the discouragement of a possibly overdue baby overwhelm and distract me from the actual gift and incredible miracle of being pregnant in general.

I was so focused on my daughter coming early that I forgot to notice the cute little kicks she was making in my belly and remember that I would be pregnant only for a few more weeks. These realities were placed on the back burner because of my own selfish desires, and when I realized I might not get what I wanted, it sent me on a dark, negative, discouraging journey that made me miss out on those last precious moments of being pregnant for just a little while longer.

Oftentimes, when we don't get what we hope for, and it is brought to our attention that things might not go as we wanted, we become discouraged. We lose hope and spiral downwards mentally and emotionally. But God tells us that He will fill us with hope, joy and peace, the complete opposite of discouragement. So, remember the journey is just as great as the prize and allow that joy and hope to enter your heart rather than discouragement as you patiently wait on all the Lord is going to do for you.

Hope in the Lord

BY KELLEY MATIERIENE

Why are you cast down, O my soul?
And why are you in disquieted within me?
Hope in God: For I shall yet praise Him,
The help of my countenance and my God.

—PSALM 42:11, NKJV

When I was in college, I met a young man two weeks after freshman orientation. He was funny, smart, protective, and had one of the best accents ever. He was also persistent. Needless to say, I fell head over heels. I remember coming home for Thanksgiving break, and he came with me. My mother's exact words were, "I sent you to college and, in two weeks, you call telling me you have a boyfriend." I think she was more surprised than anything. He fit right in with my family and got along with everyone. To say he became one of my best friends in that first year of college was an understatement.

I still remember the gut punch I felt when we broke it off. We dated on and off for four years after our initial break up. The initial breakup was the hardest; I thought I would surely never find love again. I prayed and cried and kept my other friends up all night talking. I would go on to fall in love with and marry someone else, but at that time, I couldn't imagine being with anyone but him and didn't even think it was possible.

Many times, we hold on to the thing in life that we feel we can't live without—someone or something that we feel God could never possibly replace or there couldn't possibly be anything better. We are completely wrong. The plans and places God has in store for us are oftentimes beyond our wildest dreams. How wise we would be if we would just remind our heart and souls to keep hoping and trusting in God.

It is not easy, but God never promised easy. He never said, "Stick with Me, and we will have a relaxed, easy life." No, He promises turmoil and tribulations but the best part is that He is there with us every step of the way. He will give us a song in our hearts and change our sadness to gladness if we just keep hoping, just keep praying.

I don't know where you are in your journey with the Lord but I encourage you not to lose hope. Maybe that dream didn't turn out the way you planned. Maybe that person you loved didn't reciprocate your love. Do not let the turmoil in your mind or life cause you to let go of the hand of God today.

Today, seek out a hymn that reminds you that God is your hope… that He will carry you, that you are not alone. If you need to borrow one until you find your own, try "Lord in the Morning."

The Power of the Cross

BY ANANDI MOSES

Looking only at Jesus, the originator and perfecter of the faith, who for the joy set before Him endured the cross, despising the shame, and has sat down at the right hand of the throne of God.

—HEBREWS 12:2, NASB

The death of Christ on the cross paid the penalty for every sin ever committed. Because of it, we can stand in judgment and claim righteousness. Our salvation was gifted to us through the price paid by Jesus on the cross. We could not have a place in heaven or enter eternity without the sacrifice of Jesus. Paul calls it a great salvation: "How will we escape if we neglect so great a salvation?" (Hebrews 2:3, NASB). But our salvation was not the only accomplishment of the cross of Christ.

Jesus' death on the cross was the final blow to the devil. His judgment was passed when Jesus died on the cross. He is a defeated foe awaiting his final decimation. Because of the cross, we will not have a tempter or deceiver in the new heaven and the new earth.

The other important work of the cross is that it once and for all proved the character of God to the rest of the universe. All accusation against his character by the devil was cleared when the Son of God gave His life to save His creation. The angels in heaven and the rest of the beings in the universe were able to look upon the love of God personified in Jesus on the cross.

The cross has another exciting gift to give us! We know that, in the new heaven and new earth, affliction shall not rise up the second time (Nahum 1:9). Why is this? Is it because we will have a different nature? No, Adam and Eve sinned in Eden in their creaturely perfection. Is it because there will be no tempter in heaven? No, Satan sinned in heaven when there was no one to tempt him. Then, what will keep sin from rising again? It will be the love and justice of God shining through the cross that will safeguard us and the rest of the universe from sin forever. The cross stands as a standard against sin in the breadth of eternity for all creation.

The work accomplished on the cross is enormous. The love of God is as powerful as it is sweet.

Holy Spirit

But the Advocate, the Holy Spirit, whom the Father will send in my name, will teach you all things and will remind you of everything I have said to you.

—JOHN 14:26, NIV—

Baptized by the Spirit

BY KAREEN WILSON

*Jesus answered, "Very truly I tell you,
no one can enter the kingdom of God unless
they are born of water and the Spirit."*

—JOHN 3:5, NIV

The air is full of joy and clapping. As I approach the river, I see people dressed in white going to the water's edge.

I am surprised to see how clean the water is and how prepped the area is for anyone who wishes to be baptized. It always brings a tear to my eyes to witness anyone being baptized. When that person comes out of the water, they are ready for a new way of life. They are ready to walk with the Lord.

It is remarkable to be baptized in the Jordan River, where John baptized Jesus. Sitting at the water's edge, I remember the story of Jesus coming out of the water and a dove descending over his head. God leads by example.

Today, this area of the Jordan River has been built to reflect a peaceful tourist atmosphere. Two areas are marked for pilgrims to be baptized. The area of the Jordan River that scholars believe is a holy site is called Qasr al-Yahud and sits on the eastern bank in Jordan, not Israel. This river area has been diverted for agriculture, with low water levels. This area is on conflict ground, part of the Israeli West Bank and Jordan. The river has also been affected by climate change and pollution. Hopefully, we will preserve this place where God came down and led by example on how we can be born again.

The baptism of Jesus is an integral part of the life of the Savior. This is an acknowledgment of Him being the long-looked-for Messiah. Also, He provided an example of how we can be reborn in Christ.

It is a joyous occasion to see someone rise from the water. As I watched people being baptized, I made a personal commitment to God in my own heart. A prayer of thanksgiving and praise left my heart and lips. I pray that you will commit your life to Christ, and if you have not experienced the joy of coming out of the water, what are you waiting for?

How will you be born again in the Spirit?

The Place God Calls You

BY ZORAIDA VELEZ-DELGADO

> *There the angel of the LORD appeared to him in flames of fire from within a bush. Moses saw that though the bush was on fire it did not burn up. So Moses thought, "I will go over and see this strange sight—why the bush does not burn up."*
>
> —EXODUS 3:2–3, NIV

The burning bush in Exodus 3 represents God's power, sacred light, and illumination to His children. I grew up listening to this beautiful story, imagining how God's energy was strong enough to burn a bush without consuming it.

See, my favorite part of the story is not the actual burning bush, nor the miracle of seeing a little bush involved in a powerful energy burst. It was the part of the story where Moses saw this little demonstration of God's power but had a hard time believing the same God could use him to deliver His people.

God uses that light to call on Moses, to show him His amazing power, and Moses objects. "They won't trust me. They won't listen to a word I say. They're going to say, 'God? Appear to him? Hardly!'"

So, our Mighty God gives another powerful demonstration: a staff that becomes a snake and then becomes a staff again once Moses reaches out and grabs it by the tail. God showed him His power two more times, and, even then, Moses was fearful, making excuses: "I don't speak very well." And that is when the real magic happened.

In the movie "Prince of Egypt," this scene is captured in a magnificent way. Moses says, "I stammer," and God responds with a powerful voice accompanied by thunder and wind that seems to castigate and caress Moses at the same time. "Who do you think made the human mouth? And who makes some mute, some deaf, some sighted, some blind? Isn't it I, God? So, go!"

I can only imagine that moment, a voice of thunder speaking through the burning bush and the wind caressing Moses' face with hope and love. "I'll be right there with you—with your mouth! I'll be right there to teach you what to say."

Growing up in a Christian home, I learned to see this story in many different situations of my life:

- When God calls you, He won't make a spectacle. Moses was attracted to the burning bush because it didn't act normally; the fire was not consuming the bush!
- When God calls you, He will use you to show others His wonders.
- When God calls you, He will facilitate the help you need.

Have you ever received a call from God? Have you obeyed that call? Can you recognize a call from God? The God we serve is powerful enough to provide for us as He sends us on missions that, in the end, will transform our lives. Do not doubt His calling, do not present excuses before Him. Just go! He will illuminate the way, provide you with the tools you need, and use you to show this world all His wonders.

Magnifying Glass and Binoculars

BY MEGAN BLACKMORE

Search me, God, and know my heart; test me and know my anxious thoughts. See if there is any offensive way in me, and lead me in the way everlasting.

—PSALM 139:23–24, NIV

I recently got into a nature kick. I want to read, study, and learn anything and everything I possibly can about the great outdoors, the world our Creator created.

Thus far, I've learned all types of information…from trees communicating with one another, to how important fungi is to our ecosystem, to the difference between deciduous and coniferous trees, and even how many cones per millimeter an eagle's eye has in its fovea! (I told you, a nature kick.)

But even more recently, I have found myself wanting to discover on a closer level. So, I purchased a magnifying glass and borrowed my dad's binoculars (with his permission) when I went to his house. I was bound and determined to examine this world on a "microscopic" level—and that I did.

HOLY SPIRIT

I looked at everything I could get my hands on with my magnifying glass—moss, lichen growing on trees, a three-leaf clover, a tiny insect that landed on my arm while bird watching at the park. I also examined a ton of different birds in my backyard with the binoculars.

Upon all my examinations, I noticed how intricate and detailed this world God has made. Moss looks very different up close than it does when just glancing at it as you walk by. There are so many tiny little bugs that live within its green walls—like the speck of dust in *Horton Hears a Who!* that houses an entire world.

All of this close observation I have been doing makes me think about how I view this life we have been given. Do I pay attention to the tiny little details? Do I go throughout my days not even noticing the people around me or seeing all the little ways the Lord is blessing me?

I felt as though I needed to take a magnifying glass to my life and not just to nature. I needed to examine closely all I was truly spending my time doing, or what I was thinking about or even just feeling lately. Maybe it's time for you to do the same.

Self-reflection is something we should welcome into our daily lives as we welcome in the Holy Spirit. In fact, we should call upon the Holy Spirit to examine our hearts and let us know what He found so that we can then surrender it to the Lord and grow in spiritual maturity as we walk this path of righteousness God has called us to walk with His grace.

Home

*If you say, "The L*ORD *is my refuge," and you make the Most High your dwelling, no harm will overtake you, no disaster will come near your tent.*

—PSALM 91:9–10, NIV—

Keep It Simple (Part 1)

BY KAREEN WILSON

He has shown you, O mortal, what is good.
And what does the Lord require of you?
To act justly and to love mercy and
to walk humbly with your God.

—MICAH 6:8, NIV

We humans love to make things hard. If it is not difficult, then we feel "it" is not worth it. We apply this even to the spiritual part of our lives.

The phrase "Keep it simple" can apply to many aspects of our lives. If we could just love God and love people, as the song performed by Danny Gokey encourages us to do, we would live a much more simplistic life.

Life becomes complicated when we try to interpret and deal with our relationships with our friends, family, and God. We think we know how to deal with others. But we put meaning to everything that is said and done and make assumptions. We judge, and we critique. We try to create a definition of happiness, and when we fall short, we analyze it again. Before you know it, you need a Ph.D. in psychology to deal with life.

We tend to apply this to even the spiritual part of our lives.

Throughout the ages, we have seen how people feel they need to have rituals and perform great ceremonies to attract the ear of God. God loves us regardless of the length or poetry of our prayers and liturgy. No amount of money can make God love us more.

In the Scripture for today, we see the Israelites making things complicated. They have a ritual for this and a sacrifice for that, and their way of life has become one big ritual and ceremony so much that they have lost their relationship with God.

(To be continued)

Keep It Simple (Part 2)

BY KAREEN WILSON

He has shown you, O mortal, what is good.
And what does the Lord require of you?
To act justly and to love mercy and
to walk humbly with your God.

—MICAH 6:8, NIV

Has your life been too centered around everything you must do and accomplish to be accepted by God? This is a merry-go-round with no way to jump off because you will never know when to stop. God does not take pleasure in what we can do to impress Him. God just wants our hearts.

Micah is telling the people, "Keep it really simple. Act justly, love mercy, and walk humbly with your God." We cannot do these three things if we separate from God. This requires a personal relationship with Christ.

Act in a way that is fair and kind. Be just in sharing your time and money. Know that God's mercies are new every day. Pay that mercy forward. Extend love and mercy to others.

We walk humbly when we surrender our will and submit to the way He wishes for us to go. We walk humbly when we do not need to boast or show the world how righteous and religious we are. We are walking hand in hand with God.

Are you religious, or are you spiritual? Are you keeping it real and simple and developing a loving relationship with the one who loves you the most? Find a way to always connect with the loving God who wants you just the way you are—simply you.

Thank the Lord that He is a God of love and simple things. How can you build that simple relationship with God?

Time to Slow Down for a Moment

BY MEGAN BLACKMORE

You have put more joy in my heart than they have when their grain and wine abound.

—PSALM 4:7, ESV

While writing this devotional, I am currently thirty-one weeks pregnant with my first child. To say I am eager and excited for these remaining nine weeks to go by is an understatement. I just can't wait for our daughter to get here.

I find myself counting down the days and weeks and thinking about how long I have left if she comes a week or two early. I find myself so caught up in the future rather than in the incredible, present moment.

The fact that God has blessed us with a healthy baby girl currently growing inside of me is incredible! The mere thought of life in my womb is a miracle and a blessing I truly never thought would come my way. But here I am, pushing past all of this miraculous and beautiful work of God currently going on within me and becoming excited only when I think about what will happen nine weeks from now.

I'm not saying I shouldn't be excited for her to arrive, but I am saying that I am missing so many precious moments while focusing on future joy when, at the moment, I can experience a completely different joy.

Let me challenge you to stay focused in the present. We have so much to look forward to in the future, yes, but there is just as much joy and excitement in the every day when we look for it and take the time to acknowledge it.

Did you wake up this morning with the breath of life in your lungs? Did you have the opportunity to see the sun shining or the rain falling from Heaven itself? Did you get to hug your child today or just witness their life in front of you? Did you have a good meal and even share it with others? Did you read a good book or have a Bible study?

We can find simple joy in the mundane—in the little things—but we have conditioned ourselves to look only toward the big and upcoming.

For me, I have been so focused on the "big day" that I have missed out on the little hiccups in the womb or the rolls and kicks from our little one that I will one day soon miss—those quiet moments between just my baby and me.

Take the time today to look for the sweet, gentle, and even quiet moments of pure joy and excitement that the Lord presents to us each and every day, and live in that moment for as long as you can.

The future will always be the future, but the present is what we have right now. So, yes, allow yourself to look forward to what is to come, but allow yourself to be filled with the joy and peace of what is right now.

Is Your Home Protected?

BY FELECIA D. LEE

As for Saul, he made havoc of the church, entering into every house, and hauling men and women committed them to prison.

—ACTS 8:3, KJV

I was leading a Bible study one day and drew a picture of a house on one side of a sheet of paper and a church building on the other. I gave someone a pair of scissors and asked them to cut up the picture of the house without cutting up the church on the other side. Needless to say, it was impossible, and the converse was also true. By cutting up the church, they would also be cutting up the home. The church cannot be healthy if the families that make up the church are not healthy. In the same way, you can't have a healthy marriage if the individual participants are not healthy in mind and heart; no matter how much we try to separate the two, they are linked.

"As for Saul, he made havoc of the church, entering into every house" (Acts 8:3). Now read that verse again but replace *Saul* with *the devil*. We make a mistake if we think the devil is trying to destroy the church by closing the building where believers worship. This is not the case. He wreaks havoc on the church by entering into every home.

He enters the home through entertainment. The movies, music, and television series we allow to play on our screens fill our minds with themes and messages contrary to God's Word. We are not protected from these influences by simply being aware of them. We must guard our minds against anything that does not cultivate truth, beauty, and light.

Satan enters our homes through unresolved trauma or issues from the past. Wrongs that have not been made right, sins that have not been confessed and forgiven, resentment that has not been addressed, and wounds that are not healed make room for lies and anger to fester and cause a breakdown in family relationships.

The enemy can enter through many avenues, but we have only one way to protect ourselves—complete trust in Jesus Christ. Trust the Lord and seek a vibrant, living experience with Him. Seek Him in daily prayer and devotion. Confess and repent of your sins. Consume content that will edify. Do what is necessary to address past hurts and pain. Cultivate relationships that will draw you closer to Him. Spend time studying His Word in depth.

When the disciples were huddled at home, doors bolted, terrified of the Jews after the crucifixion, Jesus Christ came twice to stand in the middle of them. Though the enemy may be attacking your home, Jesus can still stand in your midst to preserve your home and His church.

How can you invite the presence of Jesus into your home today?

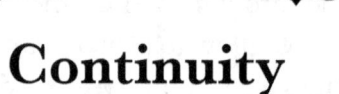

Continuity

BY EVELYN RAQUEL DELGADO MARRERO

*Start children off on the way they should go,
and even when they are old
they will not turn from it.*

—PROVERBS 22:6, NIV

My parents moved a lot. The political situation in Puerto Rico grants Puerto Ricans American citizenship. As American citizens, my family is able to travel back and forth to the US without passports or visas. So, my parents, in pursuit of the American dream, would haul their family to the United States for a year or so at a time, just long enough to work, save a little money, and then go back to Puerto Rico to continue building their dream home.

This went on intermittently throughout my childhood and into my high school years. During that time, I attended fourteen different schools. All this back and forth did not allow us, the children, to have continuity in our education. For example, I had a tough time in school with fractions. I believe that when fractions were taught in one school, I was moved to another school where the class had already covered that part of the curriculum. Because I missed those lessons, I did well in math in general but did not have a grasp of fractions until I started teaching them to my elementary school children.

I also missed out on other academic and social interactions. I don't have many childhood friends because we never stayed in one school long enough for lasting friendships to develop. It was the perfect setting for failure and unhappiness.

One redeeming point in our parents was their strong faith in God and their practice of family worship time. That family worship provided the only continuity in our education, but also in our spiritual development; it kept our family united. Every day during family worship, my father would read to us in Spanish, either from the Bible or from one of the books of the Spirit of Prophecy. If we knew how to read, we had to read a paragraph and explain what we understood from what we read. Dad would read to the younger ones who did not know how to read yet, and then ask the same questions.

New York had no bilingual programs at that time, so that was my father's way of making sure we read and understood Spanish. By doing that, he also unknowingly developed reading comprehension and critical thinking skills that were very helpful in our transient lives. As children often are, we were very flexible in adapting to new schools and new environments. I largely attribute this to our family structure. We became fluent in both Spanish and English. We were good students who excelled in academics and we all succeeded in going to college.

As a teacher, I see many students whose families also follow that pattern of moving back and forth and from school to school, and most of the time the children are not successful academically because they lack family structure and discipline. Our faith and our family unity provided the continuity lacking in our lives. God made all the difference in our lives.

Train Up a Child

BY JOAN MITCHELL

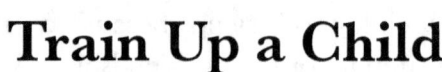

*Train up a child in the way he should go:
and when he is old,
he will not depart from it.*

—PROVERBS 22:6, KJV

The long, hot days of summer are here. School will soon be out for vacation, a time when some parents experience stress. The days can be tedious, causing parents to be overwhelmed. A day of twenty-four hours sometimes seems like twenty-six, especially for the mother who is part of the breadwinner's team. My two sons, Jack and Jackson, performed excellently in their school activities, and I told them I would buy them each a bicycle as a reward. The two bicycles were purchased, and the boys were thrilled, riding up and down the street from dawn to dusk.

I have taught my boys to pray; we had family worship and invited the Lord to lead them throughout each day. I taught them to be respectful and obedient and to respect their elders.

About two weeks after the boys received their bicycles, they were allowed to go to the store to pick up a couple of items, and, of course, ride their new bikes. It was the first time they had been allowed to venture outside of our neighborhood, so I felt a little trepidation, especially with them riding on regular roads instead of just our neighborhood streets.

About two and half hours after I left for work, I received a phone call from a number I did not recognize; I answered, and a voice I didn't recognize said, "Two boys would like to speak to you." I heard through tears, "Mom, the bikes are gone. Somebody took them…please come!"

I hurriedly made my way to the store. The boys had parked their bikes outside and secured them with locks, but someone had cut off the locks and taken the bikes. We reported the theft to the police, and I asked, "What are the chances of finding the bicycles?"

"Very slim, ma'am; it is summer. Kids are looking for a free ride on a bicycle." He told me he was sorry and that they would call if they learned anything further.

The boys' sadness was indescribable; I reminded them that, despite the officer's reply, Jesus knew exactly where the bikes were, and He could help the police find them. That night during the Prayer Meeting at church, we prayed specifically for the bikes to be found.

Two days later, our home phone rang incessantly for a long time; finally, I shouted to the boys to answer, and I soon heard a loud shriek of joy followed by, "Mom, they found our bikes!" Yes, both bicycles were found intact, leaning against a fence. This experience solidified my sons' faith and trust in God.

Today, my boys are men and have continued to trust God and have each chosen Christ for themselves. Parenting can be difficult, but God has given us the assurance and promise in Isaiah 49:25 that he will contend with those who contend with us to save our children. And he is faithful to His Word!

Our Greatest Counselor

BY STEPHANIE BLAKENEY

And it shall come to pass, that before they call, I will answer; and while they are yet speaking, I will hear.

—ISAIAH 65:24, KJV

As part of our human experience, difficulties or challenges often occur that trigger us to seek answers. For some, we start to self-assess with questions like, "What have I done?" or "What caused this current situation?" We often try to "fix it" before ever seeking help and influence from our greatest counselor and champion. Whether the situation in which we find ourselves is self-inflicted or not, He is ultimately the one with the best response—the one that will lead us to success not just in the moment but eternally.

As someone who often attempts to independently tackle obstacles as quickly as they occur, I'm striving to instead create a habit of instantly turning to my best resource. It is something I believe we all need to be disciplined in training ourselves to do. We live in a day and age where most questions can be researched by using a smartphone or app to get an answer within seconds. But something is grown and developed in us spiritually when we take the time to speak words of prayer in faith. Before I even speak the words, He knows my need. When no one else may be able to see the struggle, pain, or hurt, He does. And He will answer. Jeremiah 29:12 (KJV) says, "Then shall ye call upon me, and ye shall go and pray unto me, and I will hearken unto you."

Today, take the time, even if it is brief, to speak the words on your heart and mind in prayer. You are not alone in your struggles or your triumphs. Take heart!

Meaningless

BY EVELYN RAQUEL DELGADO MARRERO

*"Meaningless! Meaningless!" says the Teacher.
"Utterly meaningless! Everything is meaningless."*

—ECCLESIASTES 1:2, NIV

I have to admit that I was perplexed the first time I read this Bible verse. The first thought that came to my mind was *Depression. This book of Ecclesiastes is very depressing. I always thought of the Bible as a book of hope. I don't want to read a book that clips my wings and frustrates my efforts.*

Nevertheless, I continued reading, and the words of the teacher in Ecclesiastes echoed in my head. *Meaningless…vanity of vanities…* Solomon, the wisest man, expresses the futility of life as he sees it. I wondered yet again why this book that foresees no hope was inserted into the Bible. It made me question why we put so much effort into our everyday lives if it's all for naught. We set high goals in life and work hard to acquire the "best" of everything—brand-name clothing, expensive cars, and big houses. We pursue and achieve our college degrees and then our master's and some even acquire a doctorate. We value education to help us get ahead in the world. We think that others will respect us more because of all that we possess.

In Ecclesiastes 1:17 (NIV), Solomon says, "Then I applied myself to the understanding of wisdom, and also of madness and folly, but I learned that this, too, is a chasing after the wind." As human beings, we all want to have meaningful lives, and, in searching for that meaning, we experience both joy and sorrow, both accomplishment and disappointment. The interesting thing is that people in all social stratification want to achieve and experience the same things. We all go through the same cycles in life: we are born, we live for a little while, and then we die. The poor, the middle class, and the rich all have the same beginning and the same end. Ecclesiastes gives us an appreciation for our common humanity. God helps us realize that the ups and downs of life are normal.

In our struggle to find meaning in the pleasures or accomplishments of life, in climbing the social ladder, or in accumulating money and possessions, we find that each of these undertakings is meaningless unless we add meaning by including God in our lives. Ecclesiastes shows us a man who experiences life and comes out wiser because he realizes that all things are meaningless without God. The only way we get through life is to have our life anchored in God.

Have you struggled with misplaced pursuits in life? If your life lacks meaning or purpose, Solomon encourages us in the book of Ecclesiastes to add meaning to our lives by placing our trust solely in God.

Do You Hear My Suffering?

BY MAYRA RAQUEL MARINO

Honor your father and your mother, so that you may live long in the land the Lord your God is giving you.

—EXODUS 20:12, NIV

As a nurse, I see many patients who are suffering. I don't like to see anyone suffer, but that is especially true of the elderly. One patient I will never forget was a woman in her eighties who was admitted to the hospital due to memory loss, and her children felt it was too difficult to take care of her at home. She wasn't eating and was growing weaker. Even before meeting her, I knew it was going to be a difficult case for me since I have a soft spot for the elderly.

When I met her, I found that she was a very pleasant little Italian lady who was so happy to meet me. She reminded me of my grandmother, and I immediately took a liking to her. I introduced myself and told her why I was there and what I would be doing. It didn't take her long to open up to me. She was confused as to why she was in the hospital all alone, and she couldn't understand why her children had left her there. My heart ached for her; in her confusion, she felt all alone. I could tell she just wanted someone to sit with her and help her understand what was happening.

I explained to her that she wasn't feeling well because she wasn't sleeping at night, that she was losing weight from not eating, and that she was dehydrated and had developed an Urinary Tract Infection.

In return, she told me her life story. She had lost her husband the year before and life just hadn't been the same. She emphasized the fact that she had been married sixty-five years and said she didn't know how she could go on living without her husband.

Her family told me that she would call his name at night and continued to set a place for him at the dinner table. My grandmother also lost her husband and had a tough time adjusting to life without him.

My patient was depressed. She was dealing with many changes in her life in a very short period of time. She had lost both her husband and her independence. She had to move in with her sons and let them take care of her. She was lonely. She didn't know how to go on with life without her husband and became dependent on her children.

This is a huge transition that many elderly people experience, and it usually involves a lot of suffering for them. We, as sons and daughters, have a big responsibility. If we are lucky, we can stay home with our elderly family members to take care of them. But more than likely, we must rely on others to help us care for them. This is understandable since we also have busy lives and families of our own to take care of. But regardless of the situation, we need to prioritize spending time with our elderly to talk with them and listen to their needs. We want to make their golden years happy years, not suffering years.

So many elderly people today are suffering and dying alone… how different is this from how God's Word tells us we are to treat our elders? From Genesis through Revelation, we are taught in various ways to respect our parents, that it is good for godly people to reach a ripe old age, and that our elders are to be obeyed. God calls us explicitly to honor our parents.

Is there an elder that you can touch today? Who knows? You might even find that you can learn something from their lifetime of experience.

Possessions

BY ANANDI MOSES

But He said to them, "Beware, and be on your guard against every form of greed; for not even when one is affluent does his life consist of his possessions."

—LUKE *12:15*, NASB

Minimalism has been gaining popularity in the last few decades but is not a new concept. Jesus taught us to be careful about the allure of material possessions. It is important to know the priority of the soul over stuff.

Everything we own takes up mental space and causes stress, no matter how small or trivial it is. So, a minimalist chooses to live with fewer possessions. The process of executing a minimalist lifestyle requires being intentional about everything we bring into the house. Only the most valuable (though not necessarily of monetary value), purposeful, and meaningful objects are allowed in. A constant clearing away of the stuff that is already there takes place. The perceived value of various items is re-evaluated. It takes conscious decision-making to answer the questions of what and how much. In time, it becomes second nature to just keep it simple. With wise implementation, a minimalist can surround herself with beauty and meaning instead of clutter.

Like the clutter that collects in our homes and fills our basements and garages, junk and clutter can fill our minds too. Worry, anger, pride, and negative thoughts are like junk. They eat up our mental energy. There is other clutter like the internet, media, overdoing what we consider to be good things, or doing interesting but purposeless things... All of these can turn the mind into a junkyard rather than a beautiful space where God can reside.

Just as we clean our homes in the spring, how about re-evaluating what is taking up room in our minds? It takes the same process as living a simple life. It takes conscious decision-making about what we are willing to allow in our minds. What do we think and care about? What causes us to worry? What thoughts are not elevating? What can we bring into our lives that is wholesome and healing?

Is your mind clear enough to focus on God? A mind that is clear and uncluttered can hear the voice of God. It can notice the reminders of love that the Father sends from above. It can enjoy the Word of God. It can develop a sense of the simple yet profound truths that the Holy Spirit speaks to our minds. It can be quiet and still in the presence of God.

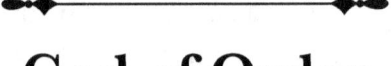

God of Order

BY EVELYN RAQUEL DELGADO MARRERO

A time to seek, and a time to lose,
a time to keep, and a time to cast away.

—ECCLESIASTES 3:6, ASV

Every now and then, ever since I was young, I would get the urge to clean—I mean really clean, declutter, and organize. I would take the time to weed out the clothes from my closet that I no longer wanted or needed. I would mend and iron the clothes that I liked but that needed fixing. I would turn my room around to the point that I would sometimes get up in the middle of the night and be unable to find my way around. I believe this happens to many women since I remember that when I was a little girl, I sometimes arrived home from school to find that my mother had completely rearranged everything. It was like coming into a new house.

When I rearrange my house now, it confuses my husband. You see, I am good at throwing away things—at least, unneeded things! My rule is, if it's old, or if it does not fit or work anymore, it's out! My husband says, "I had better be careful because, one of these days, she'll throw me out, too! Seriously, I do not like clutter. But it is not always easy to get rid of all the stuff that we accumulate.

Sometimes it is so hard to throw away the old useless things we accumulate and keep as mementos.

I would usually get a burst of energy right before my cycle began. My "friend" never arrived regularly, but I always knew when I got the urge to clean that my body was telling me it was on the way. Scientists call that urge menstrual nesting, and it's caused by spikes in estrogen levels that provide a powerful urge to tidy up even though you may feel more tired than usual. During those days, cleaning and organizing my surroundings made me feel at ease, when I would have probably been better off lying down and suffering through the cramps that heralded my "friend's" arrival. Having a tidy house gave me a feeling of control over the whole situation.

Decluttering works for our hearts also. I remember my mom saying, "God is a God of order and cleanliness." If we want Jesus to come into our "house," we need to clean and declutter our hearts. Jesus wants us to do a daily cleaning of our lives by confessing sin, mending relationships, and decluttering our minds from worldly, undesirable content. We can't let hate, quarrels, resentments, or misunderstandings clutter our hearts because, whether we want them to or not, those things will take over. Then there is no room for God to live in our hearts.

Let us remember 1 Corinthians 14:33a (NIV), "For God is not a God of disorder but of peace."

Praise Is Your Superpower

BY KELLEY MATIERIENE

Sing to the Lord! Give praise to the Lord!
He rescues the life of the needy from the hands of the wicked.

—JEREMIAH 20:13, NIV

He is the one you praise; he is your God,
who performed for you those great and awesome
wonders you saw with your own eyes.

—DEUTERONOMY 10:21, NIV

As I was dropping off my son to catch his bus that would take him to school forty minutes away from our home, I stopped at a stop sign and saw a bird flying away with a strip of what we might call trash in its beak. It kept flying back and forth, picking up items to craft into a nest for its new chicks. That bird was using someone else's discarded trash to make a nest—a home.

In life, when things happen that we don't like or understand, we need to be like this little bird—one by one, pick up the pieces and rebuild.

In today's fast-paced world, we sometimes feel discarded; but we must remember that God doesn't make trash. In His hands, we are precious. Some days, the rebuilding feels overwhelming. But on other days, we can look at how far we've come and praise God out loud, knowing that it was only by His grace that we kept picking up the pieces and putting one foot in front of the other.

The day the cabinets were installed in my new home after my divorce was one of those days. It was a new place. I was rebuilding and finding my way through the debris of my old life into a new one…into something I had envisioned. It was also a sad day because I was building something new without someone by my side with whom I could share it.

When bittersweet moments in life threaten to make me more bitter than sweet, I allow myself two things: a good cry and a praise party. The cry I allow this because sometimes that's what the mind and body need. The praise party consists of me playing my favorite hymns and gospel songs on repeat. It's a reminder to the same mind that is processing my sadness that we made it by God's grace and mercy and that He has promised not to forsake me. I mean, look how far He's brought me. Look how far He's brought you. Daily, despite the pressures and difficult circumstances, we need to remind ourselves of and take every opportunity to praise God for His blessings.

Today, amidst your trials and tribulations, cry if you need to; there is no harm in crying. But then find your favorite hymns and gospel songs and play them on repeat to remind yourself that the Lord our God is worthy of praise and that He will bring you through. Though the path may not be what you imagined, that doesn't mean He's not making a way. Praise Him as you wait!

The Best Father

BY EVELYN RAQUEL DELGADO MARRERO

See what great love the Father has lavished on us, that we should be called children of God! And that is what we are!

—1 JOHN 3:1A, NIV

One thing I remember about my dad is that he would help me with my science projects when I was growing up. As we worked on the projects, he would talk about heaven in such a real way that I looked forward to getting my wings to travel through the universe and go to heaven.

Dad was also very funny. When my sisters and I had boys over the house, he was always there with convenient though indirect reminders: "Girls, you need to go to sleep now because the guys want to leave." They were quick to take the hint and head home.

When I started my teaching career, my father helped me a lot. It was hard going into a classroom without having teaching experience. I remember him giving me advice on how to manage classroom behavior. He was a good listener, and he encouraged me not to give up. His experience as a teacher helped me through those difficult times.

When we were growing up, my father was very strict with us. If we wanted to hang out or sleepover with a friend, we could—at our house. We respected him too much to go against his wishes. Now I know that was his way of showing his love and protecting us from taking unnecessary risks. One of my friends told me "I think my parents don't love me because they don't protect me like yours protect you."

He told us that we had to chew each bite of food thirty-two times. I believe he counted while he was eating because he was always the last one to finish. We were not allowed to say we didn't like food without first trying it. We learned to eat our vegetables and all different kinds of food. Our visiting friends had to eat the vegetables, too. As adults, my friends say they learned to eat vegetables at my house.

We were privileged to have such a loving person as a father. He made us a happy family. His love showed in everything he did, especially towards my mom. To him, my mother was always the most beautiful woman, and he always told her so. They were married for sixty-five years, and they completed each other's thoughts, sentences, and life. They gave us a good example of how to have a happy marriage. He was our encourager and motivator. I was by his side when he passed away, and I was able to tell him how happy I was to have him as a father.

I am so grateful to have had such an honorable father. For those who have not had the privilege of having this experience, God in His infinite love has called us to be His daughters. We simply need to accept His invitation.

Nature

*Look at the birds of the air;
they do not sow or reap or store away in barns,
and yet your heavenly Father feeds them.
Are you not much more valuable than they?*

—MATTHEW 6:26, NIV—

God's Natural Medicine

BY KAREEN WILSON

> *Consider the lilies, how they grow:*
> *they neither labor nor spin; but I tell you,*
> *not even Solomon in all his glory clothed*
> *himself like one of these.*
>
> —LUKE 12:27, NASB

My busy bee mind and body are busy cleaning and prepping the house. I pay attention to every detail, from the dusting to the vacuuming and everything in between. I look out the window and see the bright blue sky with puffy clouds, and I can feel the warm sun through the pane. I tell myself that when I finish my household tasks, I will venture outside and hike up the hill around the house.

My neighbor has been telling me about this fantastic hike, and she says that every step of the journey inspires awe. She has told me that the view is worth the uphill climb. I convince myself that I will go as soon as I am done.

A few hours go by, and I am tired, with barely enough strength to put on my hiking shoes; but I promised myself I would make it up there today. I turned my treat into a task because I was so determined to get my work done. I complain that I should have left earlier and wasted my afternoon, but I keep walking and, after a few minutes, I begin to let go of the stress as the exercise brings fresh air into my lungs.

I turn the corner to start the uphill climb and stop in wonder. The fields on both sides of me are an array of colors with tall lupines standing tall, looking up toward heaven. I smile and thank God for their beautiful abundance. The view reminds me of the verse about how God cares to dress the lilies of the valley. I walk further, and the field turns into a street with tall, majestic trees on both sides that meet overhead and block out the sun.

What I see is so beautiful that I stop again just to take it all in. The trees provide shade, and the canopy is many shades of green. I think of how awesome God is to create all of this. Each step relaxes my nervous system. As I leave the trees, I am almost at the top of the hill, and to my right is a large pond with water as still and clear as glass. The reflection of the sun gives it an otherworldly shine. I thank God that I am so blessed to be able to experience this and thank Him for His goodness.

As I return to the house, I remind myself that since research shows that nature is the best medicine, I need to move when I feel inspired. The chores can wait. Take time to smell and see the roses, the trees, and the beauty all around. Enjoy each moment and move towards peace and beauty.

How has nature inspired you?

Nature's Therapy

BY KAREEN WILSON

*But ask the beasts, and they will teach you; the birds of the heavens, and they will tell you; or the bushes of the earth, and they will teach you, and the fish of the sea will declare to you. Who among all these does not know that the hand of the L*ORD *has done this? In his hand is the life of every living thing and the breath of all mankind.*

—JOB 12:7–10, ESV

The view in front of me calms my senses and draws out a feeling of awe. Our house in Vermont sits on a hill, the deck sits high, and the view encompasses rolling hills and trees everywhere. The sky turns various colors in the evening as the sun sets behind the hills. At night, the moon and millions of stars stare back at me. I feel and experience the wonder of God.

In the morning, I hike through the horse trails with tall trees all around me and the sun streaming through the leaves, and I feel and hear the crunch of leaves under my feet. The air is pure, and I thank God for His mercies and love. Nature heals the soul. The simple creations of God are the best therapies.

NATURE

I remember foraging in the bushes behind my school when I was a little girl in Canada. We lived in a city, and even though I had a backyard, being out in the forest behind the school brought me joy. We would make forts and also mud and rhubarb pies. Games of hide-and-seek and getting lost in the trees was our favorite pastime.

My girls had a treehouse and a few acres to explore as children. They grew up before cell phones and iPads were available to small children. They still knew how to use their imagination and create stories in the field. They know the feel of grass on their feet. They know how to climb trees. They know how to play.

Maybe that is why my mood changes for the better when I go for a run on the trails. I feel the energy of the trees and the freshness of the air. That is why my husband loves riding his mountain bike through the wilderness trails and seeing nature all around him. We were created to enjoy God's creation. The next time you need a recharge, head out to the forest. Sink your feet into the green grass. Feel the healing power of nature.

Galapagos

BY EVELYN RAQUEL DELGADO MARRERO

> *So God created the great creatures of the sea and every living thing with which the water teems and that moves about in it, according to their kinds, and every winged bird according to its kind. And God saw that it was good.*
>
> —GENESIS 1:21, NIV

My husband and I recently had the opportunity to travel to the Galapagos Islands in Ecuador. We landed in Puerto Ayora, on Santa Cruz Island, and our first stop was the Charles Darwin Research Station, where we met our guide. After that, we went to El Chato Tortoise Reserve to get acquainted with the famous dome-shaped Galapagos tortoises. We were able to get close to the black turtles to see them in action, mating and laying eggs. Although our tour guide was very protective of their habitat, she gave us an opportunity to interact with these magnificent creatures. We even met Diego, the famous Hood Island giant tortoise who is over 100 years old and has fathered more than 900 offspring. Just for fun, my husband climbed into an empty tortoise shell, and we kept a photo of that amazing sight.

We explored tunnels made of cooled, hardened lava and got to see many iguanas and crawling reptiles that roam freely around the island, unafraid of humans. We saw giant cactuses and many different kinds of plants. From there, we took a boat to get to Isabela Island to learn about the wide variety of fish and birds on the island. Although we are not aquatic enthusiasts, during our adventure, we were able to do some snorkeling and saw a myriad of colorful, tropical fish, sea horses, and even sharks face to face. On the island, we saw finches named "Darwin's Finches" because he classified the variety of their species. (I would call them "God's Finches" because He made them according to their kind.) We saw the blue-footed booby and learned that the brighter the color, the healthier the bird since the color intensifies with a good diet. The brighter blue also attracts mates who associate the color with youth and higher competence to raise offspring. We watched the males display their feet in an elaborate mating ritual by lifting them up and down while strutting in front of females.

We saw the magnificent frigate bird. This large bird has a brownish-black plumage, long narrow wings, and a deeply forked tail. The male has a strikingly red gular sac which he inflates to attract a mate.

All this variety of birds and the fascinating behaviors that I observed are attributed to an evolutionary process. I am quite certain, however, that all of this could not be the product of evolution. I believe in God's creative power even though I don't know exactly how He did it. He has never revealed that to men, but I know that human science cannot search out the secrets of the Most High. In the book *Christian Education*, EG White says in chapter twenty-four, "God has permitted a flood of light to be poured upon the world, in both science and art." But when professedly scientific men consider these subjects from a merely human point of view, they will assuredly come to the wrong conclusions. Those who leave the Word of God and seek to account for God's works of creation using scientific principles "are drifting, without chart or compass, upon an unknown ocean."

Distracted and Disoriented

BY MEGAN BLACKMORE

Let your eyes look straight ahead; fix your gaze directly before you. Give careful thought to the paths for your feet and be steadfast in all your ways. Do not turn to the right or the left; keep your foot from evil.

—PROVERBS 4:25–27, NIV

Fireflies are quite magnificent little creatures. We know these beetles from their infamous summer night glow that we tried to catch as children.

Their bioluminescent flashes are used mainly to find a suitable mate. Before the end of their lives, they light up in search of a partner to help carry on their legacy; and shortly after they reproduce, their lifespan is complete.

Why am I telling you all these facts about a quite unattractive insect?

Fireflies are incredibly sensitive. They become lost in the ways of the world, for lack of a better term. Their flashes of light are signals to other fireflies, but any artificial light source that is around them throws off their whole mating dance.

Your porch light, a flashlight, or even car headlight beams confuse and disorient them. When these lights come on, they can no longer see the other fireflies, which interferes with their mating and has a negative effect on the firefly population. Every year, fewer and fewer fireflies are able to reproduce—leaving them nearing the endangered list.

As Christians, we live with the responsibility of shining our own light in the world—a light that spreads the news of the gospel and the love of our Creator. We share this light based on the fruit we produce and the life we live.

However, just like the firefly, countless distractions throw us off course and cause us not to bear the light given to us. Any number of things can distract us—bad habits, pride, selfishness, temper, or even what we allow our minds to dwell on.

If the light given to us by God is to draw in other people to help grow the population of heaven for eternity, but we aren't producing a good enough light for others to see simply because we are distracted by other worldly glows and allurements, fewer and fewer people will be entering those pearly gates.

We have a responsibility so important that God needs us to be laser-focused. We must keep our eyes on Him and not allow the outside world to make us sway from the path at hand. We must not become disoriented and distracted like lightning bugs when outside distractions come our way. It is too easy to stray from the straight and narrow, but we have a light to shine, so let's shine it the brightest we can.

God Is in the Details

BY MEGAN BLACKMORE

> *For since the creation of the world God's invisible qualities—his eternal power and divine nature—have been clearly seen, being understood from what has been made, so that people are without excuse.*
>
> —ROMANS 1:20, NIV

I recently learned about the inner workings of trees. It perhaps sounds mundane or unimportant, but the world of trees that surrounds us has truly taught me many things—and one thing in particular. God is in the details.

Did you know that trees are actually social? They have the ability to and do, actually communicate with one another. The intricate root system allows for the trees to nurture one another, warn each other of dangers, and even care for their "offspring."

Mother trees for many species even drop their seeds right below their own branches so that they can care for their seedlings by shading them from the sun to keep them from growing too fast and provide nutrients to the baby tree's roots from their own.

NATURE

I have always been fascinated by trees but never really understood why. Though they are often a part of our everyday lives, we don't give them much thought as they rise to the sky all around us to provide shade on hot sunny days. But the more I learned about them, the more I learned how incredible the God we serve truly is.

Consider this small detail for instance. In God's perfect creation, He decided that trees were to have "taste buds" or a tree's version of them at least. When insects begin to feed off of trees, the tree can determine which insect it is from the saliva it leaves behind and, in turn, produce a bitter taste to ward off specific types of bugs. The tree can also send an airborne message to nearby trees to prepare for the insects.

If God has taken the time to create trees with such a degree of detail, what care and concern has He invested in the rest of His creation—especially us? We were formed in God's image, which in and of itself is spectacular, but our design is so complex and intricate that we can't explain it any other way besides the hand of God.

So, the next time you are feeling less than, not good enough, or simply insignificant, look outside your window and glance at a tree. Then remember that if God put such detail into trees, He put even more into you. You were created perfect, in His image, and He has plans that only you can fulfill.

Creator God

BY ANANDI MOSES

In the beginning God created the heavens and the earth.

—GENESIS 1:1, KJV

Genesis 1 is the introduction to the whole Bible. The Scriptures are the revelation of God to humanity. What does God say to introduce Himself to us? He says, "In the beginning God created." God, in His first words to us, tells us that He is the Creator, and we are His creation. As our Creator, He is above and beyond us. He is unfathomably different from us. He is from a different realm. He is utterly "other." The "otherness" of God and His power inspires awe and worship in us. Worship is our first response to God.

As the chapter continues to the creation of Adam and Eve, God created them in His image. This is our identity. We are people created in the image of God. The gap between God and us in the Creator-creature relationship is huge, but God gave us His image and moved closer to us so we can relate to Him.

Both the "otherness" of God our Creator and the closeness of God's image in us are foundational in our relationship with Him.

These tell us who God is and who we are and what the relationship is between God and us. No wonder the enemy has attacked these principles by casting doubts about the creation story. Even theistic evolution, which tries to find a place for God in the evolution theory, undermines these attributes of God.

The scientific evidence for intelligent design and order in creation is abundant. It is useful to educate ourselves about such evidence because it will help us guide the next generation which God has placed in our hands to raise for His glory.

Exquisite Arrangements

BY ANANDI MOSES

*For we are His workmanship,
created in Christ Jesus for good works,
which God prepared beforehand
so that we would walk in them.*

—EPHESIANS 2:10, NASB

A pleasant memory comes to my mind when I think of creativity. Our college chapel displayed two flower arrangements each week. The centerpiece is magnificent with beautifully cut flowers, all fresh and perfect. But the one that I always looked forward to seeing is the one by the organ. It contains a bunch of oddities. A twisted twig bent under the weight of a much stronger branch. A dried-up bean from the Mayflower tree. Flowers that grow on weeds from the uncultivated corners of the garden. Unfit flowers are thrown out of the main arrangement. Grass, seeds, and roots. All of these find their home in the curious vase. It was non-standard in every way!

But there was a transformation. A creative mind and talented fingers went to work arranging it. A mind that could picture the end result and a hand that had the talent and resources to bend, mend, and place every part of the arrangement in just the right place. When the work was done, this arrangement had a symmetry of its own that could not be duplicated. It stood out among all others as peculiar but exquisite.

Who could get more creative than the Creator of heaven and earth?

Spirits bent under overbearing circumstances and people, leftovers of the beauty and glamour of youth and strength, talents long lost and forgotten under the grind of everyday life, and unique character traits that bloom out of unique experiences. Stumps that remain after a life wasted in sin, weaknesses, inabilities…our Creator can take all these and turn them into beautiful works of re-creation…just as peculiar and exquisite as a newly cut bloom!

God already sees the result of His work! He sees a distinct vase that will decorate the heavenly courts. He sees the greatness you may achieve. He sees the character of God that you may reflect. He sees the joy of communion you will have with God Himself. He sees in you the one that will understand the love of God as it was poured out in a Savior. He sees the result of a dash of color from the grace of God, some coaxing from the spirit, and bending and mending from the guiding hand of the Savior. You are beautiful and one of a kind because of the blemishes healed under the hands of the master. And all of this takes place while we are unfit and imperfect.

Strength from the Lord

BY MEGAN BLACKMORE

I can do all things through Christ who strengthens me.

—PHILIPPIANS 4:13, NKJV

One of my favorite things to do is to take a walk while it is raining.

I love the sound of the rain pattering on my umbrella, and I love the way the rain feels, smells, and looks outside when it is raining.

On one of my rainy-day walks, spring had just arrived, and the leaves had just begun to grow. Daffodils and tulips were sprouting up. That early part of spring is one of my favorite times of the year.

As I walked along the path alone, as no one else seemed to want to walk in the rain that early morning, I took time to look around at the nature being birthed around me—and I stumbled upon a tree whose leaves were growing, but not yet fully grown. I noticed that the leaves looked weak and sad, drooping down toward the ground. I remember thinking how despondent those vibrant green leaves looked.

But then I was reminded that they weren't sorrowful at all; they were just infants. They were infant leaves that simply didn't have the strength yet to hold themselves upright.

This made me think of our life and walk with the Lord. There are times when we will not be strong enough to hold ourselves up. It's not because we are incapable or unwilling, but because we just simply lack the strength in that given moment of life.

As the branches and trunk continue to provide all the nutrients the leaves need, they will soon grow stronger and stretch up toward the sun; in the same way, the more we connect with the Lord and rely on Him for the strength and nutrients we need, we will be able to stand fully on our own two feet.

God tells us it is through Christ that we can do all things, for it is Christ who strengthens us. Therefore, in moments when we feel like that weak green leaf that is trying to grow strong but needs more time and help from its parent tree, we must remind ourselves that our weakness is because we need a further connection with the Lord. He gives us our strength—and when we have His strength, we can do anything. We can weather any storm, face any demon, or fight any battle, for we have already won with the strength of the Lord.

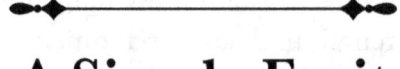

A Simple Fruit

BY MEGAN BLACKMORE

> *Do you not know that your bodies are temples of the Holy Spirit, who is in you, whom you have received from God? You are not your own; you were bought at a price. Therefore honor God with your bodies.*
>
> —1 CORINTHIANS 6:19–20, NIV

I recently learned a little bit more about a favorite fruit of mine, the peach. Besides its juicy, delicious taste that sends my taste buds on a flavorful adventure, it also brings a bit of joy to my heart when I eat one.

Now as odd as this sounds, it turns out it isn't that odd at all. The peach has a phytochemical within its peel that has the ability to work as a neurotransmitter that helps to regulate mood; it even has effects of pain relief and lifting feelings of depression. In my book, this yellow, fuzzy, fleshy fruit is a superfruit for these qualities alone! In addition to the peach's ability to satisfy a craving and fill my human need for food for survival, this fruit does even more than expected.

Many times, we look at food for one thing—its flavor. We don't necessarily pay much attention to the other qualities and health benefits particular foods bring us. For instance, I have been eating peaches all my life without ever considering that they might have the ability to lift depression.

These simple facts about peaches opened my eyes even more to the importance of what we are putting into our bodies. If something as natural as a peach can have such astounding effects on our well-being, what do "bad" foods do to us? In addition, these characteristics of the peach truly show God's perfect craftsmanship in His design for this world in which we live. Everything is so intricately designed for our well-being and prosperity if we use it properly.

So, I encourage you to pay attention today to what is going on inside your body. Do this without judgment, just as an experiment to see what you are eating or drinking. The purpose is simply to open your eyes to what you have been using to fuel this body the Lord has given you.

Then, take a few moments to look up facts about the food you've consumed today. Look up the benefits of that banana or that potato you ate for dinner. You'll be amazed by what you find. Do this for the not-so-good foods too. Sometimes we just need an eye-opener to help us put that bag of chips back in the pantry.

The Lord has designed our body with such detail, and what we put into it will either strengthen it or weaken it. The choice is ours. God has provided all the tools needed to create a strong, healthy body, and we can see an example of that in one fruit alone—the peach. Now, just imagine all the other benefits He has provided for our well-being in all that He has created for us to use to nourish our bodies…and be amazed.

One of "Those Days"

BY MEGAN BLACKMORE

*And the peace of God,
which transcends all understanding,
will guard your hearts and
your minds in Christ Jesus.*

—PHILIPPIANS 4:7, NIV

I sometimes have days when I just feel off. Everything bugs me; I am easily annoyed and don't want to be messed with. On such days, I have also realized that I am much more vulnerable, sensitive, and emotional. I find myself craving gentle, loving attention—and if I don't receive it, I feel less than, unloved, and unimportant.

I am sure I am not the only woman to feel this on certain days, and it's not only during my monthly cycles that I have such days. Times like this aren't easy to cope with regardless of when they happen.

I often seek that extra love and attention from my husband, but he falls short of what I need and desire. That's not because he isn't capable of filling up my love tank, but because I have come to understand that those days are special because the extra attention

NATURE

I need in those moments cannot be met by my husband or anyone else. They are instead a call from God that I need to spend a bit more time with Him that day.

You see, the Lord offers love, attention, and care that no earthly person, place, or thing can give us. His love and peace surpass all our understanding of what those two feelings even are. Having those needs met is something we will never experience outside of our Creator.

So, I have come to look at those times when I feel off, down, unloved, uncared for, unimportant, and easily agitated as moments to seek not earthly comfort and love, but Heavenly comfort and love.

Once I realize I am in one of those moods, I acknowledge it for what it is—emotions—and then turn to the one who can help me overcome…God.

I read through some promises He gives me, maybe listen to a bit of classical or worship music, read a verse or two from the Bible, and, of course, pray—opening up my heart to the Lord, telling Him all the horrible things I am feeling, and all about my desire to feel loved and needed in that moment.

Knowing in my heart that the Lord wants to help me feel fulfilled every day, but especially on "those days," brings me comfort that someone cares for me more than anyone on this earth can. He cares more than my husband can, more than my friends or family can, more than that last Oreo on the shelf can (emotional eaters, anyone?).

What's even more amazing is that He cares for you just the same.

Poison Ivy a Good Thing?

BY MEGAN BLACKMORE

*You intended to harm me,
but God intended it for good to accomplish
what is now being done,
the saving of many lives.*

—GENESIS 50:20, NIV

When you think of poison ivy, I'm sure you think of a toxic plant that produces a terribly itchy, not-easy-on-the-eyes rash. You might even be thinking, *Leaves of three, let them be.*

If you've ever encountered poison ivy, you might wonder why the Lord created such a wicked plant. Our thoughts about poison ivy are similar to our thoughts about mosquitos. To be fair, poison ivy was never meant to harm us in the perfect world the Lord originally created. But, if we want to entertain the fact that it has always been poisonous, we have to understand that although it is not good for us or our furry canine friends, we can find numerous benefits for other parts of God's creation in its "poisonous" goodness.

For one, poison ivy is a great food source for a lot of wildlife, including migrating birds, which love to snack on the berries this plant provides. Those berries help sustain them for their long flight ahead and give them a small source of the lipids they need for their bodies. In addition, deer and insects love to eat the leaves of this plant—the same leaves that give humans that horrible rash. Not only is poison ivy a good food source for some animals but it is also considered an early successional plant—meaning it paves the way by altering the soil for the next group of plants to grow in the same space. Poison ivy is actually a quite selfless plant—it's always thinking of others…until it comes to humans anyway!

Along the same line, we often think of the troubling times we encounter in this life as poison to our souls. We wonder why we are having to go through trials and tribulations and wonder what benefit our struggle could possibly have. *Why can't I just get over these bad habits?* we ask.

But when we look at the grand scheme of things and examine every obstacle from God's view, we see that although what we have gone through has left us scarred and maybe even a bit damaged, it is through those injuries and wounds that we are able to heal and help others.

Having overcome a struggle with pornography can equip you to help someone else defeat this demon. Recovering from an addiction to alcohol or drugs allows you to help someone else become sober. Sometimes our pain and struggles are a benefit to others. Just like poison ivy, those things can leave us with horrible rashes—but just as getting rid of the poison ivy removes the help it gives to animals and other plants, having no struggles would take away our ability to help others when they are fighting the same battles.

We must learn to accept our struggles as being something God can use both for our good and the good of others in the long run.

Simple and Quiet Life

BY MEGAN BLACKMORE

And to make it your ambition to lead a quiet life: you should mind your own business and work with your hands, just as we told you, so that your daily life may win the respect of outsiders and so that you will not be dependent on anybody.

—1 THESSALONIANS 4:11–12, NIV

My heart has been drawn to a simple and quiet life in this past year or so. The more easygoing and minimal it is, the better it is for me. I found that I am not stressed, I can think clearly, my mood is much better, and I have less and less anxiety throughout my days.

A quiet life can look different for everyone, but for me, it's all about getting rid of distractions and physical things, and lightening my daily load of tasks while, making time for what brings me peace and joy: reading, writing, being outdoors, listening to calming music, and even just sitting and doing absolutely nothing while listening to my surroundings.

In our verse for today, we are guided to live a quiet life, a life where we mind our business. We are guided and encouraged to live a life where we work simply with our hands, and when we do all of these things, we are then shown respect from those around us, and we will have all the means necessary to take care of ourselves. We won't need to depend on anyone, for we have the ability to do all we need to do.

The more chaotic a life we live, full of constant, never-ending agendas, and the more we put on our plate, the more stress we feel. This applies even to something as simple as the number of items in our home—the more clothes we acquire, the more laundry we do; the more cups and plates we have, the more dishes we must wash. The more books and toys our children have, the more that needs to be put away.

A quiet and simple life to me is also living with less, which creates less and less stress.

The guides and advice given to us in God's Word have purpose and meaning, or else God would never have placed those words in Scripture. When we read certain things, just like when we hear certain things, we tend to let them go in one ear and out the other—out of sight, out of mind. But, when we carefully consider all of the advice the Lord gives in His Word and take a moment to truly ask why He would say that, we find that it all makes sense: the Lord's Word and ways of life are truly and incredibly perfect.

What does a quiet and simple life look like to you? What's one thing you can do today to create that life for yourself and your family?

Sunflowers and Solid Food

BY MEGAN BLACKMORE

*Anyone who lives on milk, being still an infant,
is not acquainted with the teaching about righteousness.
But solid food is for the mature, who by constant use
have trained themselves to distinguish good from evil.*

—HEBREWS 5:13–14, NIV

Sunflowers are one of the most incredible flowers, in my opinion, that God has created. Their ability while young flowers to follow the orientation of the sun throughout the day is quite mind-blowing. And then, at night, they slowly reorient themselves back to be prepared for the coming Sun in the morning, only to do it all over again.

Young sunflowers are like infants, constantly needing the help of their parents to survive and grow—like a nursing baby, these baby sunflowers follow the sun to receive the most sunlight possible for photosynthesis.

However, once the sunflower reaches maturity, it no longer needs to follow the sun throughout the day. In fact, a mature flower orients itself so that it is constantly facing east. The east, you wonder?

This fact alone is fascinating. The sun rises in the east, and when the sun rises, these beautiful summer flowers attract the morning bees that begin their work at the sun's rise due to the increased warmth. So, when the sunflower faces east, it is facing the direction of the sunrise, meaning the bees have an easier time finding their flower and can begin pollinating as the day begins, which in turn helps the sunflower reproduce more easily.

Sunflowers with their big, beautiful, yellow canopy remind me of today's verses in Hebrews. We are like the young sunflower needing the sun throughout the day until we grow strong enough to do without that constant nourishment, we are like the infant needing its mother's milk until we are able to eat solid food, as infants in the faith, we are not equipped or prepared for the teaching of righteousness; but as we mature in our faith and grow stronger and wiser through the Spirit, we can ultimately understand and survive off of the "meat" or solid food of the Word of God.

The sunflower reminds me that everything works according to God's plan. We start out as infants, then through study and prayer transform into mature adults full of wisdom that we share with others. Then, once we have fulfilled our purpose, we await the return of Christ. The sunflower has a similar life plan: it starts off needing nourishment from the sun, then it builds strength as it matures so that it no longer needs constant nourishment. Now the sunflower is fulfilling its purpose for the bees and reproduction.

God's beautiful plan of salvation is for all of us. We start as infants, but through Christ and the Holy Spirit, we grow and transform into the being that God has called us to be—His righteous child, justified through Jesus.

The Bonsai Birch Tree

BY MEGAN BLACKMORE

*I am the true vine, and my Father is the gardener.
He cuts off every branch in me that bears no fruit,
while every branch that does bear fruit he prunes
so that it will be even more fruitful.*

—JOHN 15:1–2, NIV

I am always so impressed by nature in the sense of how easily and readily it connects to the Creator and the messages He has provided for us in His Word. The Bonsai Birch tree is a perfect illustration of today's passage.

I have always loved bonsai trees because of their miniature size. To me, it's truly like bringing nature indoors on a smaller scale. The bonsai tree is an ornamental shrub that can be grown in a pot—it's like having a miniature tree on your dining room table.

The Bonsai Birch is fascinating to me because, every season, this shrub rejects some of its branches. It cuts off supply to those branches so that they wither away and fall off, allowing the shrub to grow new branches in their place that are stronger and healthier and altogether better for the tree. The Bonsai Birch gets rid of the bad to make room for the good.

When we look at John 15:1–2 and Matthew 7:19, we see this same message being delivered. God tells us that He will cut off every branch from His tree that does not bear any fruit, and then after He cuts off all the "bad" branches, He will prune the good so that the tree will be even more fruitful. In other words, God weeds out the individuals who truly do not follow Him with all of their heart, and in doing so, this leaves more room for new individuals to come along who will serve Him and do His work. God, just like the Bonsai Birch, gets rid of the bad branches to make more room for the good.

Nature gives us signs everywhere we look and points us to the incredible power of our Lord, Creator, and personal loving God. We can see God's handiwork and the interconnectedness of God and His Word through the characteristics of the Bonsai Birch, but we can also see it in nature all around us. Everything always points back to the work and Word of God; we just have to take the time to notice.

Next time you're outside, take a look at the birds and how they operate, or even examine the moss or the ants like Solomon. We can find lessons in it all.

The Glass Frog

BY MEGAN BLACKMORE

Your eyes saw my unformed body;
all the days ordained for me were written in
your book before one of them came to be.

—PSALM 139:16, NIV

The glass frog is quite a spectacular little creature. Its lime-green exterior back is eye-catching in and of itself, but what is truly incredible about this little amphibian of the Central and South American rainforests is its belly.

The underside of this frog is completely see-through. You can see all of the frog's organs as well as the happenings of its inner being, almost as if you are looking through a piece of glass. You can clearly see its tiny heart beating and even the slow movement of parts of its body at work. You can't hide much when you are a glass frog.

When I first learned about the glass frog, I thought of our Creator and how He knows us even better than we know ourselves. We can hide nothing at all from Him. He knows all of our inner workings well—our thoughts, motives, intentions, fears, how many hairs we have, and even how each tiny cell aligns uniquely to make us who we are.

We are transparent in God's eyes, just like the glass frog is transparent in ours.

The Bible tells us in today's Scripture taken from Psalm 139 that the Lord knew everything that would happen on any given day of our life before one of those days ever happened. He even saw our unformed bodies before we were born or even recognizable.

We are glass humans to the Lord, and this is something we should honor and love about our Lord of Lords. Because He knows us so well, we can trust Him more deeply than we trust anyone else in this world.

The Father knows His creation. He has the ability to look inside us like we are made of glass and tell us what needs to be changed, what needs some work, and even what will make us the happiest and most content.

Because the Lord knows all of our inner workings as well as everything about us before it even happens—He knows the future—we have the honor of trusting that everything will be okay. Not only does God know all of this, but He wrote our story for us, and it is a story of prosperity (Jeremiah 29:11).

Treetops in the Wind

BY MEGAN BLACKMORE

A strong wind was blowing and the waters grew rough. When they had rowed about three or four miles, they saw Jesus approaching the boat, walking on the water; and they were frightened. But he said to them, "It is I; don't be afraid."

Then they were willing to take him into the boat, and immediately the boat reached the shore where they were heading.

—JOHN 6:18–21, NIV

I love watching treetops blow in the wind during a storm or even just a strong breeze sweeping through a lush canopy. I love seeing the leaves sway back and forth and watching the trunk sway and rock at the wind's command. Then I let my eyes travel all the way down to the base of the tree to stare at the secure trunk rooted in the ground. While looking at the base of the tree, you would never know that the top was flexing, bending, and moving at that same moment. These visuals remind me of Jesus walking on the water towards the disciples in that storm on the sea.

No one seeing Him walk calmly with such gentle strength across that violent water through the equally violent wind would have known that a raging storm was taking place. He was like the base of the tree, steady even during a storm. He was so deeply and securely rooted in His Father that no storm could uproot Him and drag Him into the rushing waters.

Jesus took that first step off the shore placed His foot on the surface of the sea and walked as if strolling through a park—as if mayhem were not taking place all around Him. He was totally and utterly unfazed, solely because His root system was grounded in His Father above.

The winds were rough, and the disciples were terrified as the storm grew in intensity. But not Jesus. He embraced the storm and overcame it.

This firm foundation in the Lord, like our gentle trees have in the ground, is the same type of anchor we must have in our Creator.

We must be so firmly planted in our faith that no matter what storm, turbulence, trials, or tribulations we face in this world, nothing has the ability to pluck us from our Roots and carry us away from the Lord.

We instead must be the seed planted in the good soil so that our roots will hold us within the Lord's embrace—so that we can be unfazed when troubling times come our way.

Like Christ, we can take that first step off the shore and walk across the stormy seas on top of the water, knowing and holding firmly to our faith that the Lord will always and forever keep us afloat.

Calming Waters of Life

BY MEGAN BLACKMORE

But whoever drinks the water I give them will never thirst. Indeed, the water I give them will become in them a spring of water welling up to eternal life.

—JOHN 4:14, NIV

I've always been drawn to water. I love any type of scenic view that incorporates any body of water: a lake, a river, the sea, a pond, or even just a small stream weaving and flowing its way through nature.

There is something so peaceful about still water- of course, but even tumbling waves and a strong current can seem so effortless and melodic with a natural rhythm that allows us to get lost in its soothing movement.

Jesus talks about life-giving water in the verse chosen for today. And I love the simplicity of the message given within those words.

Water is a life-sustaining substance, we were created with bodies that must have it to survive. We can live without food for weeks, but only a few days without water.

So, when Jesus tells the woman at the well that the water He can offer will allow someone to thirst no more, the woman gets excited. Imagine never being thirsty again, never having to be concerned about staying hydrated.

Jesus' example of using water to explain the life He could give to someone who would accept Him and believe in Him is extraordinary.

Jesus is saying that if we have faith in Him, we can live a life without need. We can live a life that is never at risk. We can live a life where all we require is provided. We will never need to search for answers, for all we will ever need is in Him.

Water keeps our bodies alive, and Jesus refers to Himself as this water. He is our life sustainer, He has purchased a gift of eternal life through His death on the cross, and He is giving us this gift for free.

Water is vital to our health. Based on this verse and others in the Bible, we see that Jesus is vital to our spiritual health. Without His sacrifice, we would perish immediately. But thanks be to our Savior who made the ultimate sacrifice for a people undeserving of such an act.

I try to remind myself when I gaze out at an open sea or a beautiful, pristine, and calm lake, that water is vital to my health and wellbeing—I can't survive without it. Then, I remind myself that Jesus is also my life-giving water, and I can't survive without Him either.

When we remind ourselves of our need for our Savior, we are humbled and eager to praise His name and His Heavenly life-giving Father.

Hiking the Appalachian Trail

BY MEGAN BLACKMORE

> *In his hand are the depths of the earth,*
> *and the mountain peaks belong to him.*
> *The sea is his, for he made it,*
> *and his hands formed the dry land.*
>
> —PSALM 95:4–5, NIV

My husband and I have the crazy goal of walking the entire Appalachian Trail (AT) at some point in our lives before we die. Averaging fourteen to twenty miles a day, it takes on average about five to six months to complete a thru-hike, and it's roughly five million steps from Georgia to Maine.

Many have set this goal, and many have also accomplished it. The distance or duration isn't what makes this goal unusual for my husband and me. What makes it a crazy goal is that neither of us at this point in our lives has ever camped or hiked more than maybe two miles at a time, nor do we know anything at all about what it means to hike the AT. However, despite all of these facts, we still have set this goal for some point in our lives.

NATURE

We told ourselves this summer that we'd start small. We are determined to buy some camping gear and periodically set out for the great outdoors to experience nature as neither of us has ever done before. The good thing is that we are both huge nature lovers; we don't mind getting muddy and dirty, we don't mind bug bites or spending the day just exploring the great outdoors. In fact, we spend most of our days outside doing just that, especially in the spring and summer. So, this goal of ours and the journey it will take to get us to the AT hiking level is actually quite exciting and invigorating.

When I read about all those who have hiked the AT or any similar long hike, I think about the people in Bible times who walked everywhere they needed to go. Sometimes, their journey was even longer than five months or five million steps.

I think about everything they saw on their journeys and the impact that kind of travel had on their lives. For us, just simply taking an afternoon stroll down the sidewalk can be mood-altering—it can completely change a day, making the sour-sweet again. I can imagine that the long journeys taken in Bible times had a similar effect.

Being out in nature and enjoying the Lord's creation in its raw and beautiful form is something God wants us to experience. Jesus often went away to secluded places in nature to pray and commune with God—far from distraction, far from the craziness of the world. Getting out to walk is what we all need sometimes. Even if it's not the entire AT, a quick stroll around the block will do.

Plans with Seasons

BY KELLEY MATIERIENE

*There is a time for everything and
a season for every activity under the heavens.*

—ECCLESIASTES 3:1, NIV

My favorite seasons are spring and fall; summer is too hot, and winter is too cold. I love the spring when the flowers start blooming and the world feels like it's waking up from a deep sleep. The daffodils always seem a bit eager as well, but they are my sign that more warm weather is coming. And though I hate the cold, autumn's cool breezes mean campfires and snuggling under my blankets. I long for hot cocoa and stories around the dinner table.

When our kids were small, their dad made them learn Ecclesiastes 3:1–8. This was especially for my son who is the joker in our family. My husband wanted the kids to remember that everything has its place and its season.

Sometimes. seasons change when we least expect it and, sometimes, we can anticipate the change and be ready. Either way, seasons change.

My son didn't like rapid season changes. He preferred to be told what was coming so he could expect it and feel prepared. To this day, he is still like that. He will ask me what the plan is and go over summer plans, school year plans, etc. Maybe he got that from me. I am a planner by nature, I planned out what age I would be when I graduated from college, and when I needed to marry if I was going to have kids by a certain age. It all seems quite humorous when I look back on it.

A lot of my life actually went according to plan, to be honest. However, what I couldn't plan for or didn't plan for are the seasonal changes within the larger picture. We all have quiet details that most people can't plan because they are unaware of them.

For example, I had my first child at twenty-seven, right on plan! Thanks, son. However, with all of my big plans, I didn't plan for where he would go to preschool or move him and his sister to a new state when he was four years old. I didn't plan for the details because I didn't know about them. The truth is, I am glad I didn't many times because that allowed the Lord to move in and surprise me, to put things in place that I could have never imagined with all my planning.

My friend, make plans. As the saying goes, if you fail to plan, you plan to fail. Just be sure to leave room for Christ to come in and shape your seasons. You will find that he does a better job at the details than you ever could. Today, write out two of your plans; then pray over them, asking God to shape them in ways only He can.

Metamorphosis

BY KAREEN WILSON

*Therefore, if anyone is in Christ,
he is a new creation;
the old things have passed away;
behold, all things have become new.*

—2 CORINTHIANS 5:17, NKJV

*"Just when the caterpillar thought the world was over,
it became a butterfly."*

—CHANG TZU

How does a caterpillar change itself into a butterfly? What happens inside a chrysalis or cocoon? The caterpillar digests itself. It turns into a soupy mess, but it is a sophisticated mess. Some of the cells are so highly organized that they regroup and remember their function from the time the caterpillar was conceived and in egg form. They remember they are to be a butterfly's legs, arms, and eyes. The new cells use the protein-rich soup to build more and more cells to create the magnificent butterfly. The precise timing and amazing perfection of the process amaze scientists today. I imagine that it is uncomfortable, with growing pains and discontent, as the caterpillar destroys itself to become something different.

Most caterpillars are pretty plain. They crawl on their belly with short little legs that don't take them very far. Some are not very colorful and pretty low on the food chain if they do not watch their back. In their mind, they may not be able to imagine that they will someday be colorful and fly to see the world. But it was written in their genes from the second they were conceived.

When we are created in Christ, we are a new creature: lovely, magnificent, able to comprehend new ideas and see new territory. Sometimes, we must rest in a cocoon and allow that cocoon to rearrange our thoughts and turn them into soup, to instill new strength and new insights. That's when we transform and become beautiful creatures in Christ.

How can you become new in Christ?

Miracles

*Jesus looked at them and said,
"With man this is impossible,
but with God all things are possible."*

—MATHEW 19:26, NIV—

Coincidences and Miracles

BY KAREEN WILSON

Now to him who is able to do far more abundantly than all that we ask or think, according to the power at work within us, to him be glory in the church and in Christ Jesus throughout all generations, forever and ever. Amen.

—EPHESIANS 3:20–21, ESV

Bethesda Medical Mission was created as a reaction to the devastation that hit the country of Haiti in 2011. This country already dealt with poverty and pain; watching the continued blows of injustice and Mother Nature was just too much.

Bethesda Medical Mission is a non-profit that provides health services to people in developing countries. BMM also helps to rebuild homes that have been damaged due to natural causes.

Every year that we travel, we organize and bring all the supplies we need for our trip. This requires seventy to a hundred large bins heavily packed with meds, dental equipment, food, and supplies to make the trip successful. Each year, we reach out to the airlines about our plans, and they provide clearance for us to bring all that we need to serve.

One year, we were flying to Haiti through New York, and as we approached the counter to check our luggage, the receptionist stated that she did not see the special clearance and that there was no way we could bring the supplies. We begged and explained, but everything we said was disregarded. Not knowing what to do, we got down on our knees. We prayed.

I approached the counter again, explained our situation calmly, and confidently, and then just stood silently to hear the verdict. For some reason, the receptionist changed her mind. She mentioned that she would love to help and told us that the new shift supervisor was from Haiti and just might allow our supplies to go through. Isn't that remarkable?!

When the new supervisor heard our story, she personally guided us, helped us get all of our bins checked and secured, and ensured that our return flight would be hassle-free. She thanked us for our efforts to help her country and blessed us.

God answered our prayers. What are the chances of a Haitian supervisor just starting shift as we are about to board a plane? Never underestimate the power of God in every situation. Believe in the miracles that will appear just when you need them.

How has God worked coincidences (aka miracles) in your life?

My Protector

BY KAREEN WILSON

*Then Jacob made this vow: "If God will indeed be with me and protect me on this journey, and if he will provide me with food and clothing, and if I return safely to my father's home, then the L*ORD *will certainly be my God."*

—GENESIS 28:20–21, NLT

We have all heard those stories that leave you wondering how that is even possible. A miracle. A strange gentleman watches over your luggage as you chase your runaway child. When you return and thank him, no one is there as you turn around. You are down to your last five dollars in the bank and your pocket, but you give it in the offering plate anyway, and the next day you receive a mystery check in the mail for the exact amount to cover your needs. Miracles leave us baffled about how they happen, but they also leave us with a warm glow in our hearts.

When I was around five years old, my parents worked opposite shifts to allow one parent to always be home with me. I was an only child then, so I was their pride and joy until my brother came along. My mother worked nights and my father during the day, and there was always a two-hour gap between their work schedules for my father to pick up my mother, bring her home, and prepare to leave the house for his shift. My dad would get me dressed early in the morning, we'd drive out to pick up my mother, then sit and have breakfast together.

One particularly cold January Winterpeg morning (I grew up in Winnipeg, which might as well be called Winterpeg because of the extremely cold winter conditions), Daddy decided to let me sleep and run out to pick up my mom without me. He figured since Mom's workplace was only 10 minutes away, that I would be safe in my warm, comfy bed, never even knowing he was gone.

However, my internal alarm clock went off, and I woke up just as he left. I looked for my dad and realized I was all alone. I clearly remember this incident because I did not feel afraid. I put on my coat, gloves, hat, and boots and decided that I was going to walk to Mom's workplace and meet them. In Winnipeg, in the winter, the temperatures in the early morning can be in the minus-degree range. Plus, we have only about seven hours of daylight in the winter months. It seemed like a great plan in my five-year-old mind, except it was dark, cold, and a five-mile walk. Also, I am sure my navigation skills at that age were not ideal. Nevertheless, I stepped out into the unknown.

My father and mother were driving back from work when they saw a little figure in the distance that caught their attention. What would such a little child be doing out in the cold at this early hour all alone? Then they recognized my coat, and I can only imagine the feeling in the pit of their stomachs.

The way Dad tells the story, I walked almost two miles all alone on the correct road to my mom's place of work. I dressed so well that I didn't get frostbite. I had even packed a snack just in case I needed something to eat.

My parents never left me home alone again until I was twenty-one.

It was a miracle that I was safe. My dad knew that God was watching over me and protecting me. I was unhurt by the weather, cars, or people.

God is our great protector and defender. He is working behind the scenes to provide miracles to show us His love. We all must believe that He will send His angels to protect us. This is just one of the ways the supernatural impacts our lives.

God's Gift Against All Odds

BY MICHELLE ANDERSON

Behold, children are a heritage from the LORD,
the fruit of the womb a reward.

—PSALM 127:3, NLT

In life's journey, we often encounter unexpected twists and turns, facing insurmountable challenges and obstacles. Yet, in our doubts and fears, God has a way of surprising us with His miraculous intervention, bringing forth blessings beyond our wildest dreams.

Let me share my story of God's gift against all odds. After struggling with fibroid tumors and receiving medical advice to remove my uterus, I turned to God for healing. Though the fibroid remained, God worked extraordinarily, shrinking it enough for me to conceive. It was a miraculous moment, defying medical odds and reaffirming God's power to grant life.

The thought of having a child hadn't crossed my mind for eight years of marriage. Yet, when man said no, God said yes! In His perfect timing, I discovered I was expecting my first child, a beautiful blessing despite the fibroid's presence. This realization reminded me of the truth expressed in Psalm 127:3. Children are a heritage from the Lord—a precious reward that He bestows upon us.

Every step of my pregnancy was a testament to God's steadfast love. Even though the fibroid continued to grow, posing potential risks, God protected and nurtured the precious life within me. I endured pain and struggles, requiring regular doctor's appointments to monitor the baby's well-being. Yet, week after week, the doctor marveled at the baby's growth and development, despite the fibroid's attempts to hinder his growth. It was a remarkable display of God's faithfulness, proving that circumstances do not thwart His purposes.

At thirty-seven weeks, I gave birth to a healthy baby, defying expectations or complications. Though the delivery was challenging and required a C-section, God's hand of protection was evident. He spared my life and my son's life, a testament to His unwavering faithfulness and loving care.

May my journey exemplify the beauty of trusting God's plan despite obstacles and uncertainties. The arrival of my precious child is a testament to the miraculous power of God's love and His ability to bring forth life in unexpected ways.

Lost and Found

BY SANDRA A. SERGEANT

*The LORD directs the steps of the godly.
He delights in every detail of their lives.*

—PSALM 37:23, NLT

The story in 2 Kings 6:1–7 is about a group of prophets who came to Elisha, the prophet and told him they needed a larger space to meet. "Let's go down to the Jordan River, where there are plenty of logs. There, we can build a new place for us to meet."

"All right," he told them, "go ahead."

"Please come with us" someone suggested.

"I will," he agreed.

When they arrived at the Jordan, they began cutting down trees. But as one of them was chopping, his ax head fell into the river.

"Ah, my lord!" he cried. "It was a borrowed axe!"

"Where did it fall?" the man of God asked. When he showed Elisha the place, the prophet cut a stick and threw it in the water.

Then the axe head rose to the surface and floated. "Grab it," Elisha told him. And the man reached out and grabbed it.

As we continue to focus on miracles in our everyday lives, I think we are often looking for someone to be raised from the dead or some illness to disappear before we classify it as a miracle. While these events have occurred, our text reminds us that God cares about the little details in our lives—such as misplacing car keys, forgetting where we parked the car while shopping, misplacing a wallet…

"Does God care about that?"

Yes. Yes, He does.

Elisha's act demonstrated God's power working through him. It highlights God's care for our lives in even small and seemingly mundane aspects—like the recovery of the borrowed axe or some item you have lost and then found. These miracles serve as reminders of God's provision and intervention in everyday matters. Thank God today for the little miracles in your life, for miracles do happen.

Miracles Happen

BY SANDRA A. SERGEANT

*"Where did it fall?" the man of God asked.
When he showed him the place,
Elisha cut a stick and threw it into the water at that spot.
Then the ax head floated to the surface.*

—2 KINGS 6:6, NLT

In this fast-paced world, where everything is measured in nanoseconds, we often overlook the simplicity and awe-inspiring nature of our existence and forget the miraculous acts of God

The series of miracles outlined in 2 Kings serve as a reminder of God's continuous involvement in our lives. These accounts showcase how God's intervention in seemingly ordinary situations can result in extraordinary outcomes. By acknowledging God's presence and surrendering control to Him, we open ourselves to experiencing miracles daily.

Miracles are defined as events that surpass natural or scientific explanations and can be attributed to the divine agency of God. They defy the limitations of our understanding and remind us of our Creator's supernatural power and love.

CONNECTING WITH GOD

When we allow God to enter our daily lives and relinquish our desire for control, we create space for His miraculous works to manifest. By slowing down, seeking His guidance, and trusting in His plan, we can witness the miraculous occurrences that unfold in our lives. Miracles can become a regular part of our existence, shaping our perspective and reminding us of the extraordinary nature of our relationship with God.

By embracing the simplicity of our existence and acknowledging God's miraculous nature, we open ourselves to experience daily miracles. Allowing God complete control in our lives enables us to witness His supernatural intervention, transforming ordinary moments into extraordinary encounters with His grace and love.

Let us embrace a spirit of wonder and gratitude as we uncover the miracles woven into the fabric of our everyday existence.

You Will Know

BY SANDRA A. SERGEANT

*You have searched me, L*ORD*, and you know me.*
You know when I sit and when I rise;
you perceive my thoughts from afar.
You discern my going out and my lying down;
you are familiar with all my ways.
Before a word is on my tongue you,
L*ORD, know it completely.*

—PSALM 139:1–4, NIV

Another story in 2 Kings reminds us that God will reveal what we need to know. The king of Aram was at war with Israel; he would confer with his officers and say, "We will mobilize our forces at such and such a place."

But immediately, Elisha, the man of God, would warn the king of Israel not to go near the place, for the Arameans planned to mobilize their troops there. The story says the king of Israel would send word to the place indicated by the man of God, warning the people to be on their guard. This happened several times.

The king became furious since his plans of attack were thwarted. He called his officers to determine who was the traitor among them. He demanded to know who it was, but they told him, "It's not us! One of the prophets in Israel tells the king of Israel, even the words you speak in the privacy of your bedroom!"

Imagine the miracle of knowing someone's thoughts and having God's guidance in every aspect of life. Because He knows what we are going to say before the word is on our tongue, what a mighty God we serve. How deeply He cares about our being known and understood by the Creator of the Universe and desires to be involved in every aspect of our lives. With such a supernatural force behind us, how could we not experience daily miracles?

To experience such miracles each day, our only function is found in Proverbs 3:5 and 6 (NIV): "Trust in the Lord with all your heart and lean not on your own understanding" because He knows us intimately. Do this and watch the miracles happen!

Changing the Filter

BY ELINETE RODRIGUES REIS

*So God created mankind in his own image,
in the image of God he created them;
male and female he created them.*

—GENESIS 1:27, NIV

Social media has changed the way we see ourselves and others. Many voices have been raised addressing its impact on our lives in general, but especially in the lives of young people. Truth be told, social media is a reality we can't avoid. It impacts our daily routine, it shapes our opinion, it consumes our time—whether we accept it or not, whether we agree or not. It's here, and it doesn't seem that it will disappear from our daily lives.

We all have been impacted by the online platforms. Social networks use several techniques to keep us "connected," "linked," and "engaged." They change interfaces and features often to keep us involved. One of their tools is filters. Filters are appearance-altering digital images, also known as beauty filters. Filters use editing tools, artificial intelligence, and computer vision to alter appearance, especially of facial features.

New filters appear every day, all in search of the "perfect symmetrical feature." Society has an unwritten rule that women especially must present a *"flawless image,"* putting women on an endless and unachievable quest for the perfect version of themselves. As a result, many studies today directly link social media behaviors to low self-esteem, mental health, and negative body image.

Nonetheless, the use of filters isn't necessarily a bad thing. We just need to look in another direction and use the correct filter—the filter of Jesus. When we put our image behind Jesus and shine through Him, our best version comes to the surface—the image of His creation, the one from which we were all made. We don't need to chase all these "ideal" templates to make us look prettier; we have already been wonderfully made (Psalm 139:14). The creator of the universe made us in His own image. No touch-ups are necessary. Jesus is the Creator of beauty, and He made you.

Today, put on your best filter —the filter of JESUS—and radiate perfect, immaculate beauty.

Marriage & Relationships

*He who finds a wife finds what is good
and receives favor from the Lord.*

—PROVERBS 18:22, NIV—

Embracing the Strength of Faithful Unity

BY AVALEY FRANCES MATIERIENE

Be devoted to one another in love.
Honor one another above yourselves.

—ROMANS 12:10, NIV

As an exchange student in the Philippines, I carried the rich heritage of my Seventh-day Adventist faith with me. Aware of the challenges and opportunities that awaited me in a foreign land, my mother provided invaluable advice—to seek out the local Seventh-day Adventist community. Following her guidance, I embarked on a journey that not only strengthened my personal faith but also fostered deep connections and a sense of pride within the community.

From the moment I stepped into the Seventh-day Adventist community, I experienced a warmth and acceptance that surpassed all expectations. The name and affiliation of Seventh-day Adventists carried significant respect within the broader community. Known for their outstanding colleges, hospitals, and dedicated service to the less fortunate, Seventh-day Adventists embodied the compassionate love of Christ in tangible ways.

Within this faith community, I found immediate and enduring friendships that have stood the test of time, spanning more than fifteen years. The bond we shared was not based merely on shared beliefs, but on a shared commitment to love, support, and uplift one another. It was through this unity that the true strength of our faith shone brightly.

Reflecting on this journey, I am reminded of the words of Romans 12:10, which encourage us to be devoted to one another in love and to honor one another above ourselves. In the Seventh-day Adventist community, I witnessed this devotion and honor in action. It was a testament to the transformative power of faith and the incredible bonds that form when individuals come together with a shared purpose.

Let us treasure the gift of community and embrace the strength that comes from walking together in faith. May we continue to honor one another, uplift one another, and celebrate the unique role each person plays in the tapestry of our faith community.

True Femininity

BY FELECIA D. LEE

*Charm is deceptive, and beauty is fleeting,
but a woman who fears the L*ORD *is to be praised.*

—PROVERBS 31:30, NIV

For many years, I struggled with Proverbs 31 (as I'm sure many women do.) It seemed to showcase an impossible standard to live up to. I thought that if I could just do these things, then I could be a virtuous woman. But this passage isn't about doing things in order to be virtuous. It's highlighting works that can come only as a result of faith in the power of Jesus. The woman in Proverbs 31 is feminine not as a result of what she does, but because of who she is in Christ.

It takes faith to practice femininity in a world that wants to desaturate the color of womanhood and produce caricatures that are an affront to all that it means to be a woman. True femininity reflects Christ by abiding in Him.

As red is to the rose, waves to the ocean, loftiness to the mountain, heat to the sun, and white to the snow, so is femininity to the godly woman.

Being a woman is not simply the wearing of pink and pumps, lace, and lipstick. It is the fragrance that a woman emanates when crushed by trials. It's the light she gives when everything around her is dark. It's the song on her lips as she goes about cleaning baby bottoms and wiping snotty noses. It's the quietness of her soul when her work or ministry—or life—is filled with turmoil.

Femininity shows itself in the art she wears and shares; a true walking temple of Solomon arrayed in the finest purple, blue, silk, and linen.

Femininity is the subduing of the soul when tempted to yell, employing wisdom and grace to convey thoughts and opinions, and using clarity to communicate needs and wants. The feminine woman shuns clamor, vulgarity, hatred, resentment, impatience, uncleanness, idleness, despondency, passive-aggressiveness, immodesty, and pride. When these thorns are found in her garden, she calls to the holy Husbandman who carefully cuts them out.

Femininity is praising instead of pouting, praying instead of pestering, shunning and rebuking gossip, raising children to be obedient to Jesus, and manifesting the fruit of the Spirit even when all the forces of hell have been unleashed against her. Womanhood stands for truth and despises the sins that led the Son of God to the cross. Femininity shines from a woman who knows she is a martyr in the making, not a doll for playing.

Femininity requires power, fearlessness, valiancy, meekness, courage, and submissiveness. It is found in a woman whose spine is made of steel and whose heart is sewn with silk. It does not come naturally. But when we submit to Christ daily, by faith, we can be what He created us to be: truly feminine women!

In what area of your life does femininity need to shine through?

My Peace I Give to You

BY MEGAN BLACKMORE

> *Peace I leave with you; my peace I give to you.*
> *I do not give to you as the world gives.*
> *Do not let your hearts be troubled and do not be afraid.*
>
> —JOHN 14:27, NIV

As a new mom, one simply cannot prepare for certain fears, worries, and concerns that will arise once you give birth.

As I sit writing this, my daughter is six days old today, and I must admit that I was not prepared for a lot of the mental battles I have experienced now that she is finally here. The first few days, I found myself paranoid, overwhelmed, constantly anxious, and restless in both mind and body—I simply couldn't relax, and my mind was so full of anxiety that everything felt daunting and scary.

Like all new moms, I wanted to make sure my daughter was breathing, that she was okay, that she was eating enough, and getting enough sleep—I would overthink everything she did, and everything she wasn't doing. The levels of anxiety I faced, especially once we arrived home with our baby girl, were through the roof high—I can't even put it into words.

But, through all the fears, worries, and anxiety, I felt the Lord pulling me and calling me towards Him stronger than ever before—almost like I instinctively knew I needed Him more now than ever to silence my fears, quiet my mind, and bring peace to my body. I knew that the enemy of lies lurked behind every corner just waiting to pounce like a lion, filling my mind with lies and doubts, planting seeds of fear—and in order to conquer and defeat Satan, I had to rely on the Lord.

The moment I felt that strong call from the Lord as He was gently pulling me closer to Him, I began to feel a peace that surpassed all understanding. My body felt lighter, my mind less foggy, and my wild thoughts were tamed. I spent time in Scripture, meditating on His Word, and in prayer. I called on His name, declared His promises of peace and strength over me, and trusted Him to do all things for me. He is the one who will keep our daughter in His hands, He is the one who will guide us in being her parents, and He is the one who will help us day by day, or even hour by hour when I feel a bit overwhelmed.

Parenting is a lifetime commitment to caring for a child the Lord entrusted to you. With it come many worries and anxieties, but we do not need to dwell on the uncertainties or the worries about the future because we serve a God who has our stories already written. He has a purpose for every single one of us, and if we call on Him and trust in His plans for us, we will be given peace that this world could never bring. We can possess a peace that can come only from the Lord, our God—our Creator. He gifts us with a peace that passes all understanding.

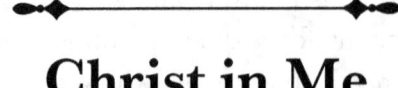

Christ in Me

BY KELLEY MATIERIENE

Let this mind be in you which was also in Christ Jesus.

—PHILIPPIANS 2:5, NKJV

When I was a little girl, I found a notebook in which my mom had written affirmations over and over. Even before it was cool, my mom was affirming herself and us as young women growing up in the world.

After I got married, since there is no school that teaches us how to be a wife or a mother, I learned by watching the women around me or the movies. As a young mother and wife, I was not always very affirming. I was easily offended and wondered why I couldn't just be me.

Then, two very important things happened.

First, my sister, who knows me well, sat me down and said, "You get to be you, but you can't control people's reaction to who you are. Just like you want to be you, rough around the edges, they get to be themselves and either respond back in the same manner or decide they don't like you." It goes without saying that I didn't like the way that felt. I wanted people to love the rough edges of me. I wasn't ready for God to smooth them out.

Then, I heard a sermon by Pavel Goia on being like Christ and having His character. He mentioned that when we are more like Christ, we aren't as easily offended by what people do and say to us. Christ lives in me, and "it is no longer I who live, but Christ lives in me" (Galatians 2:20, NKJV). That means when someone says something about me, IF—and that's a big IF—I am truly representing the character of Christ, then it's Christ they are offending. And that's between them and Christ. I don't have to teach people lessons or put them in their place because God's got me. And I can continue in the peace that is Christ's alone. I love that thought.

One of the first things I did was memorize Philippians 2:5–10 as a reminder that I want to be more like Christ—having His character, peace, and humility—and let God teach if there is an opportunity to teach and know when to walk away if there isn't.

Let me tell you that it has not been easy! Many times, I slip back into my old mindset and my former ways, but I am a work in progress—and so are you, my friend. On those days, I remember again what my friend Christ would do (not that He ever slipped up). He would go to the Father because the only way I can be like Christ is by spending time in the presence of God.

Today, choose a verse that reminds you to be like Christ. And remember He is not looking for perfection as we see it but, rather, He is looking for us to turn to Him.

Anchored in Faith: God's Faithfulness in Long-Distance Love (Part 1)

BY AVALEY FRANCES MATIERIENE

*Commit your way to the Lord;
trust in him and he will do this.*

—PSALM 37:5, NIV

Love has a way of transcending distance, stretching across oceans and continents. In the realm of long-distance relationships, I embarked on a ten-year journey with my beloved, enduring physical separation and the challenges it brought. While the path was undoubtedly difficult, it became a testament to the unshakable power of faith and the unwavering love of our Heavenly Father.

As the miles stretched between us, my heart yearned for the day when we would be united under the same roof. The distance seemed insurmountable at times, and doubts whispered in my ear. But in those moments, I turned to God, committing our journey to Him, fully trusting in His faithfulness.

MARRIAGE & RELATIONSHIPS

Throughout the years, God displayed His faithfulness in remarkable ways. He provided strength to endure the separation, granting us resilience and unwavering love for one another. Even when doubts and fears threatened to consume us, God's presence was steadfast, offering a peace that transcended the miles between us.

The journey taught me invaluable lessons about the power of patience, perseverance, and unwavering trust in God's plan. As I leaned on Him, I discovered a deeper reliance on His guidance, recognizing that His ways are higher than our ways, and His thoughts are higher than our thoughts (Isaiah 55:9).

In those long months apart, I found comfort in prayer, pouring out my heart's desires and fears to the One who understands the depths of our souls. It was through these intimate conversations with God that my relationship with Him deepened. I discovered that true contentment is found not only in the fulfillment of our desires but also in the unwavering presence of our loving Father.

As the years passed, the day of the reunion finally arrived. God's faithfulness shone brightly as we embraced under the same roof, the miles and struggles were now a testament to the strength of our love and the unwavering commitment of our Heavenly Father.

(To be continued)

Anchored in Faith: God's Faithfulness in Long-Distance Love (Part 2)

BY *AVALEY FRANCES MATIERIENE*

> *Commit your way to the* L<small>ORD</small>*;*
> *trust in him and he will do this.*
>
> —PSALM 37:5, NIV

Are you in the throes of navigating the challenges of a long-distance relationship? Hold fast to the promises of God. Place your trust in Him, knowing that He is faithful to bring His plans to fruition. Commit your way to the Lord and find comfort in the assurance that He will guide your steps.

Though the road may be filled with uncertainty and moments of longing, remember that God is with you every step of the way. He sees your sacrifices, understands your heart's desires, and walks beside you as you navigate the journey.

Today, may you find strength in God's promises. Embrace the waiting season as an opportunity to deepen your faith and reliance on God. Trust in His perfect timing, knowing that He is working behind the scenes to bring about His purposes in your life.

In the moments of doubt, turn to God in prayer, pouring out your heart before Him. Allow His presence to fill you with peace and assurance that He is with you every step of the way. Trust in His faithfulness, for He is the author of beautiful love stories and the One who binds hearts together across any distance.

May your journey be marked by unwavering faith, steadfast hope, and the joy of knowing that God's plans for your love story are greater than anything you could ever think or imagine.

Wisdom in Discerning Relationships

BY AVALEY FRANCES MATIERIENE

*Listen to advice and accept discipline,
and at the end, you will be counted among the wise.*

—PROVERBS 19:20, NIV

As we journey through life, we encounter various relationships that shape and influence us. During my freshman year at boarding school, I met a girl who quickly became a close friend. We spent time together outside of school, attending church and sharing many experiences. However, beneath the surface, her family dynamics were filled with strife and drama. As she confided in me, attempting to involve me in her troubles, I faced a crossroads that required wisdom and discernment.

It was during this pivotal moment that my dorm mother, a wise and loving mentor, observed my interactions with this friend. Recognizing the potential dangers and emotional harm that lay ahead, she graciously counseled me. She reminded me that I was just a young girl, urging me not to entangle myself in the web of my friend's family drama. Her words were like a lifeline, guiding me away from harm and towards a path of wisdom.

As an adult, reflecting upon that season of my life, I can now see the invaluable lessons embedded within that wise counsel. It is reminiscent of the way the Holy Spirit works in our lives, offering divine guidance and protection. The Holy Spirit, who knows the intricacies of our past, present, and future, provides wisdom that surpasses our own understanding. We must be open and receptive to receive this godly counsel. Proverbs 19:20 encourages us to listen to advice and accept discipline, for it is through humility and openness that we gain wisdom. The guidance of trusted mentors and the gentle nudges of the Holy Spirit serve as a compass, leading us away from potential harm and towards a path of righteousness.

In that moment of decision, I chose to heed the counsel given to me. I distanced myself from the unhealthy dynamics and protected my own emotional well-being. Looking back, I realize that this act of wisdom was not merely a human decision but a surrender to the guidance of the Holy Spirit. God's hand was at work, shielding me from the pain and turmoil that awaited. Remember that the Holy Spirit is our ever-present Counselor, offering insights beyond our own limited perspective. Trust in His leading, knowing He sees the bigger picture and desires what is best for us. Accept the protection that flows from His guidance, and humbly receive the discipline that leads to growth and spiritual maturity. ¶

The Prepared Bride

BY MICHELLE ANDERSON

*Let us be glad and rejoice, and give honor to him:
for the marriage of the Lamb is come,
and his wife hath made herself ready.*

—REVELATION 19:7, KJV

The anticipation of a wedding day is filled with excitement and joy. As the bride-to-be, every detail matters, and meticulous planning is necessary to ensure a smooth and memorable celebration. In my own journey toward marriage, I experienced the challenges of preparing for my wedding day, including unexpected obstacles that tested my resolve.

In the early stages of wedding planning, I had a clear vision of the day I desired, but time constraints and unforeseen circumstances threatened to derail my preparations. With only five months to organize an out-of-state wedding, I had to stay focused and diligently manage every aspect of the event. However, even with careful planning, I encountered a major setback: a power outage in the bustling city of New York, just days before the big event.

MARRIAGE & RELATIONSHIPS

I arrived in New York on August 12, a Tuesday evening, and spent the next two days feverishly purchasing last-minute supplies. However, on Thursday afternoon, the sudden power loss brought everything to a screeching halt. All the arrangements—the food, the printed bulletins, and essential planning notes on our laptop—were inaccessible. Panic set in as I realized that time was running out, and I had so much left to do that I couldn't complete it without electricity.

On Saturday, August 16, around 9:30 p.m., power was finally restored! Needless to say, I worked tirelessly through the night to make up for the three days I had been at a standstill. At 5:00 am on Sunday—my wedding day!—I was just lying down to sleep! The wedding was scheduled to begin at 3:30 that afternoon, but I was just getting into the limo at that point with the venue over an hour away. By the time I was finally ready to walk down the aisle, it was nearly 6:00 p.m.!

Reflecting on this challenging experience, I see a profound parallel to our spiritual journey of preparing for the marriage of the Lamb. Our relationship with Christ is symbolized as the union between a bride and her groom, and just as I had to make myself ready for my wedding day, we, too, are called to prepare ourselves for the glorious day of Christ's return.

While my earthly wedding day may have been marred by unforeseen challenges, the spiritual wedding feast with Christ is one that we should approach with preparation. We must not allow ourselves to be caught off guard or unprepared by the distractions and disruptions of this world. Instead, we are called to remain steadfast in our faith, continually seeking God's guidance and growing in our love for Him. Let us strive to be spiritually ready for the day when Christ will welcome His bride into eternity.

I Do!

BY EVELYN RAQUEL DELGADO MARRERO

That is why a man leaves his father and mother and is united to his wife, and they become one flesh.

—GENESIS 2:24, NIV

On July 30, 1978, I said, "I Do" to the man that I have been married to for over forty-five years. My husband jokingly says, "There are people who commit manslaughter and only get a twenty-year sentence," then he adds, "but these have been the best forty-five years of my life." I wholeheartedly agree with him on everything.

Like every marriage, we've had some trials, but with God's help, we have learned to navigate the adversities and embrace the blessings. We both had the best examples from our parents. His parents were married for almost seventy years, and my parents were married for sixty-five years. Their examples define for us the meaning of commitment.

I remember that someone told me soon after we married, "If you think you love him now, just wait a couple of years; you'll see how much more you love him then." I don't think that I love him more. However, I love him differently. At the beginning of our relationship, I was romantically in love with him. Now our love has grown to include other dimensions. I know that I can trust him to have my best interests in mind. We are best friends. I depend on him and confide in him in good times and in bad times. He does the same for me. I like being with him and sharing important moments. Beautiful experiences feel incomplete if he is not there to share them with me.

Yes, forty-five years is a long time, but it feels like time has flown by so quickly. Our daily lives were filled with our jobs, our children, and our routines. We dedicated our lives to raising God-fearing children. We aimed to make God the center of our family. We figured nothing is impossible with God, so we trusted Him to help us.

We both had demanding careers, but we are retired now. We raised three children who are tax-contributing members of society. They have blessed us with six rambunctious and beautiful grandchildren. We are enjoying our leisure time helping our children and spoiling our grandchildren. God has blessed our marriage, but we know that our enemy the devil prowls around like a roaring lion looking for someone to devour (1 Peter 5:8).

God had a plan. He instituted marriage in the Garden of Eden. Throughout the Bible, we see how God blesses and honors marriage. The institution of marriage is the basis for a happy family, and families are the foundation of society. The devil knows that, if he destroys the marriage institution, society will decay and fall. He is working overtime to make sure our marriages fail. We pray that God will guard and protect our marriages, our families, and our children.

Unnoticed

BY ANANDI MOSES

Then she called the name of the LORD who spoke to her, "You are a God who sees me."

—GENESIS 16:13A, NASB

My son helps out in the audio-visual department for our church service. They handle the sound and visuals that play during service and also stream the service online for people to watch on the internet.

The singers, preachers, and musicians who come up in front of the congregation depend on the AV technicians who must be constantly aware of what is taking place. They do not have the luxury of mentally signing off during church. The right mics have to be on, the camera has to move with the preacher, and the slides containing the words to the songs have to change at precisely the right time to avoid that awkward mumbling when the congregation is unsure about the next words. In short, the audio-visual can make or break the smooth operation of a worship service!

Working in AV is a unique experience. It is a background job. These technicians work behind the scenes. The AV techs go mostly unnoticed. When the service runs smoothly, everyone is focused on the platform and what is taking place there. The only time the AV team is noticed is when a glitch occurs. In that respect, it is a tough job. Their good work is barely noticed but their mistakes are glaringly public.

The work of a mother is somewhat like the job of an AV tech. The household runs smoothly, the children are well-fed and neatly dressed, the house is clean, and no one knows who is doing all the work. The mother drops the ball one day, and everyone feels the pinch.

It may sometimes seem like no one acknowledges or appreciates the work we do. But the work of a mother and a wife is watched carefully by God. He is pleased with our efforts to bring our family to the Lord. When it feels like no one knows the work you do, remember that we have a God who sees!

A Mother's Magic

BY SARA E. BAYRON

> *Her children rise up and call her blessed;*
> *her husband also, and he praises her:*
> *Many women have done excellently,*
> *but you surpass them all.*
>
> —PROVERBS 31:28–29, NIV

Isn't it funny how your family members think that mothers are magic? Maybe it's because, in their eyes, things at home get done magically. Poof!!! The dog that you promised to bathe and feed every day is magically cleaned and fed. Wow, how did that happen? Well, it was mommy. Poof!!! The dishes, plates, cups, and silverware are all cleaned and put away in the cupboards and in the cabinets, like magic. I wonder who did that? Poof!! The laundry that was left all over the floor in the bedrooms and in the bathroom hampers or in the gym bags disappeared! It is magically back on hangers in closets and neatly folded inside drawers, all clean and smelling good. That is really magic! If there were no mommy at home, the magic would also disappear. Then everyone would know that the magic is really a person who is there looking after everyone in the home.

Often, families take for granted the chores a mother does at home. We neglect to express our thankfulness so that she knows we are grateful for her magic touch.

God does beautiful, magical things for us every day of our lives. We are able to listen to the sweet songs of the chirping birds. We can see the beautiful sunrise and feel the soft, cool morning breeze. He promises to be with us through the Holy Spirit, every day of our lives. He sends His angels to be with us in our daily routines and even when we are resting at night.

Let us be grateful every day for God's blessings. Let Him know that you notice all the nice things He does for you. When we have a grateful attitude, even the tough moments will look different.

Let us walk with a smile on our lips and a song in our hearts, and magnificent things will happen in our lives.

Out of My Comfort Zone

BY GLARIBEL PINERO-AMARO

*This is my command—be strong and courageous!
Do not be afraid or discouraged.
For the LORD your God is with you wherever you go.*

—JOSHUA 1:9, NLT

My husband of eleven and a half years passed away in 2019. In the blink of an eye, my soulmate wasn't there anymore. Becoming a young widow after being happily married has not been easy. One of the most rewarding and enjoyable pastimes for us was traveling. We took cruises to the Caribbean Islands. We explored the United States, traveling to Washington DC to explore the important monuments. We visited Savannah, Georgia, and enjoyed their hospitality as we learned about their heritage. We visited different sites in Texas and many other states. My husband planned our trips meticulously, and we enjoyed every one of them.

Almost seven months after his death, COVID hit the nation and the lack of a companion added to the isolation imposed by the pandemic, dramatically increasing my feelings of loneliness. I planned a solo trip for that summer, but the social distance required by most places made me rethink going, and I ultimately canceled because I

MARRIAGE & RELATIONSHIPS

felt it wasn't safe. During the Thanksgiving school break, I wanted to get away. I needed to distract myself from everything. It was my chance to make new memories. My husband and I had planned to visit the Ark Encounter in Kentucky, a Christian theme park that features the Ark as one of its attractions, but he passed away before we were able to make the trip.

I finally made the choice to start traveling by myself, even though that was out of my comfort zone. I prayed about it and felt that God was opening a way for me to do it, so I headed out alone from Florida to visit the Ark Encounter. After stopping along the way in several different states, I made it to Louisville, Kentucky. Although I was by myself, I didn't feel alone. My friend Jesus was with me all the way.

The day that I finally reached the Ark Encounter, I felt God's blessings. Everything was perfect! The guard allowed me to go into the park a few minutes before they opened. I was the only visitor at that time, and I had the blessing of being there alone for at least an hour. I read every sign; I took pictures of everything I liked; I enjoyed the sights and smells of the place. On my way back home, I made a stop in Tennessee then drove the final fourteen hours straight through and arrived home safely with a heart full of gratitude.

That trip made me realize that I am capable of traveling alone. Although I do miss my soulmate, I am realizing that life goes on, and I can't stop doing everything I enjoy because of sadness or loneliness. After that trip, I haven't stopped. I've been traveling a lot, by myself and with friends, enjoying God's love and His messages to me through nature.

The strength that only God can give us works like an engine and pushes us to go on. Paul says in Philippians 4:13 (NLT), *"For I can do everything through Christ, who gives me strength."*

In Sickness and In Health

BY GLARIBEL PINERO-AMARO

*Two people are better off than one,
for they can help each other succeed.*

—ECCLESIASTES 4:9, NLT

I chose the most unlikely marriage partner, one very different from the man I had prayed for. I'd prayed for that husband almost my whole life. I even had a "list" of requirements that included but were not limited to tall, dark, and handsome. Interestingly enough, my requirements were dismissed, and the man I received was tall, not bad-looking, and a big plump person. However, I also received an added bonus that I'm not sure was on my list. God gave me a God-fearing man.

We needed each other. I had lost my mom three years before we met. He was divorced and trying to cope with that situation and, on top of that, he suffered from cardiovascular disease. I was 31 years old, lonely, single, and I enjoyed his company. So, we decided to get married and be a comfort to one another. Our situation reminded me of Isaac marrying Rebekah after losing his mother; the Bible says that Isaac found consolation in his wife.

The adjustment to married life is quite challenging. We were soulmates with different personalities, but God had a plan that was better than ours. We learned from each other and complemented each other.

I taught him organization and order; he taught me to be patient. I taught him to see the good in every person, but he taught me to not store hard feelings about people in my heart. I talk a lot…I mean, a lot! He taught me the blessing of silence in specific situations. He was my biggest supporter, and I learned how to embrace that big man and honor him in public as well as in private. We both made God the center of our marriage. We decided that we were going to resolve any issue that arose between us before we went to bed and succeeded in never going to bed angry with each other. That was hard, but we did it!

My parents divorced, and my father was not part of my life after that. I had vowed to make my marriage last "till death do us part." Unfortunately, that parting came much sooner than I anticipated and desired, but I did it! When he grew sicker, I stayed by his side. He died while I was holding his hand, and God's peace was reflected on his face. I haven't been able to find the words to describe it until today.

Looking back, I see that being married has been the best experience of my life. It had a powerful impact on the way that I approach life today. I enjoy every minute I have with my family, friends, and students. I want them to remember me as a caring and loving person.

"The LORD GOD said, 'It is not good for the man to be alone. I will make a helper suitable for him'" (Genesis 2:18, NIV). Happiness can be found in a marriage when we make God the center of our lives.

Love that Endures: Gift of True Friendship

BY MICHELLE ANDERSON

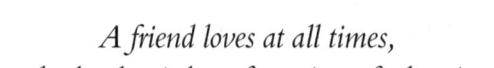

*A friend loves at all times,
and a brother is born for a time of adversity.*

—PROVERBS 17:17, NIV

True friendship is a rare and precious gift from God. It is a bond that transcends distance, circumstances, and time. When we find a friend who loves us at all times, we are blessed with a relationship that brings joy, comfort, and strength. The book of Proverbs beautifully captures the essence of such friendships in today's verse: "A friend loves at all times, and a brother is born for a time of adversity."

As a recent college graduate, I was eager to start my internship in a big city far away from home. Excitement mingled with trepidation as I faced the unknown. But amidst the uncertainties, my best friend from college made a selfless decision. Despite not having a job yet, she chose to leave her family in Boston and move to Chicago to room with me and offer unwavering support.

This act of love and sacrifice was just one of the many demonstrations of my friend's true essence of friendship. This profound display of loyalty, care, and companionship endeared her to me for life. In the face of adversity and unfamiliarity, my friend became a source of comfort and strength, a companion who journeyed alongside me through the ups and downs of life in a new city.

The bond between friends is unique and irreplaceable. Friends are there to celebrate our victories, to cheer us on, and to share in our joys. They walk alongside us during challenging times, offering a listening ear, a helping hand, and unwavering support. A true friend is someone who loves us not only when life is smooth sailing but also when we face adversity.

I have experienced the type of friend who willingly stepped into the role of a "brother…born for a time of adversity." My friend's love extended beyond good times and convenience. I persevered through the challenges and sacrifices required to be present in my life. God's design for friendship reflects His unconditional love for us. He invites us to be vessels of His love, extending grace, compassion, and support to those around us. As we love our friends at all times, we mirror the love of Christ, who is the ultimate friend that sticks closer than a brother.

Take a moment to reflect on the friendships in your life and strive to be the kind of friend that love at all times.

Banana Bread

BY MEGAN BLACKMORE

And I am sure of this, that he who began a good work in you will bring it to completion at the day of Jesus Christ.

—PHILIPPIANS 1:6, ESV

We all go through times in our lives when one chapter closes and a new journey begins. This is where I feel I am currently in my life…like an old door—or even perhaps an old house—has been closed to me, and it is time for me to take my first step into a new life, a new home, a new chapter, or perhaps even a new book altogether.

This feeling has been festering quietly within for some time in the background. Perhaps I feel it more now because big changes are occurring in my life, but during these moments I sometimes feel a bit overwhelmed even when I am excited about what is coming. I know there are plans ahead for me that I can't even begin to understand, but I think that's all part of the adventure.

Many times, we are nervous about the doors closing—it almost seems like getting an eviction notice! But in my case, I feel ready for this new embarkation in life. I sense a new me being created, and I am enjoying the process of shedding my old skin and allowing God to craft a new me entirely.

You may feel stuck, stagnant, confused, and just anticipating a change in your life, too. You're tired of the same ol' same ol'. You're eager for your life, your heart, and your mind to make a shift. You feel you've exhausted your limits in your current position and just want change. It could be a job, an unhealthy habit, or a marriage that won't grow and is dragging all you have down with it. It could be children that don't listen, leaving you at your wit's end. It could even be a spiritual battle of wanting and needing to grow closer to the Lord, but feeling that you haven't and don't really know where to begin.

So many reasons can make us feel restless and ready for a change, and to that, I say, I completely understand. I have been on this restless journey for years now—eagerly awaiting a change within to help shape and mold me into someone better, happier, and more content.

But, as I await these changes I feel brewing inside of me, I feel the need to remind myself (and you) that change takes time. When baking banana bread (my specialty), all the ingredients are placed together strategically to get the perfect batter, the pan is placed in the oven, and then the hour-long wait begins before that bread is ready to eat. If we tried to eat it before baking, we'd make ourselves sick. It's the same in waiting for change to happen. It takes time, and patience, and our one-hundred-percent submission and reliance on the Lord. So, don't give up, the Lord is putting all the ingredients together and is "baking" you into something incredible! (Like my banana bread! Trust me—just ask anyone who's eaten it!)

He Goes Before You

BY MEGAN BLACKMORE

> *The LORD himself goes before you and will be with you; he will never leave you nor forsake you. Do not be afraid; do not be discouraged.*
>
> —DEUTERONOMY 31:8, NIV

As I am writing this, I am currently about two weeks away from my due date. It's an exciting time, but also a bit nerve-racking. Not necessarily due to the labor, as I am not too anxious about that, but what comes next. Raising a child for the Lord and hoping that everything my husband and I do will lead our little one towards God so that at Christ's return we can all enter those pearly white gates together.

I often find myself thinking about these things: can I actually do this, will I be able to guide this child the Lord has blessed us with, will I be able to put away selfishness, will I be able to teach my child all that God needs me to?

As a brand-new parent, I am sure these thoughts are normal, but they can be overwhelming at times. My heart's desire is to do right by my Creator.

Whether we're moms or not, we all want to accomplish certain achievements in this life, especially for the Lord. Those can be work-related, some personal projects, or even just finishing a book of the Bible we're currently reading. Whatever the goal is that we're trying to achieve, we must remember that we are not in control.

The Lord promises us in Deuteronomy 31:8 that He goes before us, that He will be with us, and that He will never leave us—and because of these assurances, we have no need to be either afraid or discouraged.

It's easy to want to throw up our hands, raise our white flags, or throw in the towel when things are shaky or rough—when we see all that we would like to do and think about all the work it will require—like raising a child! But, in these moments when I begin to doubt my ability, it's then that I turn my attention to the ability of the Lord—and the promise in Deuteronomy that He has given me.

My husband and I are not raising this child on our own; the Lord has already forged the path for us. He went before us and cleared the trail, making a clear path for us to walk down away from the brush and wilderness on either side. God has already done this for you, too—that path has already been cleared; you just have to walk in it.

Trust in the Lord and all His promises. When you can't see the finish line, know that by walking one day at a time in the path God has cleared for you and seeking strength from promises like Deuteronomy 31:8, His moment-by-moment direction will help you reach the finish line.

The Journey of Faith

BY ELINETE RODRIGUES REIS

Keep me as the apple of your eye;
hide me in the shadow of your wings.

—PSALM 17:8, NIV

Everything was amazing…then when reality sank in and I saw my marriage in jeopardy, I was heartbroken. *What's happening and where is all of this coming from?* I used to wonder. The signs were right in front of me, but I couldn't see them. The long hours of work, never a day off, never being available to spend time together, always hanging out with coworkers that I never met, infidelity—it was all there, but I was naïve. In my mind, we were a happy couple trying to grow together. My husband seemed to be the most loving and caring person I had ever met, and I couldn't conceive of that man ever hurting me. But I had vowed to remain by his side in the good and bad times, so I was determined to stay and work to rebuild our family.

While I put my heart into rebuilding our marriage, he presented me with a list of all the reasons why we would not "make it." He wanted "freedom" to "enjoy life." Marriage was "not what he had expected," he used to say. He was "miserable and trapped in the institution." We tried prayer, fasting, counseling, and even couples therapy. Nothing seemed to help.

Finally, one Wednesday morning, he came home from work, packed, and left. What now? I had just started a new job in a field where I had no prior experience, and the integration was very challenging, in addition to my significant struggle with the language barrier. The Covid pandemic was in full swing, and fear of the unknown surrounded me. My family and friends being far away in another country just added more pain to the mixture. I felt emotionally drained.

While tempted to feel sorry for myself, I instead looked back on all the miracles in my life. I sat down and made a list of as many blessings as I could remember. I realized that God had been carrying me like the apple of His eye and in the shadow of His wings my entire life. A sense of peace surrounded me. God reminded me that I was His precious daughter. Everything was going to be alright. I just needed to keep moving on. I converted my pain into fuel to strengthen my mental, spiritual, and physical health.

I started working on rebuilding myself. I taped a note on my mirror as a reminder that I was worthy. I learned how to adjust to my new reality. I took time to understand my emotions. Realizing I couldn't go on this journey by myself, I sought a professional therapist and surrounded myself with a small group of supportive friends. I was careful about everything coming into my mind. I took time for self-care and allowed myself to be vulnerable. I learned to walk with my head held high and not be ashamed—to ignore all the pitying eyes. I put all my energy into my job and business, and God has honored me.

About three years have passed. All I can say is that God is good. He has provided me with more than I need. I lack nothing. If you're going through the same experience, listen to me, dear sister: You're going to be alright. You are God's precious daughter, the apple of His eye, and He will carry you in the shadow of His wings. Be faithful and trust HIM.

Reflection

In times of uncertainty,
we can trust in God's plan.

Trust in the Lord *with all your heart*
and lean not on your own understanding,
in all your ways submit to him,
and he will make your paths straight.

—PROVERBS 3:5–6, NIV—

Trusting in the Lord's Direction

BY MICHELLE ANDERSON

Trust in the Lord with all your heart, and do not lean on your own understanding. In all your ways acknowledge him, and he will make straight your paths.

—PROVERBS 3:5–6, ESV

In our journey of faith, there are moments when we come face to face with the true meaning and depth of the Scriptures we have heard since childhood. For me, the familiar words from Proverbs 3:5 and 6 took on a whole new significance as I navigated the path of life, learning to trust in God's direction.

I had just gotten engaged, and we were discussing our plans for where we wanted to reside to start our new life. I had already been employed in Massachusetts, but I thought a fresh start elsewhere would be best. Without seeking God's guidance or waiting for His timing, I applied for a couple of positions in various states, but only one job in Connecticut responded for an interview. After my interview in Connecticut, I convinced myself that it was meant to be and was confident that I would get the job. It seemed so perfect on paper that I did not seek God's path or allow Him to direct my steps in His time. Four weeks after my interviews, the

REFLECTION

job did not materialize. Meanwhile, the wedding date loomed closer, and frustration set in as we had no clue where we would be living. Instead of taking everything as God's will for my life, I took matters into my own hands and continued calling and leaving voice messages, even going so far as to accuse the company of discrimination. Needless to say, shortly after my desperate accusation, I was offered the job; however, it became one of the worst experiences of my life.

Instead of pausing to consider that God's hand might have been guiding me elsewhere, I persisted, thinking I knew what my path should be. Eventually, I was offered the position, but what seemed like a dream job turned out to be a nightmare. The experience served as a powerful lesson about the consequences of not trusting in the Lord's direction and leaning on my own understanding.

Part of trusting in God involves acknowledging Him in **all** our ways, seeking His wisdom, and aligning our steps with His will. It requires an intentional and continuous surrender of our plans and desires to His divine authority. When we acknowledge God in all our ways, we invite Him into every aspect of our lives, both big and small, recognizing that His ways are higher and His thoughts are greater than our own. Trusting in God means humbly submitting our plans, dreams, and decisions to His loving guidance, even when it contradicts our limited understanding.

May we continually seek His guidance, trust in His wisdom, and confidently walk in the path He sets before us, knowing that He is faithful to lead us into abundant life.

Trusting in the Lord's Guidance

BY MICHELLE ANDERSON

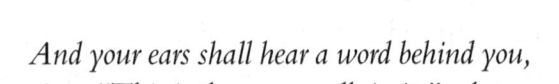

*And your ears shall hear a word behind you,
saying, "This is the way, walk in it," when you
turn to the right or when you turn to the left.*

—ISAIAH 30:21, ESV

Yesterday, I described the new employment opportunity I forced my way into in Connecticut. The story continues with me working that new job marred with stress, harassment, and constant disappointment. My manager turned out to be controlling and unkind, creating a toxic environment that quickly began to take a toll on my health and well-being. It became evident within six months that I could not remain on this job and needed to make a change.

As I contemplated my options, I began applying for other positions. Two of the positions granted me interviews and seemed to express interest in hiring me. I applied for one of the positions, as Assistant to the President, out of desperation; it wasn't something I really wanted to do long-term. The second position was a Human Resources Director role in a non-profit organization, which closely aligned with my passions and aspirations. I had completed the interview for the Human Resources Director position first and, once again, was sure it would work out. Yet again, after a few weeks of no response and receiving an offer for the other position, I began to panic. I had already determined from my previous experience not to trust in my own understanding and forge my own "path," so I made the conscious decision to allow God to direct my steps. I decided that if He was leading me to the executive assistant position, then I was willing to submit.

I was offered the executive assistant position on a Thursday, and I tried to stall by asking if I could get back to them by the following Monday. I needed to make this critical decision but desperately wanted God's path to be revealed, so I fervently prayed for direction. The following morning, on Friday, I felt compelled to reach out one last time to my desired job to let them know that I had another offer on the table. Surprisingly, they shared that they were still interested and wanted to offer me the position but had been waiting for my background check to come back. As it turned out, the agency responsible for conducting the background checks was missing a digit from my social security number, which had caused a delay. To make a long story short, they gave me a verbal offer and promised to provide the official offer by Monday morning just in time for me to respond to the other position.

Through prayer and trust, I finally figured out how to let God lead my steps. As you encounter a crossroads in your life, remember that God's voice will guide you whether you turn to the right or to the left. He will make His way clear.

A Song in Your Heart

BY ANANDI MOSES

> *The Lord is my strength and my shield;*
> *My heart trusts in Him, and I am helped;*
> *Therefore my heart triumphs,*
> *and with my song, I shall thank Him.*
>
> —PSALM 28:7, NASB

Music is a powerful way to express emotions, but music also has the power to create emotions in the listener. Have you ever tried speaking the lyrics of a song instead of singing it? It is like watching people dance with the music muted. The song loses context and meaning. The words of the song find life when put to music. Lyrics convey emotional depth when paired with appropriate music.

Songs are easier to memorize than words alone. The music seems to imprint the words on our memory longer than we can retain just words. Music is a great medium to not only convey messages and emotions but also etch those messages deeper into our memory.

Music is mentioned many times in the Bible. We read about the song of victory when the Israelites crossed the Red Sea. Moses wrote songs, and so did David; the book of Psalms is actually a songbook. Music was part of every celebration.

God gave us the gift of music for many reasons. Hymns and songs of praise are an easy and pleasurable way to worship God. Starting our day with a song helps us keep a song in our hearts the whole day. A song helps set the atmosphere for our thoughts. Songs can remind us of God's presence throughout the day. Music is a valuable weapon in times of trial and temptation, and it can bring sunshine in times of sadness.

Praise and worship are an important part of our personal prayer life. We need not relegate singing and music to corporate worship. A song or two during your daily devotional time will add joy to your worship time. Music helps express your praise and adoration for God and helps you put into words the longings and desires of your heart. It helps us to rise above the cares of this world and enter the presence of God. Music is a great way to move forward when we feel stuck in our prayer life.

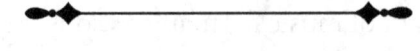

One Day at a Time

BY MEGAN BLACKMORE

*This is the day the L*ORD *has made.*
We will rejoice and be glad in it.

—PSALM 118:24, NLT

Therefore do not worry about tomorrow,
for tomorrow will worry about itself.

—MATTHEW 6:34A, NIV

If you're like every other person living in this world today, you probably feel busy, rushed, and sometimes wonder , *Where has my time gone?*

It sometimes seems as if time has jumped on a bullet train and left you standing on the platform. By the time your head hits the pillow at night, you feel as though the day has come and gone without you even being aware of it.

It is so easy to fret about time. It is so easy to worry about all that we need or even just want to do that we forget to actually live our lives.

REFLECTION

We get so used to going through each day like we are crossing tasks off of a checklist. Get up, shower, get dressed, eat breakfast, race to work, meet after meeting, squeeze in a lunch, more work, pick up the kids, go home, cook and serve dinner, go to bed, and wake up to do it all again.

When days like this hit us, our bodies have no way of relaxing, and our minds keep running even when we ask them to be quiet.

Although the Lord loves for us to keep busy in a good way, and He loves a diligent worker, He still wants us to focus on one task at a time and one day at a time.

Each day is a day He has a purpose for our lives. So, every day when your eyes open for the first time, take a few moments of quiet time to pray and ask God specifically what His goal and purpose for your life is for that given day. Not tomorrow's purpose, not next week's purpose, not next year's purpose—just today's.

Ask to hear God's voice every day as He guides you in the tasks that are required for the day at hand. Try your best not to overburden yourself with unnecessary tasks, or tasks that can be done at another time. Focus on today, and today alone.

Anytime you find your mind wandering to tomorrow's checklist, remind yourself that you aren't in tomorrow—you are in today; find something to ground you in the current moment. Take a few deep breaths, stand to your feet, and let yourself feel gravity pulling you firmly to the ground.

Tomorrow will worry about itself, next week will handle itself when it arrives, and next year has plenty of time to work itself out—we don't need to pay them any mind today.

Take life one day at a time, allowing the Lord to guide you step by step in only tasks that He is requiring of you for today.

Inhale, exhale, and begin your day afresh, starting right now.

The Gift of Silence and Solitude

BY MEGAN BLACKMORE

Very early in the morning, while it was still dark, Jesus got up, left the house, and went off to a solitary place, where he prayed.

—MARK 1:35, NIV

In a study conducted in 2014, eighteen men and twenty-four women were left alone in separate rooms with only their thoughts for fifteen minutes. These individuals were given a button that they could press that would administer a mild electrical shock to their bodies.

This study showed that twelve of the eighteen men administered at at least one shock over the fifteen-minute thinking period, and six of the twenty-four women did the same. In fact, one of the men administered a hundred and ninety electrical shocks to his body in the span of fifteen minutes of silence and solitude.

One of the conductors of the experiment found it striking that most of the individuals preferred to be shocked rather than sit alone with their thoughts for just fifteen minutes. This study on silence and solitude showed that many people do not like this type of self-interaction.

REFLECTION

These results made me think of Jesus, who the Bible says "often withdrew to lonely places and prayed" (Luke 5:16, NIV). Jesus liked being alone. He enjoyed and needed silence and solitude to connect with His Heavenly Father, to decompress and find peace. So, why would we prefer to be electrically shocked rather than withdraw to lonely places?

I believe we have become afraid of the mind, of loneliness, of memories, of sins we've committed. I believe we have become afraid of ourselves.

When we are alone in a room with nothing but our own thoughts, it seems somewhat like a nightmare. We have nowhere to hide, nowhere to run to—so an electrical shock is a great distraction from whatever might be running through our minds.

We often keep ourselves so busy that we never have time to allow our minds to wander, to allow our emotions to be heard. But Jesus didn't run from these opportunities; in fact, He sought them. He understood the importance of silence and solitude and what good it did for Him in seeking peace and connection with the Creator.

In this world today, we have forgotten to connect with self—to check in, to reflect, to spend time alone with the Lord. We are bogged down with work, household tasks, children, errands, and anything else we can think of to the point that we neglect our need to know and love ourselves, which often happens when we are alone.

Jesus understood well that, for His own well-being, silence, and solitude had to be a daily exercise, and I believe this is also necessary for us today—even if we spend only five minutes.

Power in Prayer

BY KELLEY MATIERIENE

If you then, though you are evil, know how to give good gifts to your children, how much more will your Father in heaven give the Holy Spirit to those who ask him.

—LUKE 11:13, NIV

I was there to celebrate my son's friend's birthday. As the children played various games, the parents were talking as we listened for any signs of restlessness among our offspring.

It started innocently enough. "Why don't we see miracles like we read about in Jesus' day? Didn't Jesus promise in John 1412 that we 'will do even greater things than these'?" So where are our greater things?"

My original position was that everything is a miracle. It's a miracle when we get up each day and make it home safely at night with the crazy drivers on the highway. The fact that so many of us made it through an international pandemic when others didn't, in my opinion, indicated that miracles abound. However, my friend pointed out that those are not akin to raising the dead and healing the sick or even walking on water as Jesus did. And though I tried to argue my point, it came up rather flat in the end. He had made a valid point…Ugh.

Why isn't my life full of more miracles, more amazing things? I have pondered that topic often, and I always come back to the same question: Is it that I lack the small mustard seed of faith that men and women in the Bible had? Maybe I lack the faith to say to the mountain "Move" so that it moves? I accept life's circumstances as the way that is rather than seeking God's face to really know if what is happening is His will. The whole idea is a little overwhelming and leaves me with more questions than answers. Do I have the faith of a mustard seed?

Maybe you feel like I do at times and wonder just how strong your faith really is. I am not really sure of the answer to my questions, so I take them to God. I am reminded that the people I admire from the Scripture had a walk with God. And then I am reminded of today's verses from Luke 11:13. I need to ask for the Holy Spirit. In receiving the Holy Spirit, all other gifts, and all other needs come with Him.

The sad part is that we often ask for immediate needs when we pray. We ask for what we lack here and now—help in life's sufferings or our day-to-day needs, which the Lord has already prepared a way for and promised He will take care of. Maybe it's time as Christians that we take our prayers to the next level and pray for the Holy Spirit.

My prayer for you today is that you receive the power of God's Holy Spirit and that He transforms you from the inside out. I pray that you will be able to see and accept the will of God, for with that acceptance comes peace and a change of vision for your life and the lives of those you love.

Small Moments

BY KELLEY MATIERIENE

If you then, though you are evil, know how to give good gifts to your children, how much more will your Father in heaven give the Holy Spirit to those who ask him.

—LUKE 11:13, NIV

So many conversations with my kids happen on the way to or from school or the bus stop. It's a small moment in the day but so impactful at times. I remember their father used to hate driving them to and from school...then he came home one day and said it was the best time of his day. It's funny how the smallest moments in life can change us. On this particular day, I was dropping off my daughter and was telling her how things would be wonderful again once life settled down. She looked at me and asked, "Settle down, how?"

I responded that the last few years had been hectic but that happy times were around the bend once everything settled down. And in that moment, she said, "Happy times are now, Mom, and there have been lots of happy times in the last few years."

What she said hit me right between the eyes: so often in life, we are busy trying to move past the hard times or get to that special

REFLECTION

occasion, a special date when someone returns, when we can travel back to a special place, or maybe even when a season is over. So many times, because we are focused on getting past a moment we perceive in a negative way, we miss the small moments of joy. We miss the sun shining on our faces or the wind at our backs for just a moment. The small joy of your favorite song coming on the radio unexpectedly, or that important meeting being canceled so you have one more day to prepare. What we sometimes consider the inconveniences in life can often contain little moments of reprieve or joy.

Looking back, we see so clearly what we are blind to at the moment. It's the least fun part of life—the bad day week or year. And yet, character is often shaped by that hardship. God is allowed to show up in unexpected ways, in ways we never even thought to ask Him to show up because we never imagined that situation occurring. Yet, it is in these moments in the hard times when we stop to look for that little something that brightened our day, or that couldn't exist outside of the current situation. We see ever more clearly the care of our Heavenly Father. Our hope is strengthened, and our faith is increased. And we realize that, in it all, God is working out everything for our good.

In whatever season you find yourself, I want you to look back on a recent experience and choose one to three ways that you saw the hand of God moving or a way he sent a reminder of His love and care. Write it on a 3x5 card and then tuck it away somewhere where you are sure to find it the next time you start to feel like you are in the midst of a storm.

Just Keep Going

BY KELLEY MATIERIENE

*Finally, my brethren, be strong in the Lord
and in the power of His might/*

—EPHESIANS 6:10, NKJV

It was raining when I woke up that morning. I turned over and went back to sleep; my hope was that the rain would subside in an hour so I would be able to walk the dog. Two hours later, the rain had lightened up, so I took the dog for a walk in the drizzle. I figured we had some time, so we made it a long walk. Halfway into our walk, the skies opened up, and the rain poured from the sky.

I had two choices: I could find shelter and wait out the downpour, or I could start walking back home. I chose option two. The thing is, I knew a downpour was a possibility when I left the house so I brought an umbrella. I started out as prepared as I could be. I had no idea when the downpour would come or even if it would, but if it did, I was ready.

Having the umbrella kept me dry, but it didn't prevent the downpour. Having the umbrella helped me feel prepared, but I had no sure knowledge of what would happen on my journey. I simply trusted that the umbrella I carried would be sufficient should I need it.

In this life, we will never be able to predict everything that will come our way. We can't plan for setbacks we never knew would come. However, we can be armed with an umbrella! The Word of God says, "Thy Word is a lamp unto my feet, and a light unto my path" (Psalm 119:105, KJV).

The Word of God provides hope when I am not sure how to move forward or what steps to take. It illuminates maybe not the whole way or how things will work out, but enough for me to keep trusting…to keep putting one foot in front of the other. It provides guidance and shows me that I am not alone in this world and that men and women have come before me with similar struggles and have made it by God's grace.

Today I encourage you to arm yourself with the Word of God. When the storms of life come, whether in blessings or in trials, you will be covered by God's hand and be able to keep moving forward. Read Ephesians 6:10 through 20 today and be helped.

Just Today

BY SANDRA A SERGEANT

Give us this day our daily bread.

—MATTHEW 6:11, KJV

The year 1990 was coming to a fast close, and how happy I was that the year was finally over. As I reflected, I thought *What a miserable year.* My father passed away in early spring, and that sadness lingered on for the rest of the year. My health was not the best, and I juggled between caring for my two daughters and trying to take care of my own health.

Have you ever dreaded the thought of a new day only because you did not know what lay ahead? Well, I have. Though I was glad to put 1990 behind me, I was also dreading the approaching new year which held so much uncertainty, so much unknown. How I wish I could control the hand of time.

One thought that always keeps me in line is something I remember seeing on a truck on my way to school every morning: "Time and tide wait for no man." I don't know the author of that statement, but I do know that it has stuck with me over the years, always bringing a sense of reality to certain situations.

REFLECTION

During those days of waiting for the new year to dawn, I ventured into the office of a friend who saw my sad countenance and asked what was wrong. I don't remember the details of our conversation or the details of the advice she gave me, but I do recall her telling me of her obsession with always having things in order. She said everything in her home had to meet certain specifications, but her mother-in-law taught her a valuable lesson when she moved in with the family: Worry never changes anything. My friend reminded me that life would look a lot different in just a few short years, and I felt so much better after leaving her office that I dropped by the next day with a thank you card.

In essence, she reminded me to take one day at a time. It sounds cliché, but literally, that is all I was mentally able to handle at the time. Worrying about events I could not control was futile…and exhausting. In retrospect, 1991 and the following years turned out to be pivotal years for the woman God in His wisdom was shaping me to be. He reminded me in His Word of His provision, one day at a time.

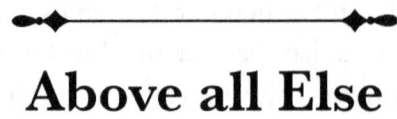

Above all Else

BY MEGAN BLACKMORE

You have let go of the commands of God and are holding on to human traditions.

—MARK 7:8, NIV

I have come to realize that humans are creatures of habit—and that includes me! We do best when things run smoothly when things go as planned, and when things for the most part play out in the manner to which we are accustomed. We like similarity and consistency, and stress and anxiety enter the room when things divert from this path.

We hold fast to certain traditions, habits, or customs for various reasons—fear, uncertainty, or just because we enjoy them. Take, for instance, Christmas traditions or weekend splurges. We have tasks that are usually done during these times, and we enjoy them.

At Christmas time every year, my family would go out and cut down our own tree. On weekends, we try to cram visits with friends, errands, chores, and other fun activities into those two days.

Although traditions and other routine practices aren't evil or bad within themselves, we must ask ourselves whether we have placed our own traditions or habits above the Lord.

REFLECTION

The weekend for which you are desperately waiting throughout the week has come; you have plans ready, tasks you want to accomplish listed out, and you even budgeted time for communion with God. But then, your family wants you to forego your day of worship and go on an outing with them. What do you do? What decision do you make? Do you forfeit your Sabbath day and go out with your cousins? I mean, it's only for a couple of hours, right? God will understand…

Now, we do serve a loving and forgiving Creator who will forgive a sincere heart, but like our Bible verse for today points out, we have gotten to a point where we have let go of the Lord's commands and instead hold onto human traditions.

This could look like a number of different things, but my point is that we must ask ourselves how far is too far. How much is too much? Are we keeping these traditions and going about our lives disregarding the Lord and what He has asked us to do first and foremost?

Have we been jeopardizing our Sabbath day, a command from the Lord, to accommodate our own selfish desires?

We often justify our actions to help us feel better, but what the Lord asks of us is very simple—to keep Him first. He isn't asking much—just, in all we do, that we do not forget Him or place anything above Him. It's time to reflect and allow the Lord to be first in our lives above all else.

Beware of the Serpents

BY JOAN MITCHELL

*Do not set foot on the path of the wicked
or walk in the way of evildoers.*

—PROVERBS 4:14, NIV

The serpents in my life came in all sizes, colors, and genders. My journey down the forbidden path began at the age of seventeen, just out of school. I was rebellious, aggressive, and frustrated—and that is putting it mildly. My mother was an excellent speaker and one who connected with intense precision. The very sight of her greatly annoyed me. To achieve peace of mind, I decided it would be best if I left home. So, one day, I did just that. I took to the streets and, sure enough, I found my first serpent.

Paula was her name. She dressed in the latest fashions, and her words left her lips like honey from a bottle. After being associated with her for a while and trying to imitate her, I was introduced to serpents of many other species. They taught me how to experiment with things I find odious today. Sadly, I encountered serpents who taught me to do pot and smoke; others took me to the clubs and offered me strong drinks, which I tasted and liked. Then there were those serpents who flattered me by saying how lovely I was, but their only purpose was to use my body. I was enjoying every bit of this lifestyle, even though it was leading me to sure destruction. (There is pleasure in sin for a season, you know.)

Still, while I was doing my own thing, I yearned for something better. I sometimes wondered how I could get out of the web entangling me, which seemed to be getting tighter and tighter. I found myself wondering: Will *I sink or will I float? Is there any hope for me? Can you like something and hate it at the same time?*

The breakthrough was coming. My situation was similar to Eve's when, in the Garden of Eden, after she accepted the serpent's invitation to eat the forbidden fruit, she realized the fatal consequences. Both she and her husband were afraid, so they hid themselves...but the Lord sought them out. I truly believe God was seeking me out. It started with a determination, against all odds, that I possessed something within myself that I could actually give to the world.

Self-esteem must be the favorite flower grown in your personal garden. As with any garden, weeds must be picked out. Let no one say to you, "You'll never make it!" Yes, you can! Philippians 4:13 (KJV) assures us, "I can do all things through Christ which strengtheneth me."

When friends see the change in your life, you may hear words of reproach spoken against you. The Bible gives us an example in Psalm 119: 133 (KJV), it's a good idea to learn and quote it often: "Order my steps in thy word: and let not any iniquity have dominion over me."

What a privilege we have in asking God to order our steps...to keep us from the snare of the serpents. The road of the serpents might seem to be built on a solid foundation, but it is sinking sand. Beware! Do not get trapped. The serpents are real.

Success

*Commit to the Lord whatever you do,
and he will establish your plans.*

—PROVERBS 16:3, NIV—

Spiritual Highs

BY ANANDI MOSES

Seek Me so that you may live.

—AMOS 5:4B, NASB

It was Friday night on Easter weekend, and I was not able to sleep. After tossing and turning for a while, I got up and walked into the living room. The house was quiet. I noticed a hymnal lying on the couch, so I picked it up and started leafing through the pages. My eyes came to rest on a hymn, and I started singing. Soon, I was singing the next and then the one after it. I sat there singing all my favorite hymns and enjoying a time of worship and peace.

By the time I got up to go back to bed, I had experienced one of the most intimate experiences with Jesus I'd ever had. My heart was filled with His love. Though this took place many years ago now, in my mind, those moments became the standard for what my worship should make me feel.

During my devotional times, when I read my Bible, a verse will sometimes speak to me in a mind-broadening manner. I can suddenly connect the dots and make sense of God's Word. I gained a whole new perspective that helped me see everything through a different lens. The scales fall off my eyes!

Before you start thinking that I have extraordinary spiritual experiences in my worship all the time, let me tell you that these experiences are not everyday events. I have learned that extraordinary spiritual experiences are just that—extraordinary. They don't happen every day. I have since learned not to look for experiences but for a consistent devotional life.

It is an error to think that we can always do what we do sometimes. Blaise Pascal called it the error of stoicism. This false expectation makes us beat ourselves up about the lack of spiritual high points in our everyday devotional life. It causes us to lose motivation to do what we should do every day, even when it does not feel extraordinary. Our everyday relationship with God is ordinary. Seeking God through reading a passage from the Bible, singing a song, praying for our needs, praising God for our blessings, and walking through the day with a sense of His presence. This is what strengthens us spiritually. If done meaningfully and sincerely, this is how God imparts life to us. This is how we maintain our relationship with God. Mountaintop experiences are exceptional, but a regular devotional life is what it takes to walk the Christian path.

Gloria May, Part 1

BY EVELYN RAQUEL DELGADO MARRERO

> *Charm is deceptive, and beauty is fleeting;*
> *but a woman who fears the L*ORD *is to be praised.*
>
> —PROVERBS 31:30, NIV

Gloria May was a long-time member of our church. I had the privilege to be asked to say something at the celebration of her life. She died a couple of months shy of her 92nd birthday. The first thing that came to mind when I thought of Gloria was that she was a woman of God. She was a generous, genuine, and God-fearing little woman. I say little because she didn't quite reach a height of five feet—but she was four feet eleven inches of condensed power.

Her generosity cannot be measured since she gave of herself, her money, and her time to so many people and causes, that it is difficult to summarize all that she did. She always had an idea or project on her mind. When God planted an idea in her mind, she would not stop until she got everyone involved in making it a success. At church, she ran a very successful Meals on Wheels program. She also organized Community Thanksgiving Dinners, to which members and non-members of the church contributed. She worked at a residential school that serviced students with disabilities, and she would organize a monthly night out for the residents and staff. She would prepare a meal and entertainment to make their night memorable.

She genuinely loved serving others. When she saw a need, she immediately acted and provided what was needed. She was an elder at the church and took her responsibility to heart. During the Covid epidemic, since we were all distanced from one another, I, and many others in the church, received a phone call from her, checking up on us and letting us know that she was praying for us.

She was a very proud woman. This pride showed in her attire and in the way she conducted herself. When she came to church, she was dressed to meet her King. We enjoyed a funny experience together once when she wore a beautiful white dress to church but noticed when she arrived that the dress was a bit more sheer than she had realized; she was scheduled to be on the platform, so she was desperate. When I got to church, she told me her predicament and asked to borrow my slip. We made the transaction, and everybody was happy!

(To be continued)

Gloria May, Part 2

BY EVELYN RAQUEL DELGADO MARRERO

Gloria often used her creativity to write poems and prose, and in light of that, I wrote something about Gloria…

>Gloria May
>By naming her Gloria May
>they allowed her the possibility of
>a glorious and celebrated future
>A possibility that she took advantage of
>and became a dignified, well-dressed,
>outstanding, self-sufficient, and impressive
>woman of God
>A woman of God who didn't let anyone
>discourage her.
>a woman of God who saw possibilities to
>do good for everyone
>Gloria May was granted a long life that
>she used to Glorify God

My dear friend, Gloria Mae, exemplified for us all Paul's words of 2 Timothy 4:7 and 8 (NIV): "I have fought the good fight, I have finished the race, I have kept the faith. Now there is in store for me the crown of righteousness, which the Lord, the righteous Judge, will award to me on that day—and not only to me but also to all who have longed for his appearing."

Don't Quit

BY BRYANA WILSON

> *"For I know the plans I have for you,"*
> *declares the Lord, "plans to prosper you and*
> *not to harm you, plans to give you hope and a future."*
>
> —JEREMIAH 29:11, NIV

When I was six, my parents made me learn the piano. I didn't have a choice. Sometimes, I enjoyed practicing, but other times I needed their encouragement. There were times when I would sit in front of the black and white keys with tears streaming down my face...sometimes from the frustration of being unable to learn a difficult piece and at other times, boredom and not wanting to practice. Often, it was because I just didn't like the song I had to play.

My parents, however, never let my tears stop me from taking lessons. Although I cried throughout my piano career, I was never allowed to quit. My mother would sit me down and find the root cause of my tears. If I were upset that a song was too hard, she would tell me to take a break and return to practicing later. If I didn't like the type of music I was playing, she would tell me to ask my teacher for music I liked.

Soon, the beginner piano player turned into an intermediate piano player. I made my way through novice piano sheet music to ear training workbooks. I started to perform in church and concerts. I was never allowed to quit. "Wilsons don't quit," my mother would tell me. She knew that learning the piano would lead to greater accomplishments in the future. She understood the big picture in a way that the younger me did not.

I was introduced to music theory, improvisation, and composition. I began to write my own music. At first, I struggled. For me, improvisation was hard. It meant I had total freedom, and ten-year-old me didn't know what to do with so much flexibility. Now, all I do is improvise. At seventeen, I received compliments on my piano skills. People admire my ability to transform musical symbols into original compositions. I have written my own music, performed at weddings, and taught other children to play piano. I have done things bigger than anything younger me could imagine. I am blessed with supportive parents and a piano teacher who allows me to express myself through music.

Like my parents, God knows the future and how different experiences contribute to a greater purpose. Even when tasks seem mundane or insignificant, they may hold hidden value. The rewards are boundless and quitting prematurely prevents us from realizing our full potential. Always be conscious that God can bless you in mysterious or straightforward ways. Pray that you will know how to see God working in your life.

Pure Joy

BY BRYANA WILSON

Rejoice, O young man, in thy youth; and let thy heart cheer thee in the days of thy youth, and walk in the ways of thine heart, and in the sight of thine eyes: but know thou, that for all these things God will bring thee into judgment.

—ECCLESIASTES 11:9, KJV

The final applause trickled away, the curtains closed, and I cried. In twenty-four hours, I would be sitting in AP statistics. But right now, I stared at the stage and remembered the actor's final bow. The realization that I would never see *The Phantom of the Opera* again at the Majestic Theater set in. The Broadway show was closing a week later, and I had just watched one of the final shows.

I had begged my parents to take me to New York City. When my mother announced I would be able to see the show, she was shocked when I jumped out of my chair in joy. Since I was a kid, *The Phantom of the Opera* was my favorite. I wasn't a theater kid, but for some reason, I just loved *The Phantom of the Opera*. I loved the orchestra, the singing, the costumes, and the plot. I was obsessed.

Finally, Wednesday, April 5, 2023, arrived. It was cloudy and slightly windy. When I walked into the theater, I was ecstatic. But it felt like the show was over in a blink. Then I walked away from the theater in a light drizzle, my vision blurred by tears.

When my mother asked me what was wrong, I told her the show was great. I told her they were happy tears. I didn't lie, but those tears meant more to me. Those tears were a realization. Life was more than deadlines, due dates, and homework.

In March, I had put myself in a cycle of schoolwork. Between studying for the SATs and doing homework, I added track practices, volleyball tournaments, and interviews. I told myself I had to do it all to get into my dream college, regardless of whether I liked doing it or not. I told myself that, eventually, life would declutter itself. The thing was, I had been telling myself life would become less stressful for months, and it wasn't happening.

Fulfilling my childhood dream of seeing *The Phantom of the Opera* made me snap out of it. Life should be filled with passion and moments that you'll remember forever. Sitting in the Majestic Theater gave me that feeling. The sad part was that I hadn't felt like that before now.

I decided to declutter my life myself. I cut out activities that lacked passion for me and focused on things that made me happy. I added experiences to my life that I would remember forever.

Life isn't about accomplishments. It is about the journey, your emotions, and your memories. Don't let the business of life take away from experiencing life the way God meant you to experience it.

Seed Among Thorns

BY ANANDI MOSES

*Others fell among the thorns,
and the thorns came up and choked them out.*

—MATTHEW 13:7, NASB

Jesus told the parable of the sower to help us understand all the different ways that Satan can hinder the working of the Word of God in our lives. The story is about a sower who went to sow the seeds. The seed fell in many places—like the wayside, on rocky places, and among thorns. The birds ate the seeds that fell on the wayside; the seeds on rocky places sprouted, but a lack of soil depth caused them to die when the temperature rose. The seed that fell among thorns grew but had no chance against the thorny weeds that choked them out. Of course, the seeds that fell on good ground gave a plentiful harvest. The seed denotes the Word of God. The sower is Jesus Christ.

The wayside and the rocky place seem to point to those not inclined toward the Christian faith. The seeds in these places don't even have roots, or they die quickly. The seed among the thorns could be pointing to a Christian. This soil is ready for the seed. The seed has all the chances to grow and flourish. Nothing is wrong with the soil itself. If not for the thorns, the seed will grow.

The world offers us thorns in every direction that can kill the Word of God. The distraction of ever-present screens, the busyness of life, and the entertainment that is readily available are all vying for the same space as the Word of God. It is challenging to keep our minds focused on God's Word when surrounded by so many distractions. We have to be intentional about pulling ourselves away from the rat race of the world to find time at the feet of Jesus, reading His Word, and allowing the seed to grow. We must intentionally safeguard the seed from the thorns that will choke it.

The soil of a Christian heart is not bad in this case. Even if the soil of your heart is good, if you don't keep the thorns under control, your heart will be transformed into a thorny place. Ask God to give you the strength and wisdom to identify the thorns and remove them so the Word of God can take root in your heart.

Faith and Works

BY ANANDI MOSES

*Therefore, everyone who hears these words of Mine,
and acts on them, will be like a wise man
who built his house on the rock.*

—MATTHEW 7:24, NASB

A constant tension exists between the ideas of faith and works. Superficially, it appears that the two terms are contradictory. For us to make sense of the relationship between the two ideas, we have first to define what the words mean in context. Faith is belief and trust in God. Work is obedience to the Word of God. Scripture says that we are saved by faith and not by works. On another note, the Bible is entirely of counsel to listen and obey and do (work). So, how are we to reconcile works of obedience and faith?

Faith and work are inseparable. We can see their interplay in every story in the Bible. The children of Israel walked into the Red Sea in faith. The people did the work because they had faith, even if it was a minor faith. After they had walked through the Red Sea, do you think they had more faith than when they started? Yes, they did. Their work of obedience increased their faith.

Faith prompts works, God intervenes when we step in faith and responds on our behalf, and this prompts faith growth. We need to repeat this cycle at every opportunity that God provides. That is how we can keep our faith and grow it.

There is a danger in using faith or works inappropriately. Faith becomes a presumption when it is not based on the Word of God. For example, if someone thinks that they can disobey clearly presented principles in Scripture and expect God to bless them. It is a presumption, not faith. On the other hand, if someone's works come from within themselves, independent of the grace of God, they become works of merit.

No matter how perfect our obedience is, it is never enough to earn our salvation. Nothing we do can match the price Jesus had to pay to redeem us. Faith helps us access this gift. Works are needed to keep faith alive. There may be other dimensions to faith, works, and salvation, but this understanding of their relationship is simple enough.

This, Too, Shall Pass

BY MEGAN BLACKMORE

I instruct you in the way of wisdom and lead you along straight paths. When you walk, your steps will not be hampered; when you run, you will not stumble.

—PROVERBS 4:11–12, NIV

You might have times in your life, or perhaps you're currently in such a time now, where you feel as though you want to give up. Perhaps life has thrown blow after blow at you, and you feel you can't take another punch. You are at your lowest and don't see how you will get back up again.

You call out to God, asking and pleading "Why?" as you wonder when these trials will finally cease. You may even be wondering if God is a God of love since nothing is working out or going according to plan.

It is in these moments, it is during these trials when I must remind you of these words by author Ellen G White: "And be assured that He will not strike one useless blow. His every blow is struck in love for your eternal happiness. He knows your infirmities and works to restore, not to destroy."

Sometimes, lessons need to be learned, bad habits need to be fixed, or wrong paths need to be straightened; and God, in all of His love and glory, is just trying to sculpt and mold us into His likeness for our eternal glory.

What does that mean though? It means that even though we feel beaten and neglected, weak and brittle, we must reassure ourselves that the Lord has greater plans. We must believe that with the strong backbone of Christ as our foundation, we can endure the trials, knowing that when we come out, we will be strengthened eternally.

As women, we love to feel secure, loved, needed, and protected. Therefore, when we go through these obstacles in life, we feel vulnerable and raw. It's not only our security that seems to be crumbling, but our hope is shaken too.

Where do we go from here? How do we get out of this? Does God even love me? All of the questions we ask ourselves point back to our fear of our security and hope being in question.

However, when we consider Proverbs 4:11-12 and the encouraging words of Sister White, we can be assured and reminded that the Lord is guiding us in wisdom, leading us to upright paths. He says we will not stumble or be hampered.

Times might be hard, and our security and hope might be tested, but even through these tests, God will never fail us or leave us. Our security in Him is a firm cornerstone. So, rest assured, this too shall pass.

Unmotivated and Lacking Confidence

BY MEGAN BLACKMORE

Commit to the LORD whatever you do, and he will establish your plans.

—PROVERBS 16:3, NIV

I am not one to be very self-motivated. I often struggle with finding the energy or even the desire to complete tasks. I don't necessarily mean tasks around the house, but more like setting goals and dreams and trying to reach them.

Unfortunately, I am one to give up easily, and I become discouraged quite frequently. I also lost the passion and drive that once fueled a ton of excitement.

This struggle has made it difficult for me as I often find myself in low spirits and battling low self-esteem. I would love to pursue my goals and even have goals that I work toward, but getting myself to accomplish them is like trying to put a feral cat in a crate to take them to the vet. It seems impossible!

The Lord tells us in Proverbs 16:3 to "commit to the Lord whatever you do, and he will establish your plans." This is a beautiful promise that we should trust the Lord to fulfill, even in times when we feel as though we might not be good enough or our ideas might not be worthwhile.

I have found that I often back down from something I have started because I lack confidence in my ability to complete it. As a writer, I have tons of book and novel ideas marching through my mind, but as quickly as they come, the doubts come too.

I second-guess my ideas and start down a spiral of negative self-talk that zaps all excitement and passion toward the original dream.

These are the moments when I must pause and remind myself of the promise in Proverbs, that not only will the Lord establish these plans for me, but He wants to establish them—especially when they align with His work that He has called me to do!

The Lord is full of incredible and powerful promises for each and every one of us, but we lack confidence in His words. We begin to doubt what He says He can do for us; this is especially so when it seems to be taking longer than we had hoped. We often expect instant success or establishment for all the goals and plans we commit to the Lord, but sometimes His establishment takes days, weeks, months, years, or even a lifetime.

What I have concluded about my lack of motivation and battling with wavering passion due to a lack of self-confidence is this: allow the goals you have to be just that. Finish the goal—do not focus on the success to follow. You want to write a book, write it, and focus solely on just that.

Why Me, Lord?

BY MEGAN BLACKMORE

Jesus replied, "You do not realize now what I am doing, but later you will understand."

—JOHN 13:7, NIV

Two years ago, my mother-in-law suffered a serious stroke that left her paralyzed on the entire left side of her body. Since then, life for her has been challenging as the road to recovery has been a hard mountain to climb.

When things like this happen, we often ask why. The famous "Why, me, Lord?" floods through our heads as we try to figure out the pieces to the puzzle.

We hear these stories all the time—something horrible happens, and then someone begins questioning God why it needed to happen to them in the first place. Now, although it is not wrong to ask why, and I'm sure countless lessons can be learned from certain troubling experiences, such questioning is a dangerous path to travel when trying to get to the bottom of the "why."

One thing my husband told me is that, while growing up, his mom would always tell him, "You'll hate me now but love me later." These words remind me of our verse for today. "You do not realize now what I am doing, but later you will understand."

We might hate what we are currently going through in the present moment: a divorce, a miscarriage, a debilitating illness, infertility, loss of a job, death of a loved one, depression. These moments seem dark and endless, and we struggle to understand them, which pushes us into the maze of the "whys" instead of focusing on the Lord.

We won't understand the why many times in life, just like John 13:7 tells us. But later on in this life, or even the life to come, things will make sense. We will look back on these moments and realize just "why" we had to endure and experience these unpleasant moments.

The why is not nearly as important as the reaction. How we react and handle our trials in this life can determine the type of life we live and how we influence others around us. If we allow the challenges of life to weigh us down as we try to figure out why, we are missing out on all the other joys God has given us and also showing others that it's okay to give up when life gets hard and just live in misery from here on out. But God tells us otherwise. He tells us that we will understand the why one day, so we don't need to spend every waking moment wondering why. Instead, we must take on the challenges life brings with the strength of God, knowing that one day it'll all make sense. Until then, we must live life with happiness only the Lord can bring. We have that promise of peace (Philippians 4:7).

He Stands for You

BY PATRICIA REED

*And he arose, and rebuked the wind,
and said unto the sea, Peace, be still.
And the wind ceased, and there was a great calm.*

—MARK 4:39, KJV

In this story, the disciples crossed the Sea of Galilee when a great storm arose. Jesus was asleep in the back of the boat when the waves began to toss the boat to and fro. These disciples were master fishermen and familiar with the seas and the storms. But this was no ordinary storm. The disciples became terrified because the boat was rocked back and forth while Jesus slept.

Have you ever been in a storm? Have you been terrified, and it seems as if Jesus is asleep? What do you do? Like the disciples, do you cry to Jesus, "Master, carest thou not that we perish?" (v. 38). The story says that Jesus arose. It was not the storm that woke Jesus, but rather the cries of His children. The disciples did not remember what Jesus had said earlier: "Let us pass over unto the other side." In other words, He had already assured them that they would make it to the other side. He told them, "Ignore what is before you. Ignore it." But how quickly we forget Jesus' words!

What storm are you going through right now? Is your marriage teetering on the brink of collapse? Are your children falling off the path of doing right? Is your job situation causing you stress? Are your finances leaving you anxious? Cry out to Him! The Bible said He stood up not because of the storm but because His children were crying out.

Jesus will stand for you when you cry out to Him! He stood up for us all when He died on Calvary's cross for our sins. And He will stand again when He comes to get His children. So, do not worry when the storms of life are raging; you WILL make it to the other side. Just call on the name of Jesus, and He will stand for you.

God's Unexpected Moments of Comfort

BY AVALEY FRANCES MATIERIENE

So do not fear, for I am with you;
do not be dismayed, for I am your God.
I will strengthen you and help you;
I will uphold you with my righteous right hand.

—ISAIAH 41:10, NIV

During the long and arduous custody battle with my son's father, the weight of the struggle sometimes felt overwhelming. Despite knowing that we have a loving God who cares for us, I experienced moments when His presence seemed distant and His movements unseen. It was during one such day, as I stood outside my son's school, that God reminded me of His unwavering presence and tender care.

As the rain began to pour from the skies unexpectedly, I found myself unprepared and disheartened, feeling that yet another thing was going against me. In that moment of vulnerability, a stranger approached me with an umbrella in hand. She explained that she was there to pick up her daughter and, without any hesitation, offered me shelter from the rain.

I had never seen this woman before, nor did our paths cross again after that day. However, the impact of her simple act of kindness resonated deeply with me. It was as if God Himself was speaking through her, assuring me that I was not alone and that He saw every moment of my struggle.

Through the unexpected encounter with the stranger and her umbrella, God gently reminded me of His care and provision. He used that simple act of kindness to speak directly to my heart, affirming that He was walking beside me every step of the way. At that moment, I realized that God's love and support can manifest through the compassion and kindness of others.

Just as the stranger's umbrella shielded me from the rain, God's love and faithfulness surround us, providing refuge and solace in our times of need. He uses people and circumstances to remind us that we are not alone in our struggles. Through these encounters, He speaks volumes of His unfailing love and care.

Today, as you navigate the challenges before you, remember you are never alone. God sees every tear, hears every prayer, and works behind the scenes on your behalf. He is with you in the rain storms of life, offering His unwavering support and strength. Trust in His faithful promises, for He will never leave or forsake you.

God's Protection in Moments of Fear

BY AVALEY FRANCES MATIERIENE

*The Lord will keep you from all harm—
he will watch over your life.*

—PSALM 121:7, NIV

Life is full of unexpected moments, some filled with joy and others with fear. As I embarked on my internship in Washington, DC, I never imagined that a routine trip to my step-sister's apartment would turn into a harrowing encounter. In that moment of darkness, however, I witnessed the unwavering protection and grace of our Heavenly Father.

Late in the evening, after a long drive from Connecticut to Maryland, I exited the car to gather my belongings. Little did I know that a stranger lurked nearby, ready to disrupt the peace we had found. In an instant, I found myself facing the barrel of a gun, the weight of fear pressing upon me.

Yet, amid the chaos, I experienced a profound sense of God's presence. Though the assailant demanded money, my stepfather and I told him we had nothing to give. And as he searched our pockets, he discovered a small amount of cash I had forgotten was there. In my frustration, I blurted out that I had forgotten about it, and the assailant snatched my purse and bag before fleeing into the night.

It is natural to question why such events occur in moments like these. We may wonder why God allowed us to face danger and loss. But as we seek His guidance and perspective, we find comfort in knowing His protection extends beyond the physical realm. God's ways are higher than our ways. His purposes are often beyond our understanding.

Though the assailant wore a mask, concealing his identity, I found solace in knowing God saw everything. He was present at that moment, orchestrating His divine protection in ways we may never fully comprehend. His love surrounded us, providing strength and courage to face the ordeal. Looking back on that unsettling experience, I am reminded of the fragility of life and the immeasurable value of God's protection. It reminds us that even in our darkest moments, we are not alone. God sees our struggles and walks with us, offering His divine comfort and unwavering presence.

Today, as you reflect on your own experiences, consider the times when God's protection was evident, even in the face of adversity. Trust in His love that never fails and find reassurance that He will always guard your life.

Surrender

Do not be anxious about anything, but in every situation, by prayer and petition, with thanksgiving, present your requests to God.

And the peace of God, which transcends all understanding,

will guard your hearts and your minds in Christ Jesus.

—PHILIPPIANS 4:6–7, NIV—

Embracing God's Perfect Plan

BY MICHELLE ANDERSON

For I know the plans I have for you, declares the LORD,
plans for welfare and not for evil, to give you a future and hope.

—JEREMIAH 29:11, ESV

In life's journey, we often find ourselves at a crossroads, unsure of what lies ahead and anxious about our future. As I approached the end of my college years, thoughts of the unknown began to fill my mind. Being a Canadian student added a layer of complexity to my search for employment, as visa sponsorship posed a challenge for many organizations. With graduation just months away and my peers securing job offers, I started to feel discouraged. Amid my concerns, however, my mother reminded me to pray to God, for He holds the perfect plans for our lives. So, I sought His guidance, surrendering my worries and uncertainties into His capable hands. Little did I know that God was already orchestrating a beautiful plan beyond my wildest dreams.

One day, as I walked into the business department building, I crossed paths with my department chair. He mentioned an internship opportunity with Adventist Health, conducting on-campus interviews for their program in Orlando, Florida. Although I hadn't heard of the internship, time was of the essence, as they would only be available for interviews for another hour! With a surge of excitement, I hurriedly changed into my business attire and stepped into the interview room, despite my reservations about competing against other highly qualified candidates.

Weeks later, I received a life-changing letter. I had been selected for the three-year internship program at Adventist Health Systems. The news overwhelmed me with gratitude and joy. However, there was one crucial detail to address—I needed visa sponsorship as a Canadian citizen. To my astonishment, Adventist Health assured me they would handle the filing and associated costs without hesitation. God's provision was evident, and His perfect plan began to unfold before my eyes.

In Jeremiah 29:11, the Lord declares His knowledge of the plans He has for us—plans for our welfare, a future, and hope. Through my experience, God revealed His faithfulness and wisdom, even when I couldn't see the path ahead. He opened doors I never imagined, and directed my steps toward an opportunity that perfectly aligned with His purpose for my life.

When we feel anxious about the uncertainty of our future, we must remember that our heavenly Father holds our destinies in His hands.

Following God's Voice

BY MICHELLE ANDERSON

The LORD directs the steps of the godly.
He delights in every detail of their lives.
Though they stumble, they will never fall,
for the LORD holds them by the hand.

—PSALM 37:23–24, NLT

This passage is a beautiful reminder of the intimate relationship God has with His followers. It assures us that the Lord not only directs our steps but also takes delight in every detail of our lives. We are not alone in our journey; God is intricately involved in every aspect of our existence.

Sometimes, however, we may feel like our connection with God is faltering, similar to a dropped call during a conversation. We may wonder why God seems silent and distant, unable to hear our prayers. In such moments, it is essential to reflect on our own obedience and willingness to follow God's previous instructions.

God's silence may not be a sign of His absence but rather a response to our reluctance to obey His previous guidance. He wants to see our commitment to following Him instead of pursuing our own desires. Before He reveals anything new to us, He desires to see that we have faithfully followed through with what He has already instructed.

In nutrition and healthy living, we often encounter barriers to making healthier choices. These barriers can be deeply ingrained bad habits that we are unwilling to release. I once had a client who weighed over 300 pounds and desired to lose weight and regain her health. She knew the excellent foods she needed to eat and even had an encounter with God where He clearly told her to stop eating meat. Unfortunately, she chose not to heed His voice and struggled in her health journey for several years. Her health declined, and she faced numerous challenges along the way.

Sometimes, like this client, we have our own agenda and expect God to answer our prayers according to our own desires. When He does not respond in the way we want, we may feel discouraged and believe that He is not listening to us. However, we must remember that God is always listening. He is attentive to our prayers and desires to align them with His perfect will.

Instead of trying to direct God or impose our own will upon Him, we should allow Him to direct us. When we are constantly conversing with Him, seeking His guidance, and obeying His instructions, He will guide our steps and protect us from harm. He desires our joy and happiness, and as we surrender to His leading, He will lead us on the path of righteousness.

This Is the Way

BY ZORAIDA VELEZ-DELGADO

Whether you turn to the right or to the left, your ears will hear a voice behind you, saying, "This is the way; walk in it."

—ISAIAH 30:21, NIV

How many decisions have you made today? According to researchers at Cornell University, it depends on the time of the day! It is estimated that the average adult makes about 35,000 choices per day. Yes, you read that right, per day!

Let's say you sleep 7 hours a day. That leaves you with 17 hours to make all those 35,000 decisions or 2,000 decisions per hour. Some of these are unconscious decisions, such as getting out of bed, going to the bathroom, brushing your teeth, washing your face, or not washing your face. These decisions are based on habits and don't seem to be important or life-changing. You make these choices automatically and don't even think about them most of the time.

Some of these decisions are poorly thought out, but you know the consequences are not dire; you took a risk and failed. Lesson learned; you move on. Next time, you will make a different decision; next time you'll do some research, and next time, it will work out.

What about the remaining decisions? The remaining decisions require a deeper look. Did you research the car you are thinking of buying? Did you read the reviews of the movie your kids want to watch? Did you give your boss the right information? Did you do your best on that report? Every action has an equal and opposite reaction.

Think about some of the decisions you have made today. The simple ones, the ones you made a habit of unconsciously. What are the opposite reactions to these actions? Your muscles must be in motion to avoid dystrophy; dental hygiene can prevent several diseases, and eating and exercising are key aspects of brain function. One could argue that unconscious decisions are as crucial as conscious ones, but we just don't pay the same amount of attention to them.

Regardless of how many decisions we have left today, or whether they are unconscious or conscious ones, we know that James 1:5 is true: "If any of you lack wisdom, let him ask of God, that giveth to all men liberally, and upbraideth not; and it shall be given him."

Before you start making decisions today, ask the Lord for wisdom. Seek wisdom to choose what's true and what's fair. Ask the Lord for wisdom to scout ahead of danger. Ask the Lord for wisdom to keep you from making wrong turns or following misleading advice. Ask the Lord to help you tune out distractions, and narrow choices, take a stand for what is right, and help you do all that again tomorrow.

Oh, His Wonders!

BY ZORAIDA VELEZ-DELGADO

He says, "Be still, and know that I am God;
I will be exalted among the nations,
I will be exalted in the earth."

—PSALM 46:10, NIV

On October 5, 1985, heavy rains caused floods that produced the deadliest single landslide in North America, killing 130 in a barrio called Mameyes, located in Ponce in Puerto Rico. The heavy rains caused not only severe flooding in the southern part of the island but it also isolated towns, washed out multiple roads and bridges, and caused about 125 million dollars in damage. I was eleven years old, watching reports on television while my mother and grandmother cried out to God, "Come soon, Lord."

That moment is still fresh in my mind, not just because it was sad but because it happened at 3:00 a.m. Most of the victims of this disaster didn't see the danger coming. A man described the moment he heard water under his house and went outside to check what was happening, only to see his house slide down the hill with his family inside. He couldn't save them. Many rescuers were attempting to find survivors. They found a little girl covered in mud, in shock, but alive. My mother placed her hand on her chest and said, "Tu eres Dios, Tu eres Dios!" (You are God, You are God) while tears ran down her strong face.

Now that I am almost the same age my mother was when this happened, I have found myself praying for someone else's children, lamenting with those who have lost loved ones, and worrying for my own children and family.

Yes, I confess that the soil under my feet often becomes saturated with fear, uncertainty, and pain. I fear seeing my house slide down the hill of depression, addiction, illness, discrimination, war, or mental struggles. Scared of the loneliness and hopelessness that loss brings, I have found myself putting a hand on my chest as my lips remind my heart repeatedly to be still because He is God. He. Is. God.

In the midst of daily challenges, when the enemy's attacks weigh heavily on you, you may feel powerless. I remind you "Be still."

Be still and know that He is the God who created the heavens and earth.

Be still and know that He is the God who healed the broken and forgives the guilty.

Be still and know that He is the God we can find forgiveness and deliverance.

Be still and know He is the God who brings peace to troubled souls and sets us free.

Be still and know that He is the God who resurrected the dead—not just those physically dead, but those whose dreams, marriages, careers, and relationships have died and, by grace, have been brought back to life again!

Be still, and He will restore your soul.

You will smile again, love again, feel again, sing again…just trust God.

Be still…be still, Be. Still,

Arms Stretched Wide

BY KAREEN WILSON

Be perfect, therefore, as your heavenly Father is perfect.

—MATTHEW 5:48, NIV

Walking down the hall toward the operating room, I am amazed at how calm I am. I am a bit elated. It has finally come. Remove this cancer, aka love bump, for me. As I walk into the room, I am amazed at how bright and large it is. At least ten people are scrambling around, preparing the room for me. Dr. King is sitting in the corner. She is her usual calm self. She is impressive as she prepares to renew me.

I observe the operating table, and it reminds me of something. The middle of the table is small and thin, with wings on both sides. It reminds me of a cross. I prayed for rebirth and sacrifice, but this was too much. As they helped me lie down, I could think only of what it must have felt when Jesus laid down willingly, face toward the heavens and arms stretched wide. My arms are spread wide, and the ceiling is my view. As they attach the anesthetic and ask me to breathe oxygen, I feel the tension in the room. The anesthesia nurse informs everyone that the anesthetic is in a puddle on the floor instead of my vein. Dr. King walks over and states that the IV should be in my left arm because she will work on the right. The anesthesiologist wants to put me to sleep and start an IV on my left arm. The pain is intense as they try to push the fluid into me. It's not working, so they all rush to insert an IV in my left arm. Now, with needles in both arms and arms stretched wide, I think again of Christ. I look up, pray for the pain to stop, and go to my happy place. I try to find something to be thankful for.

God found me in that place. The Spirit is the only thing that got me through that experience. It came to me and gave me peace. As I finally drifted off to sleep, I felt at peace with everything, and I knew that God had it all in his hands. The love of God flooded my soul. The humility of the situation brought me to a place of total surrender.

Have you ever felt total surrender to God?

God's Plans

BY KAREEN WILSON

> *"For I know the plans I have for you,"*
> *declares the LORD, "plans to prosper you and not to*
> *harm you, plans to give you hope and a future."*
>
> —JEREMIAH 29:11, NIV

Have you ever played the what-if game? What if I went to this school? What if I married this person? What if I have five children instead of two? What if I am in the wrong place in my life?

Many variations of how your life could have gone, but God knows your path.

In Jeremiah, God speaks to a group of people who have been ripped from their homes and are living in an alien world. God says that even though this is not what they saw for their future, He is always with them. Even though they cannot see a way, God's got this.

When we get desperate for a way out of difficult circumstances, we listen to people who do not know better than God. God will send the right people to help us fulfill our future. People and opportunities will come out of nowhere to help us reach our destination. It takes faith and belief in God's Word. God says that Ge will prosper us, and we will have a bright and good future. If you believe in God's promise that every word He says will not return to him void (Isaiah 55:11), then you have nothing to fear. You will succeed, and God will guide you always.

If you wish to know what God's plans are for you, then you must slow down and hear the still small voice of God leading you on your journey. When you drive to a destination that you do not know, and the GPS leads you down a dark road, do you argue with it or, worse, stop or go the opposite way? Just as you trust your GPS, trust God. Sometimes the road may be dark and lonely, but God will carry you through.

Seeking God While in Despair

BY KAREEN WILSON

Why are you in despair, O my soul?
And why are you disturbed within me?

Hope in God, for I shall again praise Him,
The help of my countenance and my God.

—PSALM 43:5, NASB1995

The last few years have been hard on me. I worked nonstop, I slept very little, and I ate when I could. Enough. It was time to take care of me. I found a naturopath. I listened and implemented everything he said to help me heal and prepare for treatment. I was ready for chemotherapy and other therapy to correct my health. I read every book on healing and mindset. I studied sleeping and eating to make the body whole. I went on a vegan no no-sugar diet. I was determined. I rewrote the program. I created the vision for my healing and how I would move forward.

Part of the plan was to deal with my past. I believe our past can affect our health, and I needed to be honest about it. Much soul-searching and forgiving took place

I became a new person. I became who I was supposed to be. Cancer is not genetic or something we are destined to develop in our bodies. Disease in any form is the body crying out for care and love. The mind connects to all of the trillions of cells in your body. What information are you teaching or feeding your cells? Stress and worry create a body that will not know how to fight off the enemy. I was living in fight-or-flight mode, which became my reality. I was also not living my dreams and intentions. I was trying to live up to what my family wanted of me. I had to pull off the face mask and be honest.

I can go where I wish to go. I can see who I wish to see. I can feel the love of the Spirit running through my veins with a desire to know and connect deeply. I am determined not to hide anymore.

There were many dark days…days of tears and despair. In my despair, I found God. I felt the Spirit enter my soul and say, "Be still; I'm here. Turn it all over to Me. I will give rest and the desires of your heart."

As I sat for days in pain from my muscles, my head, my stomach, my throat, and my bones, I felt at peace. As I emptied the contents of my stomach into the toilet, I heard the small voice whisper its peace. As I climbed out of the cave, I could see the light. I saw for the first time that my perfection was not in the world but in the smallness of just being me. My physical body just holds what is visible, but my mind and soul are the energy that is the Beloved of God.

His grace has surrounded me.

Peace and Serenity

BY MEGAN BLACKMORE

*For the Spirit God gave us does not make us timid,
but gives us power, love, and self-discipline.*

—2 TIMOTHY 1:7, NIV

I have struggled with anxiety and obsessive-compulsive disorder (OCD) from a very young age. Fears flooding my head have been a constant battle of mine, keeping me from living a life of peace and contentment. As a child, I could not attend school for days and weeks because my mind was so congested with fear that I became paralyzed by that fear.

I often wondered what was wrong with me, why my mind didn't work as it should, and why fears threatened me more than the normal ten-year-old girl. I didn't have an answer, and I didn't focus much on the why as much as I did on how to manage and cope with the mental struggles so I could be "normal."

It wasn't until more than a decade went by after I became an adult as well as a Christian and got a strong grip on my anxiety and OCD that I realized that the stronghold my mind used to have on me was just a way the enemy kept me from God and from trusting in the Lord for peace, protection, and power. I'm not saying my fears completely vanished, as even to this day I have moments where my heart races, my breathing feels shallow, and I am swallowed up in the currents of my anxiety; but I look at these moments differently now.

I calm myself with the knowledge that the Lord does not give me a spirit of timidness, anxiety, or fear—and that through Christ, I have the power, love, self-discipline, and peace my heart is longing for, and I can attain it.

Mental illnesses like anxiety and OCD can be debilitating, but ever since coming to know the Lord in my late teens, I have found a new strength to conquer my off days, to battle the enemy's voice in my mind; now, I have gained my strength from the Lord who is the author of peace (1 Corinthians 14:33).

So, whenever you feel your mind spiraling out of control, and you feel bogged down by fears, stress, or everyday worries, remind yourself that those feelings are not of the Lord—and if you call on Him, He will grant you the peace and serenity only He can provide.

Surrendering Your Will

BY MEGAN BLACKMORE

*Lord, I know that people's lives are not their own;
it is not for them to direct their steps.*

—JEREMIAH 10:23, NIV

When we get our minds set on something, it can be hard to sway us any other way. We have our plan, goals, and directions, and we see the finish line to the race we are trying to win.

Often, it is in these moments that we desert the will of God and take on the will we have for our own lives.

When my husband and I were trying to have a baby, we figured because we said it was time, the Lord would act accordingly and open my womb. We didn't realize that God had His own plans, which were a bit different than ours.

After seven months of trying, we were ready to call it quits for now. We didn't want to go through another month of disappointment. When we were ready to throw in the towel and raise our white flag, it was then that the Lord opened my womb.

SURRENDER

This world has taught us that our way is best, to follow our hearts, chase after our dreams, and never let someone tell us we can't do something. But, as Christians, this is the worst advice to follow.

If we believe that our Creator has our life written even before birth, we have to believe He has orchestrated it to flow according to His perfect story. Therefore, when we try to interject our own sentences and chapters, it only makes a mess of the flow.

Still, this is what many of us do daily—we forget the will of the Lord and attack life with our will at the forefront.

Our wants and desires seem to be perfect, don't they? I mean, what was wrong with my husband and me wanting a child seven months before when God wanted us to conceive? It seemed like a harmless desire, right? It just wasn't God's will then—and that's okay.

But it wasn't okay in my mind. I allowed the disappointment every month to weigh down my heart so much that I forgot to live my life. I allowed my wants to rule me to the point that I was angry with the . and confused about why He wasn't answering my prayers.

It is in these moments, these days, these months, or even these years when we feel unheard by God that we must pause and reflect.

We serve a God who sees the big picture. He knows the next chapter, the following sentence, to the book of our life, and we need to trust in this. We must surrender our will to the Lord.

Who Would You Be?

BY MEGAN BLACKMORE

> *"For I know the plans I have for you,"*
> *declares the L*ORD*, "plans to prosper you and*
> *not to harm you, plans to give you hope and a future."*
>
> —JEREMIAH 29:11, NIV

The question was asked of me recently, "Who would you be without fear in your heart?" The question made me pause and genuinely ponder, as I often live with fear in my heart of countless different things. But this time, it made me think of my fear of dreams held in my heart.

"Will I be good enough?" I often ask myself. "What if I fail? What if no one likes it? What if it's a waste of time or money?"

All these questions spring into my mind when presented with a new idea, business venture, or craft. These questions have the ability to stop me dead in my tracks and pump the brakes to any motivation or excitement I possessed momentarily.

So, who would I be without fear in my heart? I would say, someone who is more content with life, someone who is happier…

simply because I would allow myself to try and fail…because sometimes my trying would lead to success.

My fears have prevented me from pursuits I only dream of, and this makes me sad; I know many people are just like me—standing in the way of the potential God has already bestowed upon us. God has given us this life, and though we are here for only a short time, life is full of potential unless we allow our fear of failure to keep us from trying what is on our hearts.

In Psalm 20, we are told God will give us the desires of our hearts and make all those plans succeed. It is these words I hold onto because we serve a God who loves us and wants our plans to succeed. He wants to see our goals met and dreams fulfilled.

So, when we read Proverbs 16:3, we must begin our dreams by bringing them to the Lord—a step we seem always to forget, but a step riddled with importance.

We fear the unknown and what that unknown might do to our lives. We fear that a failed venture may be too heavy for us to bear—as we don't like being met with failure. It's also true that we don't like to always put the work in to allow something to happen if it's in the Lord's plans He is establishing for us.

But dare I say, try. Bring your idea to the Lord, no matter how big or small it might be, and take a small step each day toward that dream. Doing so means we must allow failure as an option, but it also allows success as an option, too.

We Are Set Apart for Obedience

BY ANNA JENNINGS

Blessed be the God and Father of our Lord Jesus Christ! According to his great mercy, he has caused us to be born again to a living hope through the resurrection of Jesus Christ from the dead, to an inheritance that is imperishable, undefiled, and unfading, kept in heaven for you, who by God's power are being guarded through faith for a salvation ready to be revealed in the last time

—1 PETER 1:3–5, ESV

I used to hate the word *obedience*. It is even a little bit embarrassing to realize how many years I allowed myself to believe the lie that I am resistant to obeying. I let myself be numbed by the culture around me, perhaps even lulled to sleep by some church people around me. Honestly, I did want to grow in Christ; I just somehow thought I could grow and even follow Him without always obeying. The word itself was abhorrent at first perhaps simply because of the strict environment of my upbringing.

But what I'm excited about now is that something has shifted in me! I absolutely love the word *obedience*. I am filled with genuine joy and sometimes even brought to happy tears when given the honor of obeying God. Most recently, I've been given the honor to walk alongside a younger woman who is just learning how very much Jesus loves her!

I realize how Jesus obeyed Abba because He loved Abba and the people around Him; the disciples were very precious to Him. I believe He may have cried joyful tears at the opportunity to show them His Father's love. He probably also cried some tears of frustration when they were so slow in realizing the Father's obvious delight in and love for them!

How beautiful that we, as royal priests, are set apart by the Holy Spirit for obedience! This is my prayer for all of us. Precious Holy Spirit, like a mother hen who gathers chicks under her wings, dearest Lord King of the universe through whom all things were created, Anointed One who has anointed us all by pouring out Pentecost on us daily, may every woman and man and child in Your body be filled with Your love so intensely as we all realize the beauty that it is to be holy, set apart by You for obedience. Thank You, Holy Spirit, for setting us apart for this. May we learn that our obedience is designed to show Your wisdom to the rulers and authorities in heaven, that, as we go about our daily lives and obedience, even the angels will be stunned as they are reminded of what God is doing in the universe.

Oh, God, let us learn to obey when our selfish ideas are interrupted, that we would be quick to listen to you, to hear your still small voice through Scripture and the reflections that older women in our lives who love Jesus profoundly are prompted to give us once in a while.

Embracing God's Appointed Moments

BY *AVALEY FRANCES MATIERIENE*

> *I will extol the* LORD *at all times;*
> *his praise will always be on my lips.*

—PSALM 34:1, NIV

In our spiritual journey, we often find ourselves longing for deeper connections with God, yearning for His presence, and seeking solace in His unfailing love. During such seasons, we may discover unexpected avenues through which God's grace shines brightly, leading us into moments of profound worship and revelation. Reflecting on a particular chapter in my life when I was fervently seeking God's presence, I am reminded of the power of prayer and God's perfect timing. During my courtship with my now-husband, I attended a church of a different denomination from my own. Although our theological backgrounds differed, this church offered early morning prayer meetings at 5 a.m.—an opportunity I eagerly embraced.

With a desperate hunger for God's presence, I faithfully attended these early morning gatherings, where I poured out my heart in prayer and sought His guidance for my life. On some occasions, my beloved boyfriend, who later became my husband, joined me in this spiritual pursuit, perhaps motivated by a desire to spend more time with me. However, there was one particular morning when our plans seemed to misalign. My boyfriend intended to leave the prayer meeting after the song service. My heart sank at the thought of missing the prayer segment, which held deep significance for me. Nevertheless, I silently prayed, asking God to intervene and align our desires with His purpose. To my astonishment and joy, upon our arrival at the prayer meeting, the person leading the gathering shared a divine prompting they had received. That morning, they felt compelled to have an extended song service, dedicating the entire hour to praising God through heartfelt melodies. It answered my prayer, directly confirming God's hand at work in our midst. At that moment, I realized the beauty of God's orchestration. He knew the desires of my heart and honored my longing for a deeper connection with Him. Through His divine intervention, He transformed what could have been a disappointing compromise into an opportunity for profound worship and praise.

This experience taught me a valuable lesson about surrender and trust. It revealed the importance of laying our desires before God and allowing Him to align our plans with His perfect timing. As we yield to His leading, we discover that even the most minor details of our lives matter to Him. He is attentive to our needs and faithful in answering our prayers according to His will.

God's Perfect Verse for Our Loved Ones

BY AVALEY FRANCES MATIERIENE

Trust in the LORD with all your heart and lean not on your own understanding; in all your ways submit to him, and he will make your paths straight.

—PROVERBS 3:5–6, NIV

When I embarked on dating my now-husband, I sought God's guidance and wisdom. In prayer, I asked Him to provide a verse that I could pray over him, to bless and guide him in his life. In His faithfulness, God answered my plea.

As our relationship deepened and I came to know him more intimately, I realized the divine perfection of the verse that God had given me. It encapsulated the essence of my husband and who he was becoming. It spoke of trust, surrender, and leaning on God's understanding rather than relying solely on our own limited perspective.

Through this experience, I learned that God knows our loved ones intimately and cares for them deeply. He sees the paths they are meant to walk, and He desires to guide them in every step.

The verse I received became a constant reminder for me to trust in the Lord with all my heart and to encourage my husband to do the same.

God's perfect provision in that verse revealed His intricate involvement in our relationships. It showcased His desire to participate actively in the lives of those we love. As we surrender our loved ones to Him and pray His Word over them, we invite His divine guidance, wisdom, and protection to envelop their journey.

Let this story remind us of the importance of seeking God's direction in our relationships. May we trust in His divine understanding and lean on His wisdom rather than relying solely on our own limited perspective. As we submit our ways to Him, He will make our paths straight, leading us and our loved ones closer to His perfect plan and purpose.

In our prayers for our loved ones, let us remember to seek God's Word, trusting that He will provide the perfect verses that speak to their unique journeys. May we be faithful stewards of these verses, interceding on their behalf and witnessing God's transformative power in their lives?

Embracing Childlike Faith

BY *AVALEY FRANCES MATIERIENE*

*And he said: "Truly I tell you,
unless you change and become like little children,
you will never enter the kingdom of heaven."*

—MATTHEW 18:3, NIV

In the innocence of childhood, there is a beautiful simplicity that often eludes us as we grow older. It is a time when our hearts are untainted by skepticism and doubt, and we wholeheartedly believe in the power of authority figures to make things happen. Such childlike faith is a precious reminder of how we can approach our Heavenly Father in need.

As I reminisce about my own childhood, a vivid memory resurfaces. I recall a time when I desperately desired a baby sibling. Filled with hope and determination, I approached my beloved grandfather, seeking his intervention. In my young heart, I recognized him as an authority figure who could make my wish come true. I trusted that he had the power to influence my parents' decisions. While my childlike request may seem trivial, it carries a profound lesson. It is a gentle reminder of the faith and trust we should embrace as adults before our Heavenly Father. Just as I believed in the authority of my grandfather, we are called to believe in the unwavering authority of God and approach Him with childlike faith.

As adults, we often find ourselves burdened by the complexities and uncertainties of life. We may face challenges, decisions, or desires that seem insurmountable. Yet, in those moments, we have the privilege of seeking the ultimate authority—the One who holds all power and authority in heaven and on earth. Our Heavenly Father invites us to come before Him with childlike faith, trusting His ability to make things happen according to His perfect will. He longs for us to bring our concerns, desires, and dreams to Him, knowing He is attentive to every heartfelt plea. Just as I approached my grandfather with unwavering trust, we can approach God, our Heavenly Father, with unwavering trust in His authority.

In the journey of faith, may we surrender our fears, worries, and desires to the authority of our Heavenly Father. Let us approach Him with reverence, knowing He holds the power to move mountains and make the impossible possible. As we trust in His authority, we can rest assured that His wisdom and goodness will prevail in every situation.

Embrace childlike faith, and witness the incredible ways in which God, our loving Father, will make things happen for His glory and our joy.

Illuminated by Truth: Confirming through God's Word

BY AVALEY FRANCES MATIERIENE

Your word is a lamp unto my feet and a light unto my path.

—PSALM 119:105, KJV

In a world filled with various messages, opinions, and influences, it is crucial to align the guidance we receive with the unchanging truths found in God's Word. The Holy Bible serves as our ultimate source of wisdom and a reliable confirmation of God's messages to us. Just as the psalmist beautifully proclaimed, "Your word is a lamp to my feet and a light to my path" (Psalm 119:105, NKJV).

As believers, we are called to immerse ourselves in the depths of Scripture. It is within these sacred pages that we encounter the very heart and mind of God, gaining insight into His character, plans, and desires for our lives. By diligently studying the Word, we open ourselves to a greater understanding of His ways and align our hearts with His perfect will. When we encounter a message or receive guidance, we must compare it with the truths found in God's Word. The Bible serves as a solid foundation, providing us with divine principles that guide our decision-making and discernment.

As we meditate on Scripture, we allow God to illuminate our understanding and bring clarity to our path. In the pages of the Bible, we find stories of triumph and struggle, wisdom and guidance, grace and redemption. These accounts remind us that God's Word is living and active, relevant to every aspect of our lives. As we seek wisdom and confirmation, we can turn to the Scriptures as a reliable guidepost. The Holy Spirit works through His Word to convict, encourage, and illuminate our hearts, bringing divine confirmation and assurance.

Therefore, let us diligently study the Word, seeking its wisdom and guidance in all our lives. Let us approach it with reverence, humility, and a hunger for divine revelation. In the Scriptures, we find the answers to life's most profound questions, the solace for our troubled hearts, and the guidance for our daily choices. As we immerse ourselves in God's Word, we will find clarity and confirmation, knowing that His messages are in perfect harmony with His eternal truths. As you embark on your journey of seeking confirmation through God's Word, may your heart be open to His leading, and may the Scriptures become a lamp to guide your steps and a light to illuminate your path. In the truths of Scripture, you will discover the unwavering assurance and unwavering confirmation that comes from aligning your life with the eternal Word of God.

The Favor of God: Radiating His Light

BY *AVALEY FRANCES MATIERIENE*

For the L*ORD* *God is a sun and shield; the* L*ORD*
bestows favor and honor; no good thing does he
withhold from those whose walk is blameless.

—PSALM 84:11, NIV

In a world dominated by the art of the perfect selfie, we are familiar with the rule that nothing compares to the radiance of sunlight. Capturing a photo with the sun's warm glow illuminating our features gives us a sense of favor and beauty. In reflecting on this concept, I am reminded of the favor we receive from our Heavenly Father.

Just as the sunlight shines upon us, reminding us of the goodness and blessings of God, His favor shines upon our lives. It is a reminder that we are deeply loved and cherished by the Creator of the universe. When the sun's rays touch our skin, it is as if God's favor is enveloping us, pouring down His blessings upon our lives.

Our Heavenly Father is like a sun and shield to us, providing not only light but also protection and guidance. He bestows favor and honor upon those who walk in His ways, seeking His will and following His commandments. When we align our lives with His purposes, we position ourselves to receive abundant favor from His loving heart.

As sunlight brings warmth and light, God's favor brings joy, fulfillment, and divine provision. It opens doors, clears obstacles, and brings forth blessings beyond what we can comprehend. His favor is not based on our own efforts or achievements but on His unfailing love and grace.

As we navigate the world of social media and the pursuit of recognition, let us remember that true favor comes from God alone. It is not measured by the number of followers or likes but by the depth of our relationship with Him. When we bask in the light of His favor, we radiate His love and grace to those around us.

May we seek to walk blamelessly before Him, honoring His name and following His ways. In doing so, we position ourselves to receive the abundant favor and blessings that flow from our Heavenly Father. Just as the sun shines down upon us, may we bask in the light of God's favor, knowing that no good thing will be withheld from those who trust in Him.

Choosing Between Fear or Faith

BY AVALEY FRANCES MATIERIENE

*For God gave us a spirit not of fear
but of power and love and self-control.*

—2 TIMOTHY 1:7, ESV

In the journey of life, our choices are influenced by two powerful forces: fear and faith. When we allow fear to guide our decisions, we surrender to worry, doubt, and anxiety. Fear holds us captive, limiting our potential and hindering our relationship with God. However, when we choose to walk in faith, we embrace a different paradigm—one that empowers us to step out in confidence, knowing that God is with us.

Fear can manifest in various ways, gripping our hearts and clouding our judgment. It whispers lies of inadequacy, failure, and the unknown, seeking to paralyze us in pursuing God's plans and purposes. But faith, dear friend, reminds us of a fundamental truth: God has not given us a spirit of fear but power, love, and self-control (2 Timothy 1:7, ESV).

When we live in faith, we tap into the wellspring of divine power and no longer need to succumb to fear's grip, for we have access to the power that raised Jesus Christ from the dead. This power enables us to overcome every obstacle, face every challenge, and embrace every opportunity that aligns with God's will.

Moreover, faith fuels our hearts with love. Walking in faith, we align ourselves with God's unconditional love and compassion. We become vessels of His love, extending grace and mercy to others. Love becomes the motivating force behind our choices, propelling us to seek the well-being of others and to honor God in all that we do.

In choosing faith over fear, we also embrace the gift of self-control. Fear often leads us to make impulsive, irrational decisions driven by our emotions. But faith grants us the ability to exercise self-control, to resist the allure of fear's grip, and to submit our desires and impulses to the guiding hand of God. It is in surrendering our will to His that we find true freedom and the clarity to make choices that align with His perfect plan. Choosing from a place of faith requires seeking God's guidance, aligning our hearts with His Word, and surrendering our fears and desires to Him. It is a deliberate choice to trust in His plans and promises, even when the path ahead seems uncertain. Faith beckons us to step out in confidence, knowing that God is faithful to guide, protect, and fulfill His promises.

Finding Strength in Bold Prayers

BY *AVALEY FRANCES MATIERIENE*

Let us then approach God's throne of grace with confidence, so that we may receive mercy and find grace to help us in our time of need.

—HEBREWS 4:16, NIV

During the precious journey of my pregnancy with my third son, unexpected challenges cast a shadow over my heart. It was during a routine doctor's appointment at six months that the medical team discovered abnormalities in my baby's heart. Overwhelmed by this news, I found myself in the midst of a long-distance relationship, navigating a custody case for my first son, and preparing for the NCLEX exam. The weight of these burdens threatened to consume me, and I knew I needed to turn to God in prayer.

In the midst of my stress and exhaustion, I uttered a bold prayer to the Lord. I poured out my heart, expressing my inability to handle any more difficulties, and pleaded with Him to heal my growing baby's heart. I surrendered my fears and anxieties, acknowledging that God alone held the power to fix what was broken. With complete faith, I entrusted my child's well-being into His loving hands.

In the subsequent days, I underwent a specialized examination where a skilled doctor meticulously observed the blood flow through my baby's heart in the ultrasound sonogram. It was a moment of great anticipation where my soul longed for a glimmer of hope. And then, like a gentle whisper from Heaven, came the news: everything was okay. The doctor reassured me that my son's heart was developing perfectly. At that very moment, I experienced the undeniable presence of God's grace and His answer to my bold prayer.

This journey reminded me of the profound truth found in Hebrews 4:16. As children of God; we are called to approach His throne of grace with confidence, knowing that He longs to shower us with mercy and extend His helping hand in our time of need. Our Heavenly Father is not distant or disinterested in our struggles. On the contrary, He invites us to come boldly before Him, bringing our concerns, fears, and anxieties. He is ready to hear our prayers and provide the strength to face every trial.

Transformed by His Grace: A Journey of Renewal

BY AVALEY FRANCES MATIERIENE

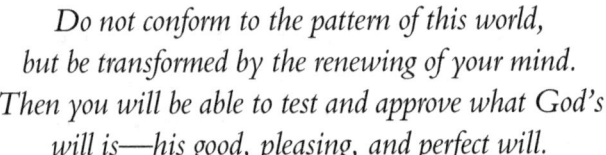

*Do not conform to the pattern of this world,
but be transformed by the renewing of your mind.
Then you will be able to test and approve what God's
will is—his good, pleasing, and perfect will.*

—ROMANS 12:2, NIV

In a world captivated by trends and fleeting fashions, it is easy to become entangled in the patterns and expectations set by society. We may find ourselves striving to fit into molds that were never designed for us, losing sight of the unique purpose and calling God has placed upon our lives. But even amid conformity, God calls us to a different path of transformation and renewal.

Just as a dilapidated house is renovated, God desires to renovate our hearts and minds. He beckons us to step away from the world's mold and embrace His transformative grace. When we surrender ourselves to Him, He begins a beautiful work of renewal, molding us into the image of His Son, Jesus Christ. Renewal is a process that requires intentionality and surrender. It requires us to let go of the old patterns, habits, and mindsets that hinder our growth in Christ. It calls us to lay down our desires and align our hearts with God's perfect will. It is through this journey of transformation that we discover the beauty and freedom found in being accurate reflections of God's love and grace.

Just as a skilled architect envisions the potential of a run-down house, God sees the fullness of our potential. He knows the purpose for which He created us, and he desires to bring out the very best in us. Through His grace, He mends our brokenness and breathes new life into our weary souls. He equips us with His Spirit, empowering us to live out His good, pleasing, and perfect will. Today, let us surrender ourselves to God's transformative grace. May we embrace the renewing power of His Word, allowing it to shape our thoughts, attitudes, and actions. As we yield to His loving touch, we will experience a profound transformation—becoming vessels of His love and agents of His kingdom in a world longing for hope.

Remember, the journey of renewal is not a one-time event but a lifelong process. Let us seek God's guidance, submitting ourselves to His transformative work. In His hands, we are made new, walking in the fullness of His purpose and experiencing the abundant life He has prepared for us.

The Tender Care of Our Heavenly Father

BY AVALEY FRANCES MATIERIENE

The LORD will watch over your coming and going both now and forevermore.

—PSALM 121:8, NIV

As a mother, I find joy and fulfillment in caring for my children. From taking them to school and extracurricular activities to nurturing their friendships and creating lasting memories, every moment is an opportunity to demonstrate love and provide a positive environment for their growth. In these moments of motherly care, I am reminded of the tender and faithful care our Heavenly Father extends to each one of us.

As I guide and bless my children, our Heavenly Father watches over us, His beloved children. His care is not limited to specific moments or activities but extends to every aspect of our lives. He is present in our comings and goings, guiding our steps and providing for our needs.

As mothers, we understand the importance of cultivating positive experiences, nurturing relationships, and creating beautiful memories for our children. In the same way, God works in our lives to create moments of joy, blessings, and divine encounters. He orchestrates divine connections and opens doors of opportunity so that we may experience His goodness and grow in our faith.

But it doesn't end there. Our Heavenly Father's care extends beyond our earthly existence. It transcends time and continues into eternity. His love is everlasting, and His watchful eye is upon us both now and forevermore. He walks with us through the highs and lows of life, offering guidance, comfort, and strength.

Just as we pour out our love for our children, let us open our hearts to receive the abundant love and care of our Heavenly Father. Let us trust in His perfect timing, knowing He has a plan and purpose for each season. His care is not contingent upon our circumstances but rooted in His unchanging character.

As we embrace His loving care, we may extend it to others. Just as we strive to create positive experiences for our children, let us be vessels of God's love and blessings to those around us. Through acts of kindness, encouragement, and compassion, we can reflect the nurturing heart of our Heavenly Father and impact lives with His love.

Letting Go of Control

BY MEGAN BLACKMORE

*Then you will know the truth,
and the truth will set you free.*

—JOHN 8:32, NIV

When my husband and I began trying to have a baby, I was 100% all in. I fell for all of the tips and tricks given to women to ensure a positive pregnancy result by the end of the month. I was sure that with my own efforts desires and knowledge, I would make this baby happen…when I wanted it to happen.

Well, that wasn't the case.

After seven months of grueling, overwhelming effort on my behalf, the Lord opened our womb. But it wasn't until I gave up and surrendered my control over the pregnancy that it happened.

If you're anything like I am, you too, struggle with giving up control, especially when it is something you passionately and deeply desire. You believe that, in your mind, you have all the ability to make whatever you want to happen. For me, I believed all the ovulation tests, frequency of marital relations, a specific diet and vitamins, etc. were going to get me the results I so desperately wanted. But it wasn't until I gave up on all my methods and decided to allow myself to re-evaluate that God said, "Now you're ready."

When one needs control over everything, it can point to insecurity and the need for security. We often seek control so that we feel powerful and in charge. We want what we want when we want it—or else.

For me, this "control" that I wanted brought me only disappointment, avoidable tension between my husband and me, and a distance in my relationship with God. It got me nothing that I wanted and everything I didn't.

It is hard to loosen the reins that we have on some areas of life—whether it is work, the children, or the way the house is cleaned. But if we are honest with ourselves (which we must be), our need for constant control over everything and everyone around us gets us nowhere fast (other than overworked and stressed), and it frustrates the people around us.

It's time we let go of the reins, step back, and allow God to be in control once and, even better, for all.

On Giving Advice

BY ESTHER PELLETIER

For God so loved the world that He gave His only begotten Son, that whoever believes in Him should not perish but have everlasting life. For God did not send His Son into the world to condemn the world, but that the world through Him might be saved.

—JOHN 3:16–17, NKJV

I remember my big-hearted brother heatedly telling my tearful sister that she should leave her abusive husband, yelling, "If he hurts you, I'll let you rot in your grave and won't come to visit you!" The irony. Sometimes we are so full of good ideas that we go into prescriptive mode with those we love. We try to protect. Unsought advice, often given "on the fly" (i.e., without preparatory prayer), is often received as painful criticism. It's like saying, "I don't trust your brain to work right. My brain's much better. Take my ideas."

To me, one of the astounding revelations of God's character in Jesus is His gentle spirit with fragile creatures. Isaiah prophesied, "A bruised reed He will not break, And smoking flax He will not quench" (Isaiah 42:3a, NKJV) and again, "[God] hath sent me to bind up the broken-hearted" (Isaiah 61:1, ASV).

The rejected woman at the well met Jesus and, in a relatively short conversation, they reached some deep territory. Soon Jesus was revealing to her that He knew she had been intimate with five men and was living with a sixth man, unmarried (John 4:17–18). If we had this knowledge about someone we just met and declared it to them, how would they feel? This woman felt elated, called Him a prophet, and couldn't wait to share with everyone she knew! (John 4:28–29).

Four chapters later, another woman "caught" in adultery also received Jesus' healing spirit (John 8:10–11). Jesus never stops short with mercy alone, though. Because covering over sin is not gentle and kind. Jesus told the woman thrown at His feet to stand and walk away into a life of freedom and true intimacy because He was providing the way—the only way—for her to know her worth and live shame-free.

Ultimately, the kindest advice we can give is to point others to Jesus. Jesus is Good Advice (God's Word) made flesh. In Jesus, truth, love, and mercy meet. He is so much more than another self-help book, another role model to try to emulate. He saves us from that exhaustion. We must have Him. There is no way we can get past the scar tissue of sin on a deep, permanent level in our own strength. Everyone, whether they know it or not, desperately longs to know that God is pleased with them. We were created to be loved by God. Even the fully human Jesus needed to know, in a big way, that He was loved by His Father to live a healthy, purpose-filled life (Mark 1:10–11).

Through patient listening, loving words, and actions sent from Heaven, we are inviting others to experience how very much God loves them. Do you know someone in need of some kind of healing? Another chapter to His epic love story?

Humble unto Death

BY PEARL SUKOU

Do nothing out of selfish ambition or vain conceit. Rather, in humility value others above yourselves, not looking to your own interests but each of you to the interests of the others. In your relationships with one another, have the same mindset as Christ Jesus: Who, being in very nature God, did not consider equality with God something to be used to his own advantage; rather, he made himself nothing by taking the very nature of a servant, being made in human likeness. And being found in appearance as a man, he humbled himself by becoming obedient to death—even death on a cross!

—PHILIPPIANS 2:3–8, NIV

I have struggled with movie/TV addiction for years. Nothing crazy, but OH the TIME I've wasted! I have been guilty of binging for HOURS. I wrestled back and forth between the knowledge that I needed to delete all the apps that made my problem available and the idea that it wasn't a problem if I could keep it under control and just stay within a time limit. I would tell myself, "Today will be different; I won't get caught up in it." I even thought, "MY WILL is greater than my temptations.

I can control this." Dear ones, the effort is nothing without Jesus.

Much of this mindset is caused by pride. In James 4, we read that pride is at the root of our desires to have what we do not have and causes us to lean on ourselves to receive it instead of on God. Verse three says, "When you ask, you do not receive, because you ask with wrong motives, that you may spend what you get on your pleasures." We are so focused on ourselves that we become a friend to the world and an enemy of God.

Fortunately for us, there is more to the story. The chapter goes on to speak about great hope! God does not just leave us flailing in the deep end of our sin; He comes near to those who draw near to Him. When we resist the devil, he will flee from us. When we are humble, the Lord "will lift you [us] up."

In the past, I had asked God to help me control my desire to spend TOO MUCH time watching my pitfalls. In the extreme, that prayer would look like this: asking God to help control a drug addiction so you don't overdose but with no intention of ending the use. A less dramatic but prevalent example is this: asking God to bless your food so it will nourish and strengthen you, but eating unhealthy food. Pride has a way of making us think we can ask God for help to do something that will lead us to harm. Here's the issue: God is NOT in the business of being the devil's advocate.

As Matthew 15:14 (ESV) says, "If the blind lead the blind, both will fall into a pit." So do not think you can teach yourself humility. For this, we must seek Jesus and imitate His ways (1 Peter 2:21), even if it means giving up our favorite pitfalls. Our sweet Jesus became humble even unto death on the cross.

What is in your life that would interfere with a Christ-like surrender?

God Made Us to Be Stars

BY EVELYN RAQUEL DELGADO MARRERO

Those who are wise will shine like the brightness of the heavens, and those who lead many to righteousness, like the stars forever and ever.

—DANIEL 12:3, NIV

One-fourth of July, while I watched and listened to a fireworks display, I was mesmerized by the beautiful display of lights and colors and a lot of noise. I thought, "God made me to be a star, but life has made me a firecracker." This thought came to me when I was just about ready to go to bed, so I jotted it down on my phone thinking that maybe I could explore it later. What does that mean to me?

You see, a firecracker is a small firework that violently explodes with a loud noise…but firecrackers have no purpose. In ancient Chinese cultures, the loud noise of firecrackers was used to ward off evil spirits. So, in reality, firecrackers just make noise; and the connotation of noise is that it is loud or unpleasant or that it causes a disturbance. Yes, they look pretty and are entertaining, but do you want to be a firecracker whose only use is to be pretty and make a lot of noise? At times we can all be firecrackers. The term *firecracker* is frequently used to refer to high-spirited women who are not afraid to speak their minds. A synonym for a firecracker personality is "feisty."

A star, on the other hand, is a beacon of hope, a shining light that guides the way. In the story of the birth of Jesus in the Gospel of Matthew, the star of Bethlehem guided the wise men to see Jesus. I want to be a star to guide others to see Jesus as well. A star is a symbol of positivity, happiness, and renewal. Have you ever been in a very dark place at night where you can look up and see the brightness of a sky full of stars? It is an exhilarating scene that gives us hope and happiness and another world without sin that we can visit someday. God created the stars to be a witness of His power and glory. "The heavens declare the glory of God" (Psalm 19:1, NIV). God wants me to be a star so that I can witness His power and glory to others. A star is a symbol of truth. Just as the light shines in the darkness, a star is the light that will bring truth to a world that is in darkness without God.

No, I don't want to be a firecracker; I want to be a star! Pray that God uses us to be shining stars in this dark world.

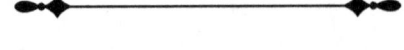

Blessed Comfort

BY EVELYN RAQUEL DELGADO MARRERO

*Praise be to the God and Father of our Lord Jesus Christ,
the Father of compassion and the God of all comfort,
who comforts us in all our troubles so that we can comfort those
in any trouble with the comfort we ourselves receive from God.
For just as we share abundantly in the sufferings of Christ,
so also our comfort abounds through Christ.*

—2 CORINTHIANS 1:3–5, NIV

My sister and I were seventeen months apart, so we were often mistaken for twins during our childhood; we looked alike, dressed alike, and were inseparable. We played together and learned to reconcile our disagreements quickly since we slept in the same bed and needed to be close to each other at night to stay warm in our cold New York apartment. We confided in each other about our secrets and crushes all the time, even into adulthood.

I remember in our high school history class when the teacher would jokingly say that he thought we had telepathic powers since we would have the same answers to the test questions, even though we sat on opposite sides.

After college, my sister married, too young, and moved away. She had three children and the perfect family—for a little while. Before long, however, that marriage became tumultuous. My sister and her husband separated and eventually divorced when their children entered their teenage years. She found herself alone raising three teenage children that she loved. They were the most important people in her life, but the situation was challenging. She remarried and tried to mend her life. After a while, her children grew up, married, and moved away.

She loved her children but was ecstatic about her grandchildren. Her first grandson took her to Michigan. He stole her heart. She found her niche in being a grandmother. My sister's daughter moved to Taiwan just before the birth of her first son. My sister traveled to Taiwan to assist her daughter in whatever she needed. She traveled to Florida, North Carolina, everywhere her daughter needed her with her four children. Then her other son had twins. She cared for the twins until they moved away to Tennessee, then moved to Tennessee to be close to them. She had full-blown Lupus by this time, but her grandchildren kept her going.

She spent the last six years caring for our elderly parents, a job that she did remarkably well. My father told everyone that she was an angel and the best nurse ever because she was so caring and sound to them.

All this time, while caring for her grandchildren and our parents, she was in chronic pain caused by Lupus and other life circumstances. Though she despaired at times, she had a great faith in God. She died of a brain bleed precipitated by a car accident and weakened blood vessels in her brain due to Lupus. In her hospital bed, the only words she could say were "I love you!" she repeated them repeatedly. Finally, she answered God's call in Matthew 11:28 (NIV), "Come to me, all you who are weary and burdened, and I will give you rest."

We can be comforted by the fact that, despite the trials of this life, what awaits us who have trusted Christ is a life of rest in the arms of our heavenly Father!

The Ladder

BY ANANDI MOSES

And Jesus turned and saw them following, and said to them, "What are you seeking?"

—JOHN 1:38A, NASB

Some days are more challenging than others. We suddenly realize how weary and lonely we are. All our weaknesses and fears seem to come into clear focus. In the Bible, we read about Jacob having one of these days. Actually, he was running to stay alive. When the evening arrived, Jacob found a stone on which to rest his head for a while, then he fell asleep and had a dream. In Jacob's dream, God repeats the covenant blessing that Jacob yearned to inherit, and then He shows a ladder full of angels going between Jacob and God!

The ladder in Jacob's dream is a representation of love and reassurance. It shows our connection with God. The Word of God and the power of prayer, the ladder rungs, will take us closer to God's viewpoint of our lives. The higher up we are on the ladder, the wider the angle of our view is, and the fewer the obstacles that impede what we can see. When we have spent time in the Word and submitted our burdens into His hands, we will have a better perspective on our lives. We will be able to see God's leading even during hard times.

The darker the clouds and murkier the shadows and gloom of the night, the more we need to cling to the ladder. We will find that these are the times when the ladder is brimming with the most activity and excitement. Plans for the future, strength for the day, provision for the unexpected, and balm for healing, are all waiting to be claimed.

Jacob exclaimed after his vision of the ladder, "The . is certainly in this place, and I did not know it…How awesome is this place!" (Genesis 28:16–17a, NASB). It was the ladder that helped Jacob realize the presence of God.

Later in the Gospels, we see Jesus making Himself the ladder for us (John 1:51, NASB). Jesus is our connection to God. We can find great comfort in knowing that we are not alone in this path that we walk. Jesus is walking with us. He is the ladder right beside us.

Got Decisions?

BY SANDRA A. SERGEANT

*There is a path before each person that
seems right, but it ends in death.*

—PROVERBS 16:25, NLT

*I will guide you along the best pathway for your life.
I will advise you and watch over you.*

—PSALM 32:8, NLT

It was a pivotal time when I decided to leave my nine-year-old marriage. As a mother of two small children, I had built a life I thought would last. At this very difficult time, my friend, who thought she was encouraging me, quoted the verse in Proverbs 16:25 (NKJV): "There is a way that seems right to a man, But its end is the way of death." As she planted that thought, it led to many doubts in my mind. *What should I do? Should I stay and endure the abusive treatment of the last nine years? Should I allow my girls to grow up in this environment? Should I leave and start over to make a new life for us?* It was a long, arduous process, with many sleepless nights and long conversations with God in prayer. Eventually, I ignored the implications of that verse and migrated to the United States, and my girls followed six months later.

In retrospect, the verse highlights the deceptive nature of human perception and warns against relying solely on our understanding. It was meant to encourage me to seek God's guidance and discernment to avoid paths that could lead to harmful consequences. Looking back, I made the best decision and have no regrets.

Over the years, in my walk with the Lord and a deeper study of God's Word, I found solace in Psalm 32:8 and embraced it as my mantra. I learned to trust God's promises and allow Him to lead me. While our natural inclinations may lead us astray, His love and guidance are constant, and He never fails those who trust Him. I implore you to continue to rely on His promises as you navigate your journey through life.

Thankfulness

*Give thanks to the LORD,
for he is good; his love endures forever.*

—PSALM 107:1, NIV—

Gratitude, Pure Gratitude

BY KAREEN WILSON

> *Rejoice always, pray continually,*
> *and give thanks in all circumstances;*
> *for this is God's will for you in Christ Jesus*
>
> —1 THESSALONIANS 5:16–18, NIV

Certain things are a dichotomy. Living in poverty in the United States. A narcissistic person. Living in the presence of God and ingratitude. Not a good mix.

Gratitude and thankfulness are two of God's characteristics. Unfortunately, gratitude is not one of mankind's strongest suits. It does not come naturally. Giving thanks when you receive desired gifts is easy, but it is a different response when you are given something you do not want. The sense of gratitude is to be nurtured every day because complaining and worrying are usually our first responses. Murmuring our way through issues in our lives tends to be our first reaction, but that doesn't comply with God's command in the Scripture today, which says to be thankful in all circumstances.

This is hard for me. I am learning, so I have created a method to help me adhere to the passage. Be grateful for the issue or problem

THANKFULNESS

that is there in the first place. The car won't start? I am thankful that I have a car. Money is low in the bank account? I am thankful I have an account and a business or house to manage money. My loved one died? I had a loved one with whom I shared memories, someone who loved me when I was with them. See the blessings. I firmly believe that what we pray about allows more of those things to appear.

Gratitude is a practice. Each day, find things for which and in which to rejoice. Create a habit of thankfulness by making a daily written list of everything for which you are grateful. This habit will be a blessing to you repeatedly, and you will eventually be able to "rejoice always."

What are you grateful for today?

Fix My Eyes on Jesus

BY KAREEN WILSON

I keep my eyes always on the LORD.
With him at my right hand, I will not be shaken.

—PSALM 16:8, NIV

I determined that if I were going to receive chemotherapy, I would also use it as an opportunity to complete something profound in me. If modern medicine injects a substance into a person to kill and attack rogue cancer cells in the body, I wanted to use that as a stepping stone. The medicine (which is also a poison) kills unwanted cells, but it also destroys healthy cells. The good, the bad, and the ugly are all the same as chemotherapy drugs. As the cancer in my body was changed by destroying cells, I decided to change and become a new person in my mind as well. I wanted to be a new person when everything was said and done.

I lost my hair a couple of weeks into the treatment. It reminded me of God assuring us that the very hairs of our head are all numbered…and that we don't need to be afraid, for we are worth more than many sparrows.

THANKFULNESS

I lost my sense of taste a few days into treatment. I allowed that to remind me that I am the salt of the earth: But if the salt has lost its saltiness, how can it be made salty again?'

As a result of the suffering brought on by the drugs, my mind spiraled into depression, and I wondered *Why me?* Then I was reminded that the Spirit says in John 16:20 (KJV), "I say unto you, That ye shall weep and lament, but the world shall rejoice: and ye shall be sorrowful, but your sorrow shall be turned into joy."

God asks us to fix our eyes not on the seen (the pain and the body), but on what is unseen since what is seen is temporary and what is unseen is eternal. My mind came to know God on a supernatural level and was transformed by the renewal of my mind. That is when I can prove what is the good, acceptable, and perfect will of God. So, when I left behind the robes of who I was before my trial, I left everything behind. The guilt, resentment, small mindset, striving, pain, anger, selfishness, and superficial layers are all gone. Beautiful things are being planted in my mind. Love, peace, understanding, and joy are my new emotions.

Along with my physical being, God is being shown in my spirit, and His light shines through as a testimony of the change He has made within me. This journey has refined me.

List what you are thankful for today and see how it changes your life.

Signs that Save a Life

BY KAREEN WILSON

*Ask thee a sign of the L*ORD *thy God;
ask it either in the depth or in the height above.*

—ISAIAH 7:11, KJV

The body will get your attention in the most peculiar ways as you go about your day if you ignore the signs that tug at your mind or your cells and organs. We keep busy denying what we feel, but they are called feelings for a reason.

The pain in my right side was so intense that I could feel it pulsing. It pulsed until I felt nausea setting in. *I don't have time for this now; I* thought as I gripped the shopping cart handle. I was determined to put the groceries away as I drove into the garage, but the pain hit me again. I crawled upstairs and would have been content to lie on the carpet and nurse my pain, but my husband saw me and insisted I go to urgent care.

My mind is spinning. *I have to return to work.* As I stood at the intake window at the urgent care clinic, the receptionist barely looked at me as she demanded my insurance card. By now, tears were streaming down my face, and I was using both hands to hold myself up at the counter. When she finally looked up and saw that I was on the verge of hitting her for her inattention or falling to the ground, her eyes popped open, and she told me to walk right in.

In the treatment room, the Physician's Assistant took one look at me and was determined to call an ambulance to carry me to the emergency room. As he left the room to make the call, the pain lifted from my side. It just disappeared. I was still in shock from the misery of the last hour of pain, but it was gone.

When he returned, I apologized for wasting his time, concluding that it was probably spicy food or an upset stomach from the night before. He was very caring but insisted he had not seen someone in so much pain in a long time. He was adamant that I have an ultrasound just to ensure I was in good health. We were able to get an appointment that day, so I went. I felt that it was pretty routine.

The pain never returned, but I am thankful for signs that protect me.

Sleeping Beauty

BY KAREEN WILSON

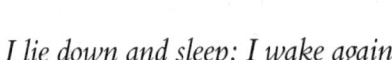

*I lie down and sleep; I wake again
because the LORD sustains me.*

—PSALM 3:5, NIV

My eyelids felt as if a fifty-pound weight was bound to my eyelashes. I wanted to curl up into a ball and just sleep. Anywhere. Anyhow. I was so tired that I could feel my heart forcing blood through my veins. I need sleep like I need air.

Have you ever felt that way? Sleep is such a vital part of our lives that after seventy-two hours without it, your body will send you vivid warnings that you are in trouble. We spend a third of our lives in bed. Sleep is a major part of our lives.

The research shows that not sleeping for a week will leave you unable to function. Amnesty International lists sleep deprivation as a form of torture. So why do we give up an hour of sleep each night and think we gain an hour of productivity? It is proven that lack of sleep can impair our learning ability and weaken our immune system. I like my memory, and I like to stay healthy. Therefore, aim for seven to eight hours a night, which is the average for everyone. Plan your bedtime like it is an official business meeting because you mean business.

Our Lord created the heavens and earth in six days and rested on the seventh day. God wants us to be rested and renewed in Him. We need to believe that we can run to Him and have rest that casts our cares in His arms and that He knows we need to recharge. In the verse today, the power of sleep and the faith that we will wake again show how He offers us rest and protection.

Be thankful for your time to rest. What goals will you create to ensure you sleep sufficiently and well?

Divine Provision in Paris

BY AVALEY FRANCES MATIERIENE

Take delight in the Lord,
and he will give you the desires of your heart.

—PSALM 37:4, NIV

In the bustling city of Paris, amidst the enchanting allure of its timeless beauty, I yearned to visit the magnificent Palace of Versailles. On our last day in Paris, with our evening flight looming, my heart was set on exploring the grandeur of this historical marvel. However, my husband doubted, believing time would slip away before we could embark on this much-anticipated adventure. Nevertheless, I held onto hope, trusting that if it were meant to be, God would make a way.

As we stepped outside our hotel, a remarkable sight greeted us—a tour bus, unmistakably marked with the words "Palace of Versailles," parked right before us. With a surge of anticipation, my husband seized the opportunity and approached the driver, inquiring if he would be traveling to the palace and the cost for our family of four. To our astonishment, the driver revealed that he had just dropped off his last passengers and was heading back to the palace's terminal, offering us a free ride—just for our family!

At that moment, it was evident that God was at work, orchestrating the perfect alignment of circumstances.

God's timing is impeccable. When we surrender our desires to Him and trust in His plan, He faithfully opens doors we could never open on our own. The divine encounter with the tour bus affirmed that God sees the desires of our hearts and delights in fulfilling them. As we delight in the Lord, He aligns the circumstances, molds the timing, and unveils His blessings in ways we could never imagine.

Reflecting on this extraordinary experience, I am reminded of Psalm 37:4, which encourages us to find joy and satisfaction in the Lord. As we prioritize our relationship with Him, cultivating a heart that seeks after His will, He graciously grants us the desires that align with His purpose for our lives. Just as God opened the doors for our family to visit the Palace of Versailles, He longs to grant us the desires of our hearts, aligning them with His divine plan.

The Transformative Power of Gratitude

BY AVALEY FRANCES MATIERIENE

*Give thanks in all circumstances;
for this is God's will for you in Christ Jesus.*

—1 THESSALONIANS 5:18, NIV

Expressing gratitude is not merely a polite gesture; it holds profound significance in our lives. Beyond its social and relational implications, gratitude brings many mental and physical benefits. Scientific studies have revealed its remarkable effects on our overall well-being.

Gratitude can improve our sleep, enhance our mood, and strengthen our immune system. When we cultivate a grateful heart, we invite a sense of contentment and peace into our lives. It diminishes the grip of depression and anxiety, lifting the weight of negativity from our shoulders.

Moreover, gratitude has been shown to alleviate the challenges of chronic pain and reduce the risk of various diseases. It fosters resilience and fortitude in the face of adversity, enabling us to navigate life's difficulties with greater strength and grace. In the realm of relationships, gratitude plays a vital role. It fosters deeper connections and encourages us to recognize and acknowledge the blessings we receive from others. Gratitude cultivates humility, kindness, and empathy, enhancing our interactions and nurturing a sense of community.

Above all, gratitude aligns our hearts with the truth that every good and perfect gift comes from above. It redirects our focus from what we lack to the abundance surrounding us. As we develop a habit of gratitude, we become more attuned to God's loving provision and grace, finding joy in even the simplest blessings.

Let us, therefore, embrace gratitude as a transformative practice. In our prayers, let us offer heartfelt thanks to our Heavenly Father, expressing gratitude for His abundant blessings. And in our daily lives, may we cultivate a spirit of gratitude, acknowledging the goodness around us and uplifting others with words of appreciation.

As we embrace gratitude, we open ourselves to a world of blessings. We invite God's peace to dwell within us and experience the profound benefits that gratitude brings to our mental, emotional, and physical well-being. Let gratitude be a cornerstone of our lives, radiating love, joy, and thankfulness to all those around us.

Awe and Gratitude in the Journey

BY AVALEY FRANCES MATIERIENE

The heavens declare the glory of God;
the skies proclaim the work of his hands.

—PSALM 19:1, NIV

As a travel nurse, I live a life often marked by long hours on the road, traveling from one destination to another. In the midst of the constant movement, I have come to appreciate the travel mercies that God bestows upon me. Yet, it is not only the safety and protection for which I am grateful; it is the breathtaking beauty of the skies that captivate my heart and remind me of the majesty of our Creator. In the quiet moments of my journeys, I have been privileged to witness the magnificence of night and morning skies. Away from the distractions of screens and the rush of daily life, I have been able to truly see and appreciate the glorious displays of colors, the twinkling stars, and the radiant sunrise that paint the canvas of the heavens.

It is easy to get caught up in the busyness of life, constantly on our phones, consumed by our to-do lists, and rushing from one place to another. Amid our hurried lives, we may inadvertently overlook the beauty that surrounds us—the beauty that whispers of God's presence and creative power. The night sky, adorned with countless stars, reminds us of the vastness and infinite nature of God. It humbles us and invites us to ponder the greatness of our Creator. As we gaze at the stars, we are reminded that we serve a God who holds the entire universe in His hands, yet He knows each of us intimately. Similarly, the vibrant colors of the morning sky awaken our souls to the promise of a new day. The hues of gold, pink, and orange serve as a gentle reminder that God's mercies are new every morning (Lamentations 3:22–23). With each sunrise, we are offered a fresh start, an opportunity to embrace God's grace, and embark on a journey filled with purpose and meaning. As you travel through life, may you be open to the divine invitation to slow down and behold the wonders of God's creation. May the night skies and morning dawns remind you of His presence, power, and faithfulness. And may you carry the beauty of these encounters with you, allowing them to inspire and refresh your spirit along the journey.

Today, remove the distractions and busyness that often consume us. Take a moment to appreciate the skies above, knowing that they are not merely a cosmic spectacle but a glimpse into the heart of our Heavenly Father.

Having a Child Amidst a Pandemic

BY MAYRA RAQUEL MARINO

Be strong and courageous. Do not be afraid or terrified because of them, for the LORD *your God goes with you; he will never leave you nor forsake you.*

—DEUTERONOMY 31:6, NIV

The second I saw that positive pregnancy test, I was both excited and terrified simultaneously. It was 2021, and I had been stuck inside my house with my two-year-old daughter for her entire life. The COVID-19 pandemic was a very frightening thing to live through with a toddler, and now I was carrying another person that I needed to keep safe. Although I was lucky enough not to have to work and was able to be home with my child, I was far away from family and friends. I was isolated and pregnant with another child.

As the pregnancy progressed, I felt more at ease, knowing that I was healthy, and so was the baby. For my first delivery, I had a C-section. My daughter was breech, and doctors could not perform an inversion safely since my amniotic fluid was low. This second time around, I was hesitant to have a vaginal birth, so I scheduled C-section just in case. Two days before my scheduled C-section, I tested positive for Covid. This added more stress to my life. My world came crashing down. I would not be able to have visitors, and the ones who were allowed to be with me would also have to be tested for COVID-19. A positive test meant they would not be allowed to be with me, including my husband. I was trying to be strong, but I felt defeated. I wondered why this was happening to me, and I was ready to give up.

Wednesday morning when I woke up, I didn't feel the baby moving. I panicked and went in to get the baby checked. His heart rate was dropping with every contraction, and he needed to come out right away.

At that point, we rushed to the hospital. By God's grace, my husband did not have COVID-19, nor did my mother, so they could both be there with me. Our baby was born via C-section that night. He was a healthy, hungry, loud baby boy. I, however, was not doing well at all. I was in so much pain. I could not even blow my nose let alone cough. Covid hit me hard after his birth.

Once we got home, I couldn't lie flat to sleep due to pain and the inability to breathe. I was so dehydrated that I barely made enough milk to feed my baby. During all this ordeal, I realized that my mother was an angel sent from heaven. God had not abandoned me. My mom would take the baby from me at night so I could rest. She would help with everything I needed in the house. When I needed to spend time with my daughter alone, she would help me with that, too.

I truly believe she was sent by God as a reminder that He is always with us in times of trouble. We should never forget that and even in times of sorrow and pain, we have to be strong and courageous, knowing that God will never leave us or forsake us.

It Doesn't Last Forever

BY MEGAN BLACKMORE

> *However, as it is written: What no eye has seen, what no ear has heard, and what no human mind has conceived— the things God has prepared for those who love Him.*
>
> —1 CORINTHIANS 2:9, NIV

I was thirteen years old when I saw my parents hold hands for the first time. We were taking a family vacation, something we hadn't done in years, and we were staying for a long weekend at a beach resort in Connecticut at a beautiful hotel with ocean water right outside our window for us to enjoy.

It was also on this trip that I not only saw my parents hold hands for the first time but also when my mom told me she was divorcing my dad as we walked into an outlet mall. I remember being taken aback at her random comment at such a random time, but in my heart, I didn't think their marriage would last forever—but then again, maybe I did.

The dysfunction and toxicity of their marriage were something I was used to. The constant arguing, the tension in the house, the walking on eggshells—I grew up viewing it as the norm. So, did

THANKFULNESS

I think their marriage would last? Yes, because I knew nothing different. But I believe I also knew that theirs was not a healthy marriage and that it could end.

My dad struggled with alcoholism for most of his life—including during my entire life and the lives of my siblings. The show we had to put on made it even more difficult since he worked in high positions in big companies. What seemed like hell when he came home on the weekends after being away on business all week was our way of life that no one else knew about.

So, when I saw my parents hold hands while lying on the bed watching a movie our first night at that hotel, it felt awkward and uncomfortable to me; but I also remember a feeling of joy and happiness in seeing that occur. However, knowing what I know now, it was far from a beautiful moment in the heart of my mother. After years of physical, verbal, and many other kinds of abuse, she was done. And I understood.

When I look back at this memory and a ton of others from my childhood, I am reminded of God's promises for those who love Him. He has plans for us of what He will do for us in this life and the one to come that no one can ever fathom. So, yes, I had a lot of rough moments as a child growing up, but I have a new freedom knowing that those hard times didn't last. As my husband and I prepare for our little one on the way, I am reminded of the Lord's blessings and how He can change a life and create in us a new heart. And if He can do that here on this sinful earth, I can't even imagine (like in today's Scripture) what He has in store for us all in eternity.

Trust

*But blessed is the one who trusts in the Lord,
whose confidence is in him.*

—JEREMIAH 17:7, NIV—

Divine Discernment

BY SANDRA A. SERGEANT

But the Lord said…I don't make decisions the way you do! Men judge by outward appearance, but I look at a man's thoughts and intentions.

—1 SAMUEL 16:7, TLB

According to Webster's dictionary, *discernment* means *the ability to judge well.* However, in the biblical context, it is the ability to perceive, understand, and judge things clearly, especially those that are not obvious or straightforward.

Our focus text reminds us that God's perspective and judgment differ from human perspectives. Samuel displayed the initial human response before he penned the above words. God sent him to anoint the new king for Israel; Samuel initially considered Eliab, Jesse's eldest son, a potential choice based on his impressive appearance. However, God revealed to Samuel that He looked at the heart and chose David, the youngest and least likely choice among the sons, because of his character and inner qualities.

Have you ever done that? One of my functions at work is to conduct interviews with prospective employees. One experience stands out. A young lady came in well-attired for an interview as a caregiver; I was impressed by her appearance since most people would not take the time to present well for that position. The interview went well; she was well-spoken and answered all questions appropriately... In my mind, I thought she was a good candidate and would represent us well in the community.

The follow-up segments in the interview process were a background check and a five-panel drug test. We proceeded to run the background check. You can imagine my surprise when the background check results came back with eight pages filled with felony and burglary charges at various times spanning five years. In addition, during the interview and on the application, there is a section to state if you have ever been arrested, to which she responded no.

I am reminded that while humans judge based on what is visible, God sees the heart. He sees beyond the external façade and understands an individual's motivations, desires, and character. An inward look is also essential to be mindful of our thoughts and intentions, recognizing that God sees and evaluates the motives behind our actions. Psalm 139:1 (TLB) reminds us, "O Lord, you have examined my heart and know everything about me." Verse 4 further states, "You know what I am going to say before I even say it."

1 Samuel 16:7 reminds us to align our lives with the One who knows us intimately. By doing so, we are compelled to cultivate pleasing qualities, such as integrity, humility, and a heart fully surrendered to Him. Only through Him can we acquire divine discernment.

GO!

BY SANDRA A. SERGEANT

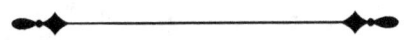

Now the Lord had said to Abram: "Get out of your country, From your family, And from your father's house, To a land that I will show you. I will make you a great nation; I will bless you And make your name great; And you shall be a blessing. I will bless those who bless you, And I will curse him who curses you, And in you, all the families of the earth shall be blessed." So Abram departed as the Lord had spoken to him, and Lot went with him. And Abram was seventy-five years old when he departed from Haran.

—GENESIS 12:1–4, NKJV

It was 2016, and after much resistance, my daughter Kelley coerced me to get out of my comfort zone and, instead of running 5K races, join her and run a half marathon—13.1 miles! I reluctantly agreed and began the process of training for the race which was a couple of months away. I joined a running club, changed my diet, ran several miles a week, procured all the needed running gear, and talked with other runners. I was ready for race day… the second Sunday in November.

What excitement at the starting line, with thousands of people lined up, Ready, Set, Go! At the sound of the starting gun and the word "GO," I joined a throng of other runners in this race. I am here to report that three hours and twenty-three minutes later, I stumbled across the finish line with my daughter, who finished an hour and a half earlier and came back to join me.

What a gruesome experience! I walked, ran, prayed, and questioned myself several times. What *was I thinking when I signed up for this?* The road seemed endless, and I learned that physical strength must be coupled with the mental fortitude necessary for such a venture. I thought when I started that I was ready for that race...but was I really?

While the world continues with this mantra of "Ready, Set, Go," God calls us to do just the opposite. He tells us to "Go, Set, Ready."

He said to Moses, "Pack up all that you have and GO to a place I will show you," and the Bible tells us Moses did. We are not told whether Moses consulted his family, friends, or pastor; we simply know that he obeyed the voice of God. Going is the act of trusting God implicitly even when we don't know where and how; it is then that we seek God's direction every step of the way. We need His guidance because we may not be truly ready to take on that new job, end that relationship, start that business, or venture out and start that ministry. We are rarely "ready" for what God has called us to do. This does not mean we are not prepared or qualified...God does not call the qualified; He qualifies the called.

God called Abraham to "go," but he did not tell him where. Yet in Hebrews 11:8, we are told, "By faith, Abraham obeyed when he was called to go out to the place which he would receive as an inheritance. And he went out, not knowing where he was going."

When Abraham took the first step, he did not know his final destination, but it did not deter him from taking the first step. What is the first or next step you must take in your journey? Today, I challenge you to GO!

SET

BY SANDRA A. SERGEANT

So is my word...It will not return to me empty but will accomplish what I desire and achieve the purpose for which I sent it. You will go out in joy and be led forth in peace; the mountains and hills will burst into song before you, and all the trees of the field will clap their hands.

—ISAIAH 55:11–12, NIV

In the world's perspective, we often associate the word *set* with being ready. However, when the Lord is directing our paths, He takes a different approach. He frequently calls us to go without any requirement of readiness.

When we make the decision to go and follow God's calling, it is essential to place our complete dependence on Him. We must acknowledge that the task at hand is beyond our own capabilities. It may even necessitate us giving up prestigious jobs, relocating to different places, ending relationships, or stepping out of our comfort zones. Whether it's pursuing the dream of writing a book, starting that business, or visiting that place you have secretly admired. All of these actions require complete trust and faith and a willingness to be obedient to the call to GO.

I can guarantee that if you take the first step in faith, God will reveal the subsequent steps to you. He has guided countless others in the past, and He will guide you as well. God honors your first step. However, the idea of being "set" in our minds often deceives us into thinking that everything needs to be perfectly aligned. We believe that plans must be established and specific conditions met before moving forward, especially when it comes to stepping out in faith. We long to have a clear understanding of our destination and the timeline for getting there. But God doesn't operate according to our desires. He reveals enough information, grace, and strength to get us started because He wants us to depend on Him daily. Just as the Lord taught His disciples to pray, emphasizing the request for daily bread, He teaches us to rely on God's revelation and seek His guidance for each step we take.

So, I challenge you today to GO! Step out in faith, fully trusting that God will SET everything in place. Embrace the uncertainty and let go of the need for a detailed plan. Instead, rely on God's guidance and provision, knowing that He will provide what you need along the way.

READY

BY SANDRA A. SERGEANT

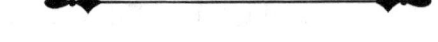

Also I heard the voice of the Lord, saying:
"Whom shall I send, And who will go for Us?"
Then I said, "Here am I! Send me."

—ISAIAH 6:8, NKJV

Sometimes we spend our entire lives getting ready for what we believe God has called us to do, and we fail to realize that we will never be ready. That is where many of us get stuck. Our failure to act on what we know God has called us to do not only breeds doubt and discouragement but it is also a form of disobedience. The old adage—ready, set go—is built on the importance of preparation, but I believe it is contraindicated to God's call of FAITH. We are never ready, and we will never be set. Sometimes we need to just go…Faith changes the sequence to Go, Set, Ready.

What is your vision for yourself, your church, or your community? When Jesus came 2,000 years ago, He commissioned us to GO. We were given the green light then, so why are we waiting for the green light we have already been given?

As Christians—or better yet, Christ-followers—we are called to take a "why not" approach to life. This approach challenges us to dream, and it is an approach that requires action. And the words *can't* or *try* are not in our vocabulary. I am not advocating a careless, haphazard approach to life; it is difficult to discern God's will for your life. It will involve prayer and fasting and will mean making tough decisions. But if God calls us to devote our lives to missions, we need to take the internship offer, quit our job, or make the move. Let us first examine our motives and make sure we are not so afraid of doing what is wrong that it inhibits us from doing what is right.

Faith is not faith until it is acted on. By faith, I went on to run several half marathons, each time decreasing my time. We are created for holiness, happiness, and usefulness. We are created to be creators. Help us, by God's grace, to be great daughters, mothers, wives, and sisters as we "Go. Set. Ready."

Rough Patches

BY SANDRA A. SERGEANT

*But now, this is what the L*ORD *says—he who created you, Jacob, he who formed you, Israel: "Do not fear, for I have redeemed you; I have summoned you by name; you are mine. When you pass through the waters, I will be with you; and when you pass through the rivers, they will not sweep over you. When you walk through the fire, you will not be burned; the flames will not set you ablaze.*

—ISAIAH 43:1–2, NIV

On a recent flight to a major city, the pilot warned there would be turbulence but gave the assurance that we would arrive at our destination safely. As I looked around, everyone sat quietly in their seats. No one was concerned by the warning and continued to do whatever suited them on this short flight.

True to his prediction, the fight encountered turbulence as we were about 130 miles from our destination. The flight was rough, with dips and rises, taking away any pleasant memories I had of my childhood seesaw rides. We did arrive safely, but it caused me to reflect more deeply on our focus text in Isaiah 43:2.

Just as the pilot assured the passengers that they would arrive safely despite the turbulence, God's promises offer the same assurance with even greater certainty. When we face difficulties, whether the fires of trials, the floods of overwhelming circumstances, or the valleys of despair, we can find comfort and peace in knowing God is with us.

Isaiah 43:1, which precedes this promise, sets the foundation for this assurance. It reminds us that we belong to God; we are His, and He has redeemed us. Therefore, we can trust in His faithfulness and unwavering presence.

Internalizing and resting on these promises requires a deep trust in God and His Word. It involves consciously believing and holding onto His promises even when circumstances around us may seem turbulent or uncertain. It is also a reminder that, as believers, we are not exempt from facing challenges in life. However, we have the assurance that God is with us every step of the way. He promises His presence, protection, and deliverance as we navigate the deep waters and fiery trials. We can find comfort and strength in knowing that we are not alone and that God's power is more significant than any circumstances we encounter. As we journey through life, let us hold onto the promises in Isaiah 43:2. May it continue to bring reassurance and confidence in God's persistent presence and protection throughout the various seasons of life.

Jireh – "God Will Provide"

BY KAREEN WILSON

*Abraham named the place Yahweh-Yireh
(which means "the Lord will provide").
To this day, people still use that name as a proverb:
"On the mountain of the Lord it will be provided."*

—GENESIS 22:14, NLT

The song *Jireh* by Maverick City fills my heart with hope as the words reference Matthew 6:26–28:

> *Look at the birds. They don't plant or harvest or store food in barns, for your heavenly Father feeds them. And aren't you far more valuable to him than they are? Can all your worries add a single moment to your life? "And why worry about your clothing? Look at the lilies of the field and how they grow. They don't work or make their clothing.*

Think of the ways God has provided for you. Every step of your life has been touched and blessed by the hand of God. He desires to provide for you and, even when you don't ask, He is providing.

I moved from Canada to attend Loma Linda for my undergraduate degree. I stepped out in faith and believed God had a reason for me to be in California. By my second year at Loma Linda, the funds to finish my education had run out. As a Canadian student, I was not privy to government loans and grants. I met with the admissions counselor, and it looked like all avenues were blocked. Just as I was about to give up hope, miracles happened in threes.

I had been particularly polite and thought well of the switchboard operator at the school, and she took a liking to me. Though there was no job opening, she felt she needed to work fewer hours, so she offered them to me. Secondly, I was the class chaplain, so the university offered a "scholarship" for the student who led the class closer to God. It was the first year they offered it. Third, my mother's tax return arrived and was just enough to keep me enrolled in school. All of these situations occurred without any of the people having prior knowledge of my situation. They were brewing in the background and coming together to serve me in my time of need.

The beautiful part of this story and many others is how God knows our needs before we even know them and crafts a way for us to succeed and thrive. As Maverick City puts it, "Jireh, You are enough. You've always been enough, And I will be content in every circumstance, Jireh, You are enough."

Think of a time when God was your provider.

God Can Be Trusted

BY PATRICIA REED

And as he entered into a certain village, there met him ten men that were lepers, which stood afar off: And they lifted up their voices, and said, Jesus, Master, have mercy on us. And when he saw them, he said unto them, Go shew yourselves unto the priests. And it came to pass, as they went, they were cleansed.

—LUKE 17:12–14, KJV

When I was a little girl, a gentleman owned and operated a general merchandise store in my neighborhood. Even though he genuinely loved people, he had a skin disease. At that time, I didn't know what was wrong with him, although I knew his skin did not look like mine. My parents, as well as others in the community, purchased a variety of goods, exchanged money, and never thought of not going to his store for things we needed. No one alienated, marginalized, or ostracized him. He cheerfully served us and would always say, "See you next time." It was only as I grew older that I realized that Mr. Chase had leprosy.

When I think of today's story from Luke 17, I am reminded of how these men stood afar off because of their leprosy. However, when they saw Jesus and cried unto Him to have mercy on them,

Jesus immediately approached them and came to their rescue. The exciting part of this story is that they were cleansed "as they went." They trusted Jesus completely and did not wait to obey Him until they were made fully whole. They were made whole while they were already obeying.

Just as the community in which I lived accepted Mr. Chase, so did Jesus. He accepted and loved the lepers into healing. This story reminds us that when we fully trust God, we can be assured that He has the power to cleanse us from anything that is holding us in bondage. Remember, God can be trusted!

Trusting in the Invisible Fence of God's Protection

BY AVALEY FRANCES MATIERIENE

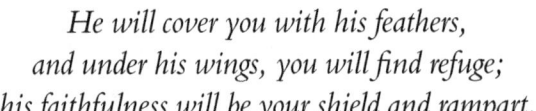

*He will cover you with his feathers,
and under his wings, you will find refuge;
his faithfulness will be your shield and rampart.*

—PSALM 91:4, NIV

As I embarked on my morning walk, I found myself passing by a house with a seemingly fierce dog. With every step, the dog's barking grew louder, its angry demeanor evident. Though my heart quickened, I continued walking, keenly aware of the dog's presence.

Unexpectedly, something incredible happened. As the dog charged toward me at full force, it abruptly stopped at the edge of the property. It was as if an invisible barrier held the dog back, preventing it from reaching me. At that moment, I was reminded of the power of God's protection in our lives.

Just like the dog was halted by the unseen fence, our Heavenly Father establishes a divine shield around us. He surrounds us with His love and faithfulness, guarding us against the attacks and threats that come our way. Though we may face adversity and danger, God's unseen protection is steadfast.

In our journey through life, we often encounter situations that fill us with fear and uncertainty. It may seem as though there is no way out, and we become overwhelmed by the challenges before us. However, we can find solace in knowing that God's invisible fence of protection is ever-present.

The dog's sudden halt serves as a visual reminder that God's power is greater than any opposition we face. Just as the dog's aggression was restrained, God's hand is mighty to shield us from harm. He is our refuge and fortress, a place of safety in times of trouble.

Let us place our trust in the unseen but unfailing protection of our Heavenly Father. He covers us with His feathers, enveloping us in His tender care. When the storms of life rage around us, we can seek shelter beneath His wings, finding peace and security in His presence.

Trusting God's Guidance in Every Challenge

BY AVALEY FRANCES MATIERIENE

I can do all this through him who gives me strength.

—PHILIPPIANS 4:13, NIV

As I reflect on my teenage years and my time at the boarding academy, a vivid memory resurfaces—a moment of academic struggle that turned into a profound encounter with the living God. It was during a challenging algebra class when I found myself sitting alone in my dorm room, wrestling with complex equations and feeling overwhelmed by the weight of my homework.

The frustration built up, and I realized I couldn't solve these mathematical puzzles on my own. In that moment of vulnerability, I turned my heart toward heaven and offered a simple prayer for help. I poured out my worries and anxieties, seeking God's guidance and understanding.

To my amazement, as I bowed my head and opened my heart to the Lord, a remarkable peace enveloped me. It was as if a gentle whisper assured me that I was not alone in my struggles. In the midst of my academic challenges, God's presence became palpable, and His peace filled the room.

As I embraced that moment of divine peace, something incredible began to happen—I started to understand the homework. Concepts that had seemed elusive suddenly became clear. Equations that had caused me great confusion now made sense. It was as if the light of understanding had been switched on within me, and I could see the path forward.

That experience instilled within me a deep conviction that God is real, present, and actively involved in the details of our lives. It taught me the power of prayer and the importance of seeking His guidance in all circumstances, both big and small. The struggles we face may vary, but God's unwavering love and support remain constant.

Let this story serve as a reminder that God's presence and guidance are available to us in every area of life, including our studies. As we lean on Him, He will grant us the understanding, clarity, and wisdom we need to overcome challenges. Trust in His faithfulness and know that you are never alone in your struggles.

Scripture assures us that God is near to all who call on Him in truth (Psalm 145:18). Approach Him with a sincere heart, and He will meet you in your struggles, providing the guidance and peace that only He can give.

Trusting God's Strength in the Midst of Unanswered Prayers (Part 1)

BY *AVALEY FRANCES MATIERIENE*

But those who hope in the L<small>ORD</small> will renew their strength. They will soar on wings like eagles; they will run and not grow weary, they will walk and not be faint.

—ISAIAH 40:31, NIV

Have you ever poured out your heart to God, fervently praying for something that aligns with His will and is morally right? Perhaps you have interceded for the protection and deliverance of your loved ones or for the cessation of sinful acts in your life and in the lives of others. But what happens when the answer seems elusive or when God's response appears to be a resounding "no"?

In those moments of uncertainty and longing, we may find ourselves questioning God's plan and His apparent silence. We may wonder why our prayers have not been answered according to our desires. Yet, amidst the struggle, there lies a profound truth: God gives us the strength to endure.

TRUST

For nineteen years, I have carried a burden upon my heart—a situation about which I have diligently sought God's intervention. The answer has not come in the way I expected or desired. The weight of uncertainty has tested my faith, yet in the midst of it all, I have found solace in the unwavering strength that God provides.

When faced with unanswered prayers, it is natural to feel disheartened, frustrated, and even discouraged. But it is during these very moments that our faith is refined and our dependence on God is deepened. We must remember that God's ways are higher than our ways, and His thoughts are higher than our thoughts (Isaiah 55:9).

Though the journey may be arduous, we are called to stand firm and trust in the strength that God imparts. It is through endurance that our character is molded, our emotional fortitude is strengthened, and our faith is fortified. As we wait upon the Lord, we learn to rely not on our own understanding but on His unfailing wisdom and sovereignty.

(To be continued)

Trusting God's Strength in the Midst of Unanswered Prayers (Part 2)

BY *AVALEY FRANCES MATIERIENE*

But those who hope in the LORD will renew their strength.
They will soar on wings like eagles; they will run and
not grow weary, they will walk and not be faint.

—ISAIAH 40:31, NIV

As we reflect on the story of Joseph in the Old Testament, we see an example of enduring faith.

Joseph was unjustly treated, betrayed, and imprisoned, yet he remained steadfast in his trust in God. In the midst of the darkness, Joseph maintained an unwavering hope, believing that God's plan would prevail in due time. Indeed, God's faithfulness shone forth as Joseph was elevated to a position of authority and used to save his family and the nation of Egypt.

Through the journey of enduring faith, we discover that God's strength is made perfect in our weakness (2 Corinthians 12:9). He equips us with the resilience to persevere and the courage to face each day with hope. In His perfect timing, He will bring forth His purposes, aligning our hearts and circumstances according to His divine plan.

Today, let us find solace in the strength that God provides, even when our prayers seem unanswered. May our enduring faith be a testimony of His faithfulness and a beacon of hope to those around us. Trust in the Lord, for He will renew your strength and lead you forward, bringing glory to His name.

Embracing God's Timing: Time and Clarity in His Providence

BY AVALEY FRANCES MATIERIENE

"For my thoughts are not your thoughts, neither are your ways my ways," declares the Lord. *"As the heavens are higher than the earth, so are my ways higher than your ways and my thoughts than your thoughts."*

—ISAIAH 55:8–9, NIV

In our journey of faith, we encounter moments when we receive a message from God, yet its meaning may not be immediately clear or fully understood. It is in these times that we must exercise patience and trust in the providence of our Heavenly Father. His ways and thoughts surpass our limited human understanding, and His timing is always perfect. Time becomes a significant element in discerning the messages we receive from God. Similar to how a seed takes time to grow into a flourishing plant, the revelations and plans from God may require time to unfold in their fullness. We must not be discouraged if immediate clarity eludes us. Instead, we are called to surrender our impatience to God and trust in His divine timing.

As we navigate through the passage of time, we are invited to wait upon the Lord patiently. This waiting is not a passive inactivity but an active posture of seeking His guidance, listening for His voice, and surrendering our desires to His sovereign will. In the waiting, God works in ways that surpass our comprehension, aligning circumstances, molding our hearts, and orchestrating divine appointments. It is during these seasons of waiting that our faith is refined, our character is shaped, and our trust in God is deepened. The process may sometimes be uncomfortable, stretching our faith and testing our patience. But as we remain steadfast, we grow in our dependence on God, realizing that His timing is always perfect, even when it does not align with our own. In the stillness of waiting, we find solace and strength in the assurance that God is in control. He sees the bigger picture, and His plans for our lives extend far beyond what we can envision. He is not bound by our limited perspectives or constrained by our human timelines. Instead, He works according to His eternal purposes, woven with threads of love, grace, and wisdom.

Walk with Me

BY TANIA FUENTES-DAVITT

When you pass through the waters, I will be with you; and when you pass through the rivers, they will not sweep over you. When you walk through the fire, you will not be burned; the flames will not set you ablaze.

—ISAIAH 43:2, NIV

God set me up. My journey with God had been troubled by the fact that I wanted God to be more tangible in my day-to-day life. I had spent many of my prayers begging God to show up, and to show up in the way that I wanted Him to show up. The funny thing is, God did show up in response to my prayer but in a God-way rather than in the way I was expecting.

My answered prayer came in the form of me standing in a hot, un-air-conditioned chapel down the river of the Amazon in the middle of telling my personal testimony to our mission team. Our vacation Bible school story for the children who lived along the river that day was about Jesus sleeping in the boat as the disciples were panicking and then Him calming the storm.

As I was giving my personal testimony, God connected the dots for me in a powerful way. He lined up the stories so that I realized that the children's story of Jesus sleeping in the boat was not just a small story for the children, but it was what I was feeling in my own personal life. God touched my heart at that moment, and as I was giving my testimony, I broke down in tears. I had felt that God was sleeping during my storm as if He didn't care, but He did care. He loves us in a way that we will never fully understand. He loves us more than a mother or father ever could, and He promises to go through our struggles with us.

We want a God that will make the storm disappear so we don't have to face the mountain ahead of us. When it seems that a life-threatening tempest could be almost overtaking us, that doesn't mean God has left us. Sometimes God doesn't take away the struggle or the storm; He just promises that He will come along with us and make a way through it so that it doesn't overwhelm us.

Think about the struggles you can trust to God's care this week, realizing that when He doesn't take away the challenge, He will be with you and make a way through it.

Look Up and Live

BY TANIA FUENTES-DAVITT

*"For I know the plans I have for you,"
declares the* L<small>ORD</small>, *"plans to prosper you and
not to harm you, plans to give you hope and a future."*

—JEREMIAH 29:11, NIV

I really struggled with depression when I was in graduate school. Every day, I called my father on the phone, crying, because it was the only way I could cope. I am usually a person who hides their pain and tries to put on a good face, but at a certain point, I can't do it anymore. I was thousands of miles away from my family, missing family events and toiling away in a laboratory at the university. I was four years into my graduate research project, and I had no idea if I was even close to finishing. The despair was palpable. I wondered how I could continue.

That same year, I decided to be part of a musical called *Pilgrim's Progress*. It was a great outlet, and it brought a lot of fun and joy to a dark time. One of the scenes in the play really struck me. Christian, the main character, is thrown into prison, and a big Ogre keeps beating him up. In the play, they really made this a comedic musical number with a very obviously fake stunt double puppet of Christian that just gets thrown around by the Ogre. (It was one of my favorite scenes).

Right after this song ends, Christian turns to his sidekick and says, "You know what? I have had the key to get out of this the whole time!" Then he pulls out a key that is God's promise. Watching that scene, I really resonated with that feeling of life just beating me up and me taking it and feeling that I am stuck in a situation, a prison that I can't escape. It is so easy to forget God's promises in dark moments, but they really are the key to freedom. God promises to be with us, to never give up on us and calls us to not be afraid.

Sometimes God leaves little nuggets of truth for us or builds us up before we go through a hard time. At the Christian college I attended, the school handed out Bibles to every student during my freshman year. A personalized note had been written in each Bible, and mine said, "Look up and live." This message was a beacon for me in the years that followed and a reminder of the key to perseverance in adversity. If we are looking up to God and trusting in His promises, we can trust that we do not journey alone and that He has not given up on us.

Take time today to remember God's promises for your life and that He has not given up on you regardless of what you are going through.

In God's Hands

BY EVELYN RAQUEL DELGADO MARRERO

Trust in the Lord *with all thine heart;*
and lean not unto thine own understanding.
In all thy ways acknowledge him,
and he shall direct thy paths.

—PROVERBS 3:5–6, KJV

Is it always easy to trust in the Lord? In 2001, my friend had a big decision to make. She lived in Romania and had just broken up with her boyfriend of five years. She was working as an elementary school teacher and studying at the same time, but desperately needed a change of scenery. In her quest for a little break, she found out that she would be allowed to travel to the United States for the summer on a work visa. She asked God to direct her in the way she should go, and she took a leap of faith. She did not know anyone in the U.S. Nevertheless, she started the visa application process but was not entirely confident that she would be granted a visa since she was only twenty-one years old and the Romanian government frowned upon young people leaving the country. She applied to work as a counselor at summer camps. Thinking it would work in her favor to work as a teacher or counselor, she put both options on her visa application.

The day that she had her visa review, she had to travel to Bucharest, an eight-hour trip, where she then waited in a room with about forty other applicants. Usually, the officers review the applications and allot the visas with very few questions asked. If they had questions, they would call out your name on the loudspeaker. After a while of waiting, the officers called out her name. In all the time she was there, hers was the only name called. They questioned her about why she had two work options. She assured them she was returning to Romania after the summer to finish her education, and she was granted her visa.

She was accepted as a counselor at Camp CONNRI, a summer Christian camp for underprivileged kids in Connecticut/Rhode Island, run by the Salvation Army. At camp, she met a handsome, God-fearing gentleman who corresponded with her after she returned to Romania, and they got engaged the next year and were married soon after.

Trust and faith are essentially the same thing. If we fail to trust God, we lose the connection with our Creator. That connection with God can be established only by faith. We trust in God, knowing that He has our best interests in mind. We are not taking a leap into the unknown but a leap toward the one who is all-knowing. So as the verse says, "In all thy ways acknowledge him, and he shall direct thy paths."

The Sound of the Trumpet

BY BRUNIE QUINONES

For the Lord Himself will descend from heaven with a shout, with the voice of an archangel, and with the trumped of God. And the dead in Christ will rise first.

—1 THESSALONIANS 4:16, NKJV

During the writing of this meditation, my heart is heavy with sorrow. A few days ago, I received the devastating news that a very good friend—one I have worked with, laughed with, and cried with—suddenly passed away. After the initial shock, I started asking myself questions. When my time comes, will I be ready? Do I know God well enough to trust in His promises? Have I done everything the Lord asked me to do? Am I completely and totally sure I will hear the sound of the trumpet and go to heaven to be with Him?

I stayed in reflective meditation for a long time. Suddenly, like a lightning bolt, a thought came to me: "If you have efficiently used and treasured every blessing given to you for your journey on a daily basis, have believed in Me, repented of your sins, and have followed Me, there's no need to worry. You will be with Me in my Kingdom." It was clear to me. I believe in Him, repent of my sins daily, and have followed Him since I received His invitation. Now, it is simply a matter of using my daily blessings to strengthen my relationship with Him.

When Mary and Martha faced their brother's death, they were not ready for it. Jesus had been a close friend, a blessing to them; yet they didn't see Him as a blessing at that crucial moment. Martha's reaction proved it. Her first words were a complaint to Jesus. "Lord, if You had been here, my brother would not have died" (John 11:21, KJV). This is a natural response from a person in pain, in need of a good shoulder to cry on. This also indicates Martha needed to strengthen her relationship with the only One who could provide answers and comfort during her greatest trial.

Whenever we are facing difficult times, it's imperative that we cling to God's promises. Remember what He promised Joshua when he faced a time of trial with the Israelites: "I will be with you. I will not leave you nor forsake you" (Joshua 1:5b, KJV). This promise is also offered to us today. Claim it daily. Cling to Jesus. Talk to Him. Call on Him. He will carry you through. I assure you the results will be life-changing.

If you are facing the loss of a loved one, trust Jesus. He has promised that the dead in Christ will rise up at the sound of the trumpet. Trust in Him, and the trial will turn into a blessing for your journey.

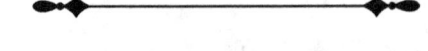

Light in Darkness

BY ZORAIDA VELEZ-DELGADO

Then they cried to the LORD in their trouble, and he saved them from their distress. He sent out his word and healed them; he rescued them from the grave. Let them give thanks to the LORD for his unfailing love and his wonderful deeds for mankind.

—PSALM 107:19–21, NIV

I was seven years old when Child Protective Services removed me from my home. I don't remember much about what happened before, but that day is very clear in my mind. After I was removed from the arms of my mother, literally, I was placed in a car with three officers and shown a gun to stop me from screaming, which I had been doing. This was in the eighties; I'm sure there would be a huge lawsuit if that happened today. I feared for my life and for the life of the only person I loved, my mother. I was taken to a judicial building to wait for my father, whom I had never met. He never showed. Instead, I spent more than an hour under a desk, waiting to be taken away by who knows who. An hour later, a woman I recognized came to the rescue. It was my mother's sister. They didn't have a good relationship, and the only time I had seen her was when she came to visit and slapped my mother across the face for some reason unknown to me. I was very afraid, but I had no one else. That night, my aunt gave me a nice meal, and a hot shower, and put me to bed. I was alone in the dark, and deeply afraid when my aunt asked me if I wanted to pray with her. She proceeded to talk to an invisible person who was supposed to help me sleep.

This new life of mine included many new experiences—new foods, clothes, shoes, school, family, and toys. Among these toys was a Big Wheel. Riding it became therapeutic for me. I'd ride up the hill on our street with difficulty, and then ride down as if I were flying! I had played alone my whole life, so when a group of boys approached me with a friendly tone, I was skeptical. One of them asked to ride the Big Wheel and, when I refused, he threatened to take it anyway. Then, he grabbed a rock and threw it at me, hitting my forehead. I started bleeding profusely, and I panicked. I was about seven houses away from where I lived, and yet I couldn't process enough to get there. I started to cry for my mother, and I was hit with the cruel reality that she was not coming. I found myself alone, bleeding, and hopeless. I couldn't move, and I was shaking.

I felt a soft touch on my shoulder, and a sweet voice followed: "You are going to be okay." I looked up and saw a young woman with a beautiful smile and reassuring eyes. She cleared the mix of tears and blood that covered my face and asked if I knew where my house was. Only then was I able to see outside of the fear of my situation. She told me to go home, and she promised to watch me until I got there safely.

Once in front of my house, I waved at her, and she waved back, and that was the first and last time I ever saw this woman. Was she an angel? I believe she was!

I stayed with my aunt for many years and, during those difficult days, I learned how to pray to God, asking Him to keep and protect me. Truly, I cried to the Lord in my distress, and He saved me. Even though my life was not perfect, God rescued me from the grave. I give Him thanks for His unfailing love and wonderful deeds toward me.

Nothing Left

BY ZORAIDA VELEZ-DELGADO

*They will receive blessing from the L*ORD *and vindication from God their Savior. Such is the generation of those who seek him, who seek your face, God of Jacob.*

—PSALM 24:5–6, NIV

It is five o'clock in the morning, and I am ready to leave the house to go on another business trip. This time, I am visiting a church in Cleveland, Ohio where Pastor Max leads a ministry serving unhoused individuals who are HIV-positive. Yes, that is still a thing! And, today, I want to learn how God is moving among those who are in great need.

We live in a chaotic world, facing many uncertainties. For many Americans, uncertainty triggers fear, then fear triggers hate, rejection, and condemnation. For the unhoused, uncertainty is their daily bread; they have lost so much that they are not fearful anymore. How can this pastor restore their faith to bring them back to Jesus? As I walked in, I saw him speaking love into their hearts. Standing there in simple jeans and a t-shirt, he had a Bible in one hand and a handkerchief in the other. It is a hot summer morning, and the air conditioning is barely working, but that doesn't stop Pastor Max. He has a message for this group of about thirty people. As his assistants pass cups with ice water, he shares the Word with them. He quotes King David, in Psalm 24. He reminds them that God created this earth and has claimed it and everything in it, including them. "Be a God-seeker, become a God-quester. Because the King of Glory is here, and he wants to transform you!"

(To be continued)

Nothing Left (Part 2)

BY ZORAIDA VELEZ-DELGADO

They will receive blessing from the Lord and vindication from God their Savior. Such is the generation of those who seek him, who seek your face, God of Jacob.

—PSALM 24:5–6, NIV

I saw smiles, many of them. The message was getting through. He brought a young lady named Rose to the front. She was a beautiful young lady, well dressed, and collected. Then she shared her story. She came to the ministry five years ago, sick, unhoused, unloved, hopeless. The ministry opened its doors and provided her with medicine, housing, love, and eventually a job. Today, Rose leads the housing department of the ministry, and she was ready with a laptop to take the information of every person in the room so that they can be provided with what they need. "God has the power to heal your soul, to bring you back to life, and He is using this ministry to accomplish that." She proceeded to show them a table where they would get food and, if they were interested, they could get a free Bible from another table.

I sat down as I saw every single one of these people register for the program, grab a plate of food, and then pick up their free Bibles.

All thirty Bibles were gone. "People want to believe in the power of God because they have nothing left,"

That night, this phrase kept bugging me. "They have nothing left." God didn't come to this earth to seek those who are full. He came to find those who had nothing more to offer, those who were empty inside because only those people had space to be filled. So here's the souvenir I brought with me from that trip: When I feel I am losing and have nothing left, get ready because the Bible teaches that He came to heal the broken, to find the lost, and to fill those who are hungry and thirsty. Yes, He came to fill the hearts of those who have nothing left, and when we have nothing left, God is enough.

A Story of Courage and Trust

BY MICHELLE ANDERSON

*I am leaving you with a gift—peace of mind and heart.
And the peace I give is a gift the world cannot give.
So don't be troubled or afraid.*

—JOHN 14:27, NLT

Finding peace can be challenging in a world filled with turmoil and hostility. We encounter situations that shake us to our core, leaving us anxious, afraid, and uncertain. However, the words of John 14:27 remind us that Jesus offers a different kind of peace—a peace that surpasses understanding. This peace can calm our troubled hearts and bring comfort in adversity.

Let me share my story of an experience I had working for an organization that claimed to value diversity and inclusivity. One day, at work, I came out of the bathroom and found a letter folded on the floor. The letter looked to have fallen out of someone's pocket. It was filled with racial slurs targeting me as the Human Resources Director. I brought equity and diversity to the organization in my role based on their communicated goals. One director in particular was not happy with the changes taking place and was not shy about expressing disapproval to me in both her tone and words.

Nevertheless, after finding the letter, my sense of security was threatened, and I was left feeling vulnerable and afraid. Anger and frustration welled within me in the days that followed as management engaged in cover-up and avoidance instead of attempting to investigate and determine the author of the letter.

The incident affected me deeply, disturbing my sleep at night, and the mere thought of going to work each day filled me with anxiety. During my turmoil, I made the decision to take some time off. I began to experience a gradual transformation in my mind. God's peace, which surpasses all understanding, started to envelop my heart and mind. The more I leaned on Him, the more I discovered newfound courage to face each day. As I continued to trust God's provision, I found the strength to return to work. Although the scars of the incident remained, I clung to the assurance that Jesus had left His peace with me.

In times of adversity and injustice, may we remember the words of John 14:27. Let us hold onto the peace that Jesus offers, knowing that it is not peace like the world gives. It is a peace that empowers us to stand firm, confront injustice with courage, and seek reconciliation and understanding amidst the chaos. May we trust God's faithfulness, allowing His peace to guard our hearts and minds.

A Story of Redemption and Restoration

BY MICHELLE ANDERSON

> *Beloved, never avenge yourselves,*
> *but leave it to the wrath of God, for it is written,*
> *"Vengeance is mine, I will repay, says the Lord."*
>
> —ROMANS 12:19, ESV

In our journey through life, we often encounter situations where injustice prevails. We may find ourselves mistreated, overlooked, or betrayed, leading to anger, bitterness, and a desire for justice. However, as followers of Christ, we are called to a different response. Romans 12:19 reminds us to trust God's divine justice, leaving vengeance in His hands.

Continuing with my story from yesterday, after enduring weeks of distress and lacking support from my workplace after the hate letter was found, the stress was immense, prompting me to take a medical leave. Uncertainty loomed over my future at work, and anger and bitterness threatened to consume me. It seemed as though justice was far from being served, and I questioned how I could ever find resolution and peace.

But in God's perfect timing and mysterious ways, He orchestrated a series of events I could never have foreseen. Shortly after returning from my medical leave, I received unexpected news: I was being "laid off" from my position. Though initially disheartened, I soon realized this turn of events was an opportunity for a fresh start.

As I navigated the aftermath of my departure, I pursued legal action against my former employer, seeking justice for the discrimination and mistreatment I had endured. Through God's provision and guidance, I won a settlement that compensated me for my suffering and served as a testament to His faithfulness in restoring what was lost.

I learned a powerful lesson about God's divine justice through it all. I understood that vengeance was not mine to seek but belonged solely to the Lord. Though the path was arduous and filled with obstacles, God repaid my faithfulness, granting me a measure of justice and allowing me to move forward in freedom.

In our own lives, when we encounter situations of injustice and betrayal, it can be challenging to release the desire for vengeance and trust in God's divine justice. However, as Romans 12:19 reminds us, vengeance belongs to the Lord, who is faithful to repay in His perfect way and timing.

God Is in Control

BY ANANDI MOSES

The LORD has established His throne in the heavens,
And His sovereignty rules over all.

—PSALM 103:19, NASB

Our world is very complex. The human body is made of complex and incredibly fine-tuned systems. The natural world around us like our environment and weather, other organisms with which we live, our complicated ecosystem, and our intricate systems of economy and technology are all complex. Our social system is multifaceted. Our homes, cars, and computers are not simple. Add to it communication, which is extremely complex.

Every morning, when we get up and go to work, we interact with all these systems, and they work together in our favor! Given the infinitesimal processes and layers of complexity, our world should be unmanageable and disordered. Anytime there is a disruption in any of these systems, it can produce a ripple effect that can collapse the organization of our world. Yet, we navigate through these systems, use them, and interact with them smoothly. It amazes me that we experience stability and order rather than chaos and unpredictability.

People offer many theories to explain how our lives feel well-ordered given the complexity of our world. However, the best theory is found in Psalm 103:19. In essence, this verse assures us that the Lord is the king, and He rules over everything.

God is sovereign. God is in control of our world and our lives. His power keeps the planets in orbit and our world in order. He knows everything due to His omniscience, He holds everything in place with His omnipotence. Nothing escapes His notice. Nothing spins out of His control. He spoke and it was done, He commanded, and it stood fast. (Psalm 33:9, NKJV).

When life seems to be out of control and unmanageable, we can rest assured that God, who is in control of this vast and complex world in which we live, can bring order and harmony to our lives. When we surrender our life to Him, He will be the ruler of it. The beauty and order that we see in God's creation will be reflected in the life that is fully surrendered to God.

What Do You Seek?

BY ANANDI MOSES

And Jesus turned and saw them following, and said to them, "What are you seeking?"

—JOHN 1:38A, NASB

We are created to move towards something. We feel satisfied when we know the purpose of our actions. We may not even be aware of it, but our hearts are fixed on things, and we work towards them. Jesus once asked two men, "What are you seeking?" It is important to God what we are moving towards, what we seek after, and what drives us. The answer to this question can determine our eternal destiny and the quality of our life here on earth. It is worth our time to contemplate the answer to this question.

Moses in the Bible was a great leader. God saw him fit to lead a whole nation of people for forty years in a journey to find their freedom and home. Moses had a huge responsibility that he worked to fulfill. On the surface, it may seem like that was his goal desire, and purpose, but if we look closer, we will find where his heart was really fixed.

At the burning bush, Moses asked God, "What is Your name?" During his conversation with God in the wilderness, he asked, "Please let me know Your ways so that I may know You" (Exodus 33:13). He said, "If Your presence does not go with us, do not lead us up from here" (Exodus 33:15). He asked God, "Please show me Your glory" (Exodus 33:18). Time and time again, we see through Moses' petitions that his heart was fixed on knowing God. He was seeking God Himself and His presence.

Reading the book of Psalms, we can easily see the center of David's life. He said, "One thing I have asked from the LORD, that I shall seek…To behold the beauty of the LORD"(Psalm 27:4, NASB). His heart was fixed on the person of God. He writes, "Delight yourself in the LORD; And He will give you the desires of your heart"(Psalm 37:4, NASB).

These giants of faith in the Bible had a heart seeking and desiring after God Himself and not just what He provides. Jesus said, "But seek first His kingdom and righteousness, and all these things will be provided to you" (Matthew 6:33, NASB). Like Moses and the Psalmist, pray for a glimpse of God's beauty and His glory. God will help you fix your heart on Him. Then, all your other desires will be sanctified. God will reveal Himself to you, and all your desires will be fulfilled.

Slow Down

BY ELINETE RODRIGUES REIS

Therefore I tell you, do not worry about your life, what you will eat or drink; or about your body, what you will wear. Is not life more than food, and the body more than clothes? Look at the birds of the air; they do not sow or reap or store away in barns, and yet your heavenly Father feeds them. Are you not much more valuable than they? Can any one of you by worrying add a single hour to your life?

—MATTHEW 6:25–27, NIV

We live in a fast-paced society. Our generation, especially the youth, is used to having everything right here, right now. We have fast food, high-speed internet, expressways, overnight postal services, "Prime," "Gold," "Platinum" or whatever special club we can sign up for to obtain the fastest results.

We have self-checkout lines everywhere. We can't waste time waiting in line at a grocery store. We pay extra for priority boarding at the airport— which I think is especially silly considering that the aircraft won't take off until all passengers have completed boarding. We're in a rush. We pride ourselves on "saving time." No time to spare.

Yet, we're tired. As a matter of fact, we're exhausted. For some of us, it is accurate to say we're overwhelmed. We live a busy life with a strict schedule. We manage to fill every hour of our lives with activities. Parents go around with the family schedule planned months ahead. The more we try to save time, the busier we become. We're not available.

When was the last time we reached out to that old friend? When did we last have time to catch up with the relative who lives far from us? When was the last time we invited people to come over for dinner? When did we have a relaxed conversation with our neighbor? When was the last time we took a day off? For some of us, this may not be possible; and you may think, *I would do it if I could.* That's a fair point. In that case, when was the last time you had the chance to have a mental break? To look around, to breathe?

Jesus was always calling the disciples to rest. To slow down. In Matthew 6:25–34, he reminded them that there's nothing we can do to add a day to our lives. Jesus is telling us that we're allowed to rest. These verses are a reminder to trust Him—to rest our bodies and minds, to find peace regarding tomorrow. He will be there. He's got us…no need to rush.

Look for the Bright Side

BY MEGAN BLACKMORE

*And we know that for those who love God,
all things work together for good,
for those who are called according to His purpose.*

—ROMANS 8:28, ESV

Life isn't always a bunch of sunny days. Sometimes dark clouds cover the skies, and we are standing in the midst of the storms of life. These storms can take different faces from childhood trauma, financial issues, marital conflicts, and parenting struggles to depression and anxiety.

These dark, rough patches in life can feel numbing and paralyzing. The heaviness can weigh us down so it is hard to take steps to move forward or even to get through each day.

When we experience hardships in life, it can often feel like torture. We even begin questioning, "Why me?"

Once we go down that rabbit hole of asking why, we have a negative outlook on life. We allow what we are going through or have gone through to define and rule our lives, casting a dark shadow over everything around us.

However, when we look at God's Word, and He reminds us that all things work together for good to those who are called according to His purpose, we have to re-evaluate the struggles we are facing and leave room for God to move in whatever way He desires.

When we look at the life of Job, trauma after trauma and hardship after hardship found their way into his life. However, Job kept pressing forward; he didn't turn from God, and he didn't give up on his life entirely. At the end of the day, God had a purpose for Job's life and a reason for all he went through, as heart-wrenching as it all was.

However, thanks to Job's life, we are encouraged and helped thousands of years later. Simply reading about Job's endurance could have saved or given another soul the courage to keep going.

We often look at our situations as having everything to do with ourselves. We have the victim mentality, or the "woe is me" mindset while God is looking at our adversity as something good even when it is terrible to go through. I am sure He has shed many tears along with you, but He also sees the good that will come from all of it.

Maybe this is what will save your soul in the end, and maybe this is what will save another soul, or maybe this is what will give you the strength needed to keep pressing forward. Whatever it may be, look for the bright side, and trust that God can see a more extensive, wider picture—and we must trust and stay in tune with God, just like Job did. Keep pressing on, and keep your feet firmly planted on the promises of God.

Jesus Weeps with Me

BY KELLEY MATIERIENE

Therefore, when Jesus saw her weeping, and the Jews who came with her weeping, He groaned in the spirit and was troubled. And He said, "Where have you laid him?" They said to him, "Lord, come and see." Jesus wept.

—JOHN 11:33–35, NKJV

Just imagine for a second that you are weeping over some significant loss, and Jesus sees you, and His spirit is moved to tears. The King of the universe, who knows the end from the beginning, who knows how long it will take for your sorrow to turn into joy, who knows the road you have traveled to arrive where you are. He sees you; He feels your pain, and it moves Him.

It's tough to imagine! It's challenging to grasp what that truly means, yet the Bible tells us Jesus wept. The day I realized my marriage was over, I wept. I can't say I was hit with the thought that Jesus was weeping with me. However, looking back, I know only that He provided the strength I would need over the years that followed. Only He could have carried me on the days I didn't want to get out of bed. And only He could have given. me the peace I needed to go on.

> *I, like Mary, was accusatory in my demeanor, tone, and thoughts.*
> *Lord, if only (fill in the blank).*
> *You saw this coming,; Lord couldn't You have warned me?*
> *Why would You let this happen to me?*

We all have our own subtle accusations that only God hears us say. Yet, He understands just like He did with Mary. Just like He does with you. When life doesn't play out the way we hope, Jesus sees us. In an honest and visceral way. Not in the way we often read this text or the way kids spit out "Jesus wept" when you ask them for their favorite verse.

Jesus knows and understands our pain, our hurt, our sorrow. He, too, has lost a loved one, been betrayed, and received a diagnosis that leads to death. He understands our response; rather than chastise or scold when these things happen to us, His spirit is moved, and He cares for us. We may not see it entirely as a big miracle as being raised from the dead, yet we can see His care and comfort in the people He sends our way. We see His care in the small mercies we experience when we least expect it, in the unexpected kindness of a stranger. We can trust that, in His mercy, the awful pain of that experience you had wasn't meant to break you. It was meant to show you God weeps with you. He sees your pain, and it moves Him at times to weep, but always in the direction of care and compassion.

ABOUT THE CONTRIBUTORS

Michelle Anderson is a wife, mother, and daughter of God. Born in Toronto, Ontario, Canada, she resides in Connecticut. Michelle is passionate about health ministry, particularly in helping women achieve whole health—emotionally, spiritually, and physically. She is a registered dietitian in a private practice specializing in emotional eating and plant-based nutrition for chronic illnesses. She enjoys traveling and spending time with her husband and son.

Linda Barton is enjoying the golden years with her retired physician husband of fifty-three years. She is a mother of four married children with ten precious grandchildren. She lives in Deer Park, Washington, on her oldest daughter's twenty-acre farm. Her hobbies include making colorful quilts and reading Christian literature.

Sara E. Bayrón is a lifetime active member of the SDA Church. A retired teacher and medical office administrator, she lives in West Palm Beach, Florida.

Megan Blackmore graduated from Central Connecticut State University with a degree in English and writing. She is a freelance editor and published author. Living in Connecticut with her husband and daughter, Megan is pursuing writing more books in the future.

Stephanie Blakeney is a wife and mother to five children; her oldest just turned sixteen, and her youngest is three. Stephanie was born and raised in New Jersey and spent some time in New York and Florida before marrying her husband and eventually moving to the remote wilderness of Brownfield, Maine. She currently lives on a 100-acre, off-grid farm. She spends her time working remotely, homeschooling her children, and helping to maintain their farm. She loves to cook and bake and enjoy time with her wonderful children.

Tania Fuentes-Davitt is a wife and mother of an eight-month-old. Her family is from Puerto Rico, and she has lived in many different locations across the United States over the course of her life. Tania earned a Ph.D. in microbiology and molecular genetics from Loma Linda University. She lives with her husband and son in the White Mountains of New Hampshire.

Sylvia Gobel Registered Nurse, graduated from Walla Walla University and lives with her husband in Spokane, Washington. She is a Christian who believes and loves God with all her heart.

Anna Jennings grew up in Bonners Ferry, Idaho, studied writing at Whitworth University, and served as a missionary in Germany for the Salvation Army. She currently lives in Spokane, Washington, where she grows and sells radishes, writes poetry and music, cares for children as a nanny, teaches preschool part-time, and participates in several ministries.

Felicia D. Lee is a wife and full-time homemaker. She is also a speaker, radio host, content creator, communication specialist, and founder of the New Wives Club, a ministry that supports newly married women through biblical mentorship. Her message of femininity and faith resonates with many as she encourages women to pursue a relationship with Christ that has depth and produces long-lasting change in their everyday lives. Felecia lives in New Hampshire, USA with her husband, Stephen.

Mayra R. Marino is a nurse practitioner with Marino Cardiology. This mother of two enjoys spending her afternoons at the beach

ABOUT THE CONTRIBUTORS

with her young children and Encarnación, her dog. Mayra resides in Hampton, New Hampshire.

Evelyn R Delgado Marrero received a D.Ed. in educational leadership and is a retired school teacher and administrator. This mother of three adult children and grandmother of six enchanting grandchildren stays busy enjoying her family; she lives in South Windsor, Connecticut.

Avaley Frances Matieriene is a wife who wears many hats with grace and dedication. She is a loving mother to four boys and a dog mom to a delightful Goldendoodle. Professionally, Avaley is a registered nurse; with her creative flair and eye for design, Avaley also runs an interior design business. Above all, Avaley's love for God is the foundation of her life.

Kelley Matieriene is a child of God who loves to share her love for God with others. She is a daughter and friend, a mother of three well-behaved children, and a CPA. She resides in the Northeast with her two children, a dog, and Cat the cat.

Adrienne McClain was born and raised in New York and resides in Dallas, Texas. She is the mother of two adult children, Denae and Winton. Adrienne is a gifted and talented elementary teacher and an adjunct professor at one of the community colleges in the Dallas area. She leads the women's prayer line for her church each week and loves to tell the stories of Jesus.

Joan Mitchell is a wife and mother of five adult children. Joan loves the Lord and is an excellent caregiver for elderly clients. She lives in Boston, Massachusetts.

Anandi Moses is a wife and mother of two. She enjoys homeschooling her children and spending time with her family. When she needs to recharge, she likes to read, write, and sing. Her curiosity fuels her reading and writing.

Esther Pelletier is so grateful that the Holy Spirit pursued her relentlessly and has brought her back into a growing faith in Jesus. She recently moved from New Hampshire to Maine to care for her mum. Esther has taught all grade levels and volunteer-traveled in Thailand, Cambodia, New Zealand, and Australia in 2010 and 2011 teaching English, homesteading, and exploring. Esther praises God for His astonishing creativity and love shown in nature.

Glaribel Piñero-Amaro, B.A.Ed., is a young widow who loves to travel and occupies the rest of her time teaching her kindergarten students. Glaribel lives in West Palm Beach, Florida.

Brunie Quiñones was born and raised in a Christian home. She is a retired teacher who lives in Hope Mills, North Carolina and enjoys traveling as a pastime.

Raquel Quiñones is happily retired from the SDA Educational Department where she served in several capacities as a teacher, principal, and superintendent. She lives in Moca, Puerto Rico.

Patricia Reed resides in Dallas, Texas, with her husband of thirty-five years. She has one daughter and one stepson. Together, she and her husband Roderick, have eleven grandchildren. As a special education teacher, she loves working with children with exceptionalities. She is actively involved in her local congregation and enjoys participating in activities that uplift women.

Elinete Rodrigues Reis was raised in Northeast Brazil in a large and beautiful family. She comes from a rural community surrounded by unique landscaping and direct contact with nature. Living miles away from the nearest school, her mother, a single mother of six girls, allowed her to live with relatives to attend school. With that family, Ellie learned about the Bible and the Seventh-Day Adventist faith, being baptized when she was twelve. Elinete grew up involved in the community and church activities, taking leadership roles at a very young age. She became Pathfinder Director at the age of sixteen. She attended Sao Paulo Adventist University for five years, obtaining a Law Degree in 2011. She is a member of the Order of Attorneys in Brazil. In 2016, Elinete migrated to the United States, living in Connecticut ever since. She divides her time between running her business and her job in the Dentistry field. She enjoys traveling, learning new languages, and sunny weather.

Sandra A. Sergeant is the mother of two adult daughters who have blessed her with seven amazing grandchildren. Sandy is a Registered Nurse who operates a home care company for the aging population. She is involved in her local church and does not shy away from challenges, either physical or intellectual. Sandy loves to travel and spend time with her family. She currently resides in Enfield, Connecticut.

Pearl Sukou is a wife and mother of four. Her oldest son was recently married. Two of her children are adopted, and her youngest has unique needs. She currently is a busy homemaker living in south central Tennessee with her husband and her youngest three children, whom she homeschools.

Sara Tabtabai MD, FACC, Regional Director of Heart Failure and Population Health for Trinity Health of New England, Assistant Professor UCONN School of Medicine. Sara is a wife and mother of three who resides in Glastonbury, Connecticut.

Zoraida Velez-Delgado M.Ed. is a leadership development and motivational speaker who lives in Grand Rapids, Michigan.

Bryna Quiring Walker was born and raised in British Columbia, Canada, before moving to the U.S. after marrying her husband, Joshua. They live in Ohio but are willing to go wherever God may lead them. Bryna enjoys her Bible study group, engaging in outreach, making smoothies, baking, and doing organizational projects. She works in the early childhood education field and loves to make learning fun and meaningful for the children she teaches. She also enjoys collecting and digitizing children's audio stories and songs to use with kids and also to share with others.

Bryana Wilson is a senior at Hartford Magnet Trinity College Academy. She has received multiple academic awards and serves as the vice president of the school's National Honor Society and captain of her volleyball team. She has worked as a communications and marketing intern for the Blue Hills Civic Association and plans to attend college to study health science.

Kierra Wilson is a junior in high school and hopes to pursue a career in the medical field. Her hobbies include art and music; she has studied the violin for ten years. As an avid believer in Christ, Kierra is grateful for the opportunity to contribute her writing.

Kareen Wilson is a Registered Dental Hygienist (RDH), MS, with a Master's in Organizational Leadership. Kareen contributes editorial articles and media presentations to national TV and co-founded Bethesda Medical Mission, Inc. She enjoys long-distance running, skiing, mountain climbing, traveling, and raising two amazing daughters. She is also into anything that helps people live healthy, satisfying lives.

BIBLE REFERENCES

Contemporary English Version (CEV) copyright © 1995 American Bible Society. All rights reserved.

Easy-to-Read Version (ERV) copyright © 2006 by World Bible Translation Center.

The Good News Translation (GNT) copyright © 1976 by the American Bible Society.

King James Version (KJV), Public Domain.

The Message (MSG) copyright © 1993, 1994, 1995, 1996, 2000, 2001, 2002. Navpress Publishing Group. All rights reserved.

The New American Standard Bible (NASB) copyright © 1960,1962,1963,1968,1971,1972,1973,1975,1977,1995 by the Lockman Foundation. All rights reserved.

American Standard Version (ASV), Public Domain.

Amplified Bible (AMP) copyright © 2015 by The Lockman Foundation, La Habra, CA 90631. All rights reserved.

Christian Standard Bible (CSB) copyright © 2017 by Holman Bible Publishers. All rights reserved.

English Standard Version (ESV) copyright © 2001 by Crossway Bibles, a publishing ministry of Good News Publishers.

Easy-to-Read Version (ERV) copyright © 2006 by Bible League International.

New American Bible (Revised Edition) (NABRE) copyright © 2010, 1991, 1986, 1970 Confraternity of Christian Doctrine, Inc., Washington, DC. All Rights Reserved.

New International Version (NIV) copyright ©1973, 1978, 1984, 2011 by Biblica, Inc.® Used by permission. All rights reserved worldwide.

New Living Translation (NLT) copyright © 1996, 2004, 2015 by Tyndale House Foundation. Used by permission of Tyndale House Publishers, Inc., Carol Stream, Illinois 60188. All rights reserved.

New King James Version (NKJV) copyright © 1982 by Thomas Nelson. Used by permission. All rights reserved.

New Life Version (NLV) copyright © 1969, 2003 by Barbour Publishing, Inc.

New Revised Standard Version, Anglicised copyright © 1989, 1995 the Division of Christian Education of the National Council of the Churches of Christ in the United States of America. Used by permission. All rights reserved.

Living Bible (TLB) The Living Bible copyright © 1971 by Tyndale House Foundation. Used by permission of Tyndale House Publishers Inc., Carol Stream, Illinois 60188. All rights reserved.

Tree of Life Version (TLV) copyright © 2015 by The Messianic Jewish Family Bible Society.

www.ingramcontent.com/pod-product-compliance
Lightning Source LLC
Chambersburg PA
CBHW052128070526
44585CB00017B/1748